IMAGES
of America

JOSEPHINE COUNTY

On the Cover: Maude and William Bigelow enjoy the natural beauty of Josephine County. (Courtesy of Lloyd Smith.)

IMAGES
of America

JOSEPHINE COUNTY

Margaret LaPlante

ARCADIA
PUBLISHING

ISBN 978-1-4671-1543-8

Published by Arcadia Publishing
Charleston, South Carolina

Printed in the United States of America

Library of Congress Control Number: 2015946906

For all general information, please contact Arcadia Publishing:
Telephone 843-853-2070
Fax 843-853-0044
E-mail sales@arcadiapublishing.com
For customer service and orders:
Toll-Free 1-888-313-2665

Visit us on the Internet at www.arcadiapublishing.com

Contents

ACKNOWLEDGMENTS

All the historic photographs in this book are courtesy of Lloyd Smith.

Introduction

Long before pioneers settled in Josephine County, the Takelma tribe called this part of southern Oregon home. The valley was divided between the Upland and Lowland Takelmas, with mostly Upland Takelmas in Josephine County. The Taltuctuntede tribe lived in the Galice area, and the nearby area of Applegate was home not only to the Takelmas but also to the Dakubetede tribe. Occasionally, fur trappers or members of exploration teams passed through the area; one group of fur trappers found the Takelmas to be rather troublesome, referring to them as "rogues." Soon, the entire valley was known as the Rogue Valley.

The Takelmas lived in pit houses. They dug 18 to 24 inches into the ground along the perimeters of the house and erected posts in the corners. They then used sugar pine planks to create siding and roofs. Takelma women wore knee-length deerskin skirts adorned with fringe made of white grass, while men wore deerskin shirts and leggings tied with a belt. Members of the tribe made robes, blankets, and hats from deerskin and bearskin and lined their moccasins with grass or fur. During the cold months, they wore sleeves made from fox skins. Their garments were embellished with various shells, white grass braids, and buckskin tassels.

The Takelmas wove baskets from tree roots, vines, and other natural resources. These baskets, often dyed using natural elements, were used for gathering, preparing, and serving food. Takelmas also wove basket cradles to carry newborns. Implements made from stone were very important to the natives, who used a stone mortar and pestle to process acorns, camas bulbs, nuts, and seeds. Members of the tribe gathered acorns throughout the valley in the spring and shelled them with the mortar and pestle. They then sifted the mashed acorns into a shallow basket, which was then placed on clean sand; they poured hot water over the mixture twice to remove the bitter taste from the acorn. Next, they would place hot stones in a basket and add the acorn mixture and water to cook it thoroughly. Camas bulbs were a staple food. The Takelmas dug the bulbs out of the ground with a sharp stick and placed them in an earth oven to cook. A layer of alder bark separated the hot stones in the bottom of the pit from the bulbs on the top. Once finished, the mixture was mashed into cakes that could be stored for the months ahead or consumed right away.

The Takelmas relied on the seeds, nuts, berries, and bark from sugar pine trees to supplement their diets. They also ate grasshoppers, yellow jacket larvae, snails, insects, the meat from birds, deer, and elk. While employed by Hudson's Bay Company, Peter Skene Ogden made several trips through the area beginning in the 1820s. He wrote about how the Takelmas ate raw meat by "devouring the entr[a]ils as they were taken out of the body without even attempting to clean them, the blood they drank with the same avidity." Titian Ramsey Peale, a member of the US Exploring Expedition, wrote in his diary about the "piles of Mussel shells" near what is known today as Grave Creek. He also wrote that large quantities of land snails were "found in piles where they had been roasted."

The Rogue River supplied the Takelmas with an abundance of salmon. It could be cooked and eaten or smoked and dried for later consumption. While on an expedition for the US Army, Rodney Glisan wrote in his diary, "One haul with a seine at the mouth of the Rogue River would yield sufficient salmon to feed 1,200 Indians a fortnight." Ogden wrote, "The natives are busily employed in collecting dead salmon, no doubt for food. They may find them palatable; even go so far as to select them in a putrid state, giving them the preference. What a depraved taste." Traveling the Rogue River, however, has always been a challenge. The Takelmas made rafts from logs or created canoes. Ogden wrote that one of his trappers found a native canoe and used it to explore the other side of the river. Charles Wilkes, who was with the 1841 US Exploring Expedition, referred to the canoes used by the Takelmas—which were squared off at each end—as "quite rude" in craftsmanship.

For entertainment, the Takelmas played shinny. This game involved making a ball from two pieces of wood tied together with stitched buckskin, and the shinny stick was a long pole with a bent end. Goals were constructed from branches stuck in the ground. To begin a game, the players tossed the ball in the air in the center of the field. The strategy was to move the ball upfield toward the goal without letting the opponent steal it. The Takelmas also sang songs and held ceremonies for important events such as births and marriages. Ogden recounted an honorific dance performed by the Takelmas by writing, "Amused the camp with a dance. In this they acquitted themselves as well as Indians ever did. About midnight they took departure well pleased."

After observing a Takelma burial in the area that would later become Josephine County, Ogden wrote, "Amongst the different Indian Tribes that I have seen, those in this quarter are the first who come as near to our mode of inter[r]ing their dead . . . their Graves are sunk from five to six feet deep, the Body carefully wrapt in Deer Skins and at the Head and Feet square Planks are erected, the Head, as is almost invariable the plan with all Indians, placed towards the East."

When white settlers first began arriving in the area in the 1840s, there were few problems between the pioneers and the natives. However, by the 1850s, as more and more settlers arrived, tensions rose between the groups. The natives felt the land they had relied on for many thousands of years was being destroyed, and their natural habitat and sources of food were being depleted. It was not long before actual wars broke out between the two parties. In September 1853, both sides signed the Rogue River Treaty in an effort to end the Rogue River Wars, and there was peace for a period of time, but in 1855, war broke out again. Between 1853 and 1855, representatives from a number of tribes signed multiple treaties that ceded most of the tribal lands to the federal government. On November 9, 1855, Pres. Franklin Pierce signed the executive order that established the Coast (or Siletz) Reservation near the Oregon coast. The Oregon Territory government gave the final order that all of the Takelma, Taltuctuntede, and Dakubetede Indians were to be relocated to the Siletz Reservation. In 1856, the last of the Native Americans who had called this land home were forced onto the reservation.

One

Life in the Country

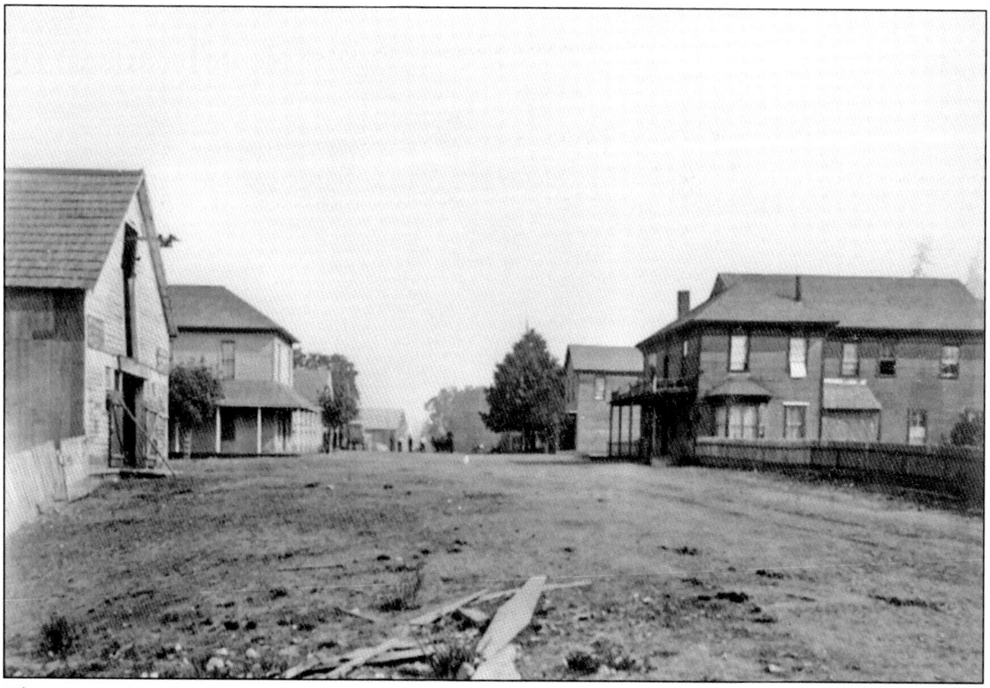

The town of Kerbyville is pictured here. Kerbyville—named for James Kerby, who arrived in 1853 and took out a Donation Land Claim—was the second county seat in Josephine County, with the first being the town of Waldo. The town's name was eventually shortened to Kerby.

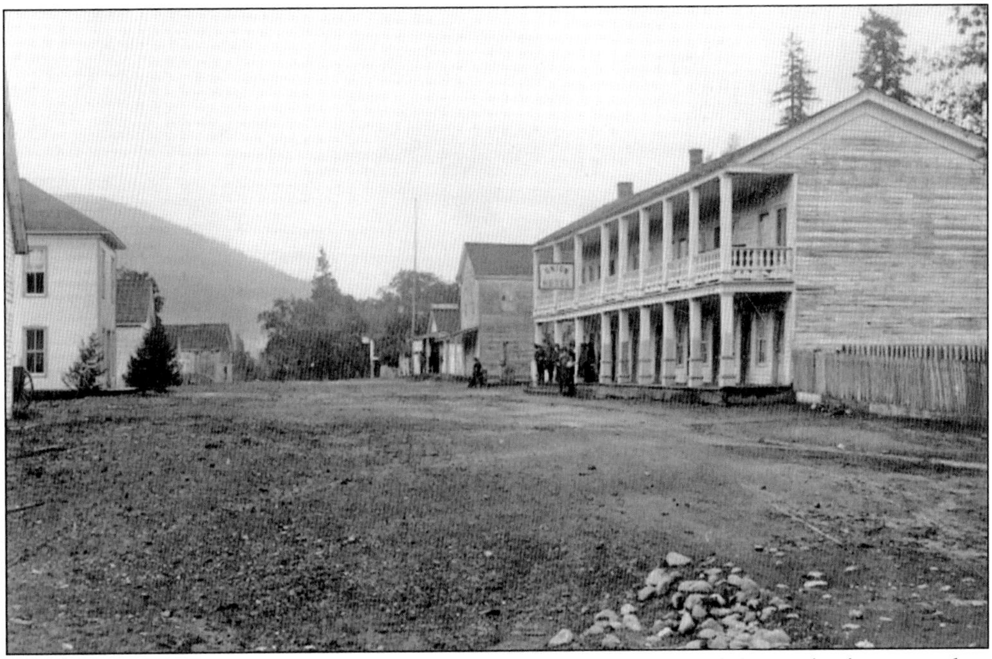

On October 6, 1904, the *Rogue River Courier* boasted, "Kerby supplies all the needs of an up-to-date community. We are very centrally located on the main road leading to Holland on the one side, Waldo and Crescent City on the main county road. New people are locating in the immediate vicinity and causing new enterprises to rise up to meet the demands of an up-to-date town. We have one of the oldest mining settlements in our county. We have splendid post office facilities, combined with a large merchandise store run by the post master, Mr. F. Smith and his assistant. We have a first class hotel. Stages leave Kerby for different places each day."

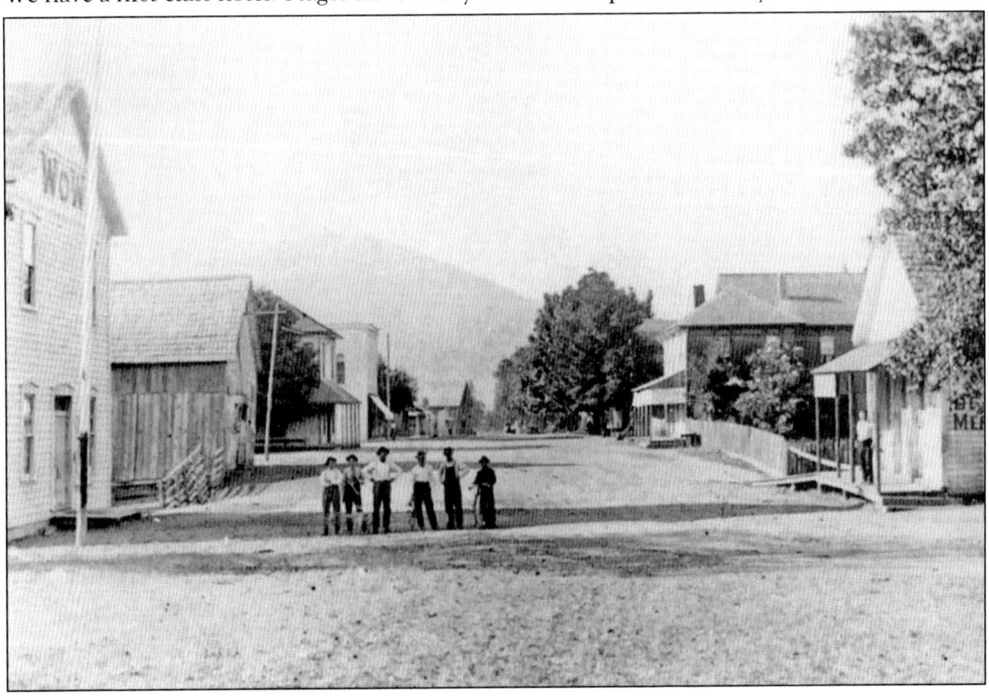

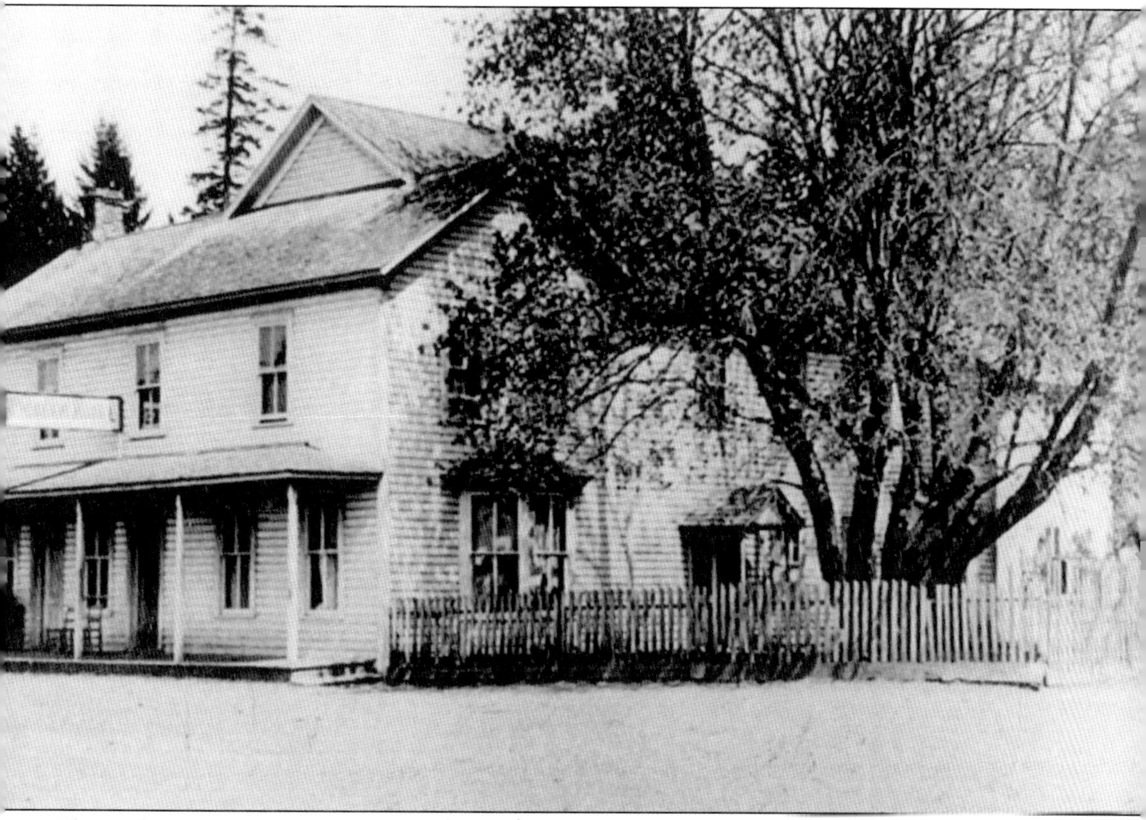

This is the Pioneer Hotel, which was located in Kerby. The Sawyer brothers, William and Sam, built the hotel in the 1850s. The brothers also operated a store in Kerby. William and his wife, Agnes, ran the hotel. They were pioneers from Biddleford, Maine.

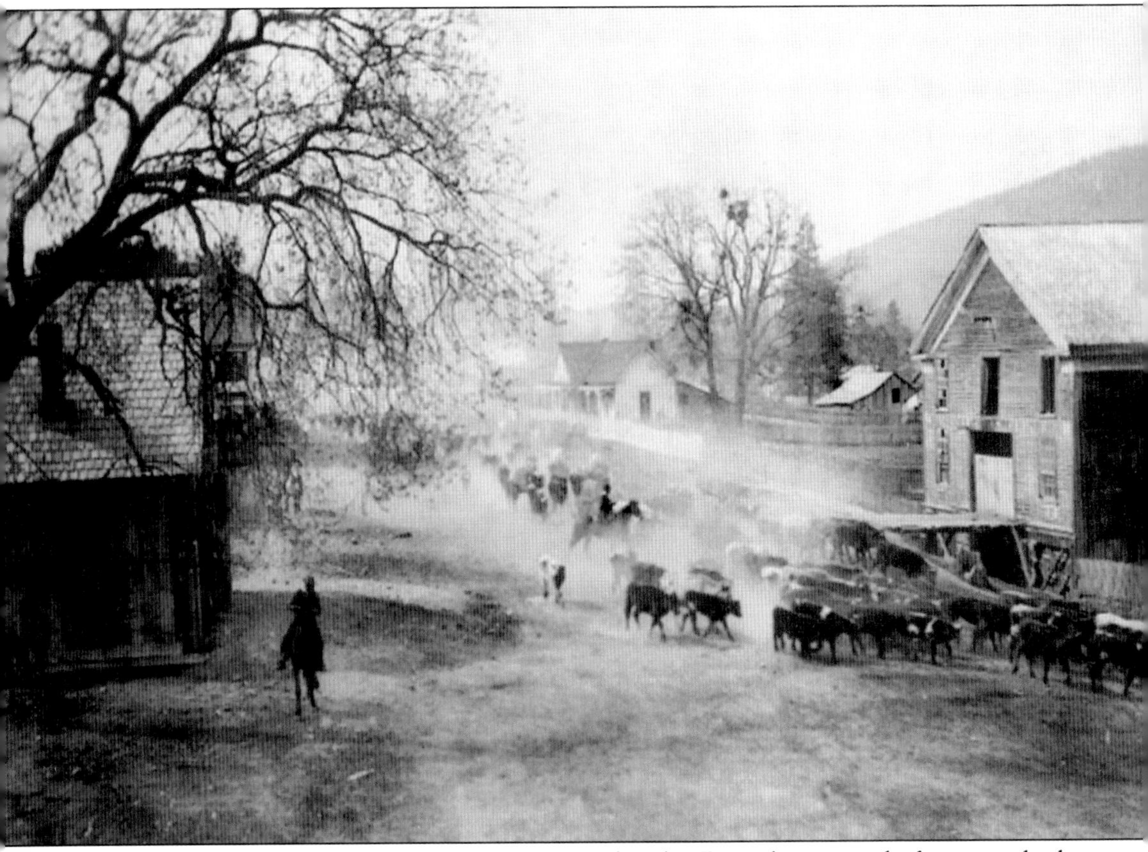

A cattle drive runs straight through the town of Kerby. For a short period of time in the late 1850s, Kerby was called "Napoleon" because the locals thought that Josephine County should have a Napoleon, but the name was short-lived.

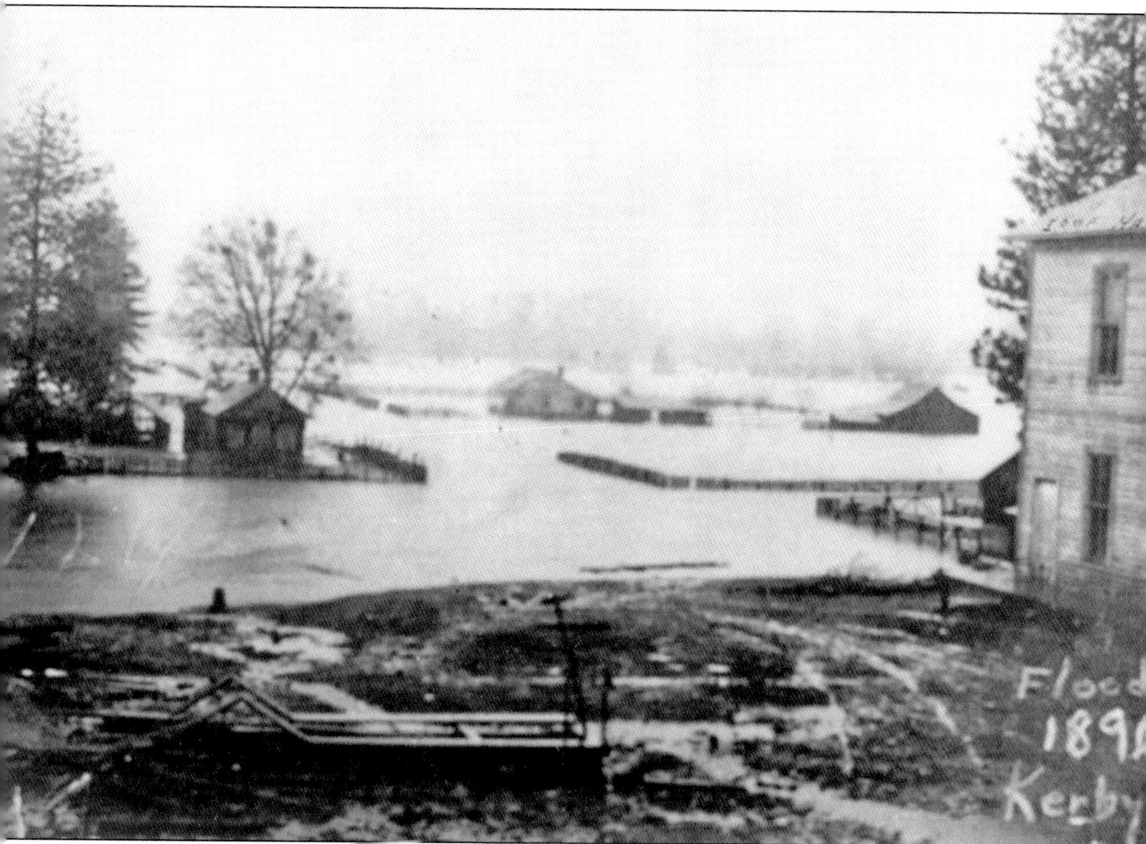

The flood of 1890 was devastating to southern Oregon and northern California. During the flood, the Rogue River, no longer contained, was flowing freely, and entire houses were washed away, farms were destroyed, and the tailings of upper mines were demolished. For decades after the flood of 1890, all other storms were compared to this one. In the center of this photograph, the Holtons' house—the first residence built in Kerby—is surrounded by water.

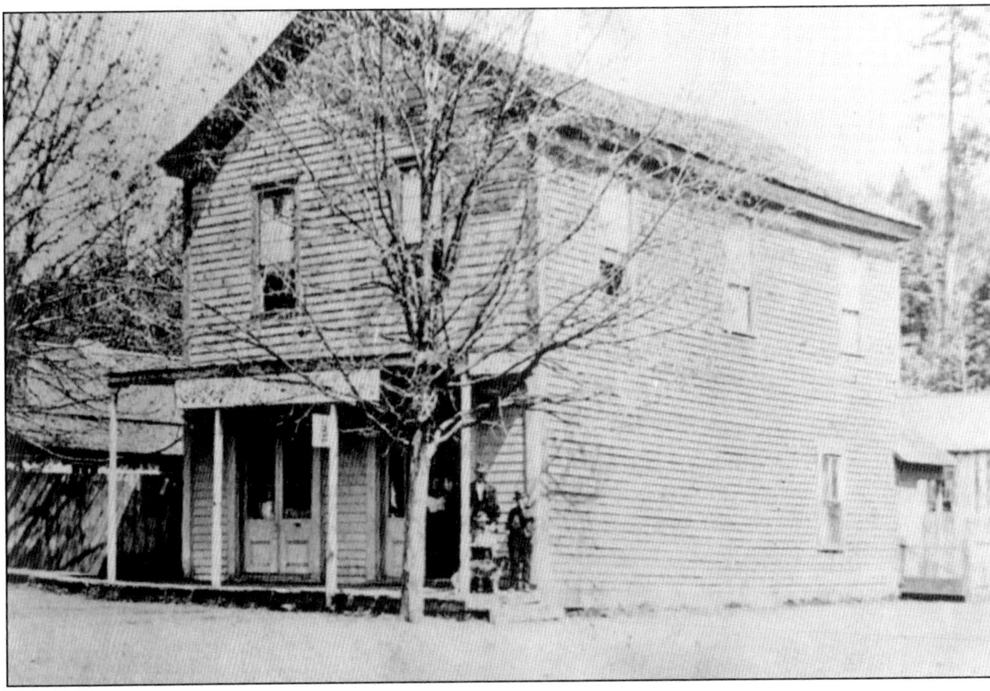

Fraternal organizations were a very important part of American life in the 19th century. Above is the Masonic hall, and below is the building that housed the Independent Order of Odd Fellows (IOOF); the people gathered in front of the IOOF building are preparing for a parade.

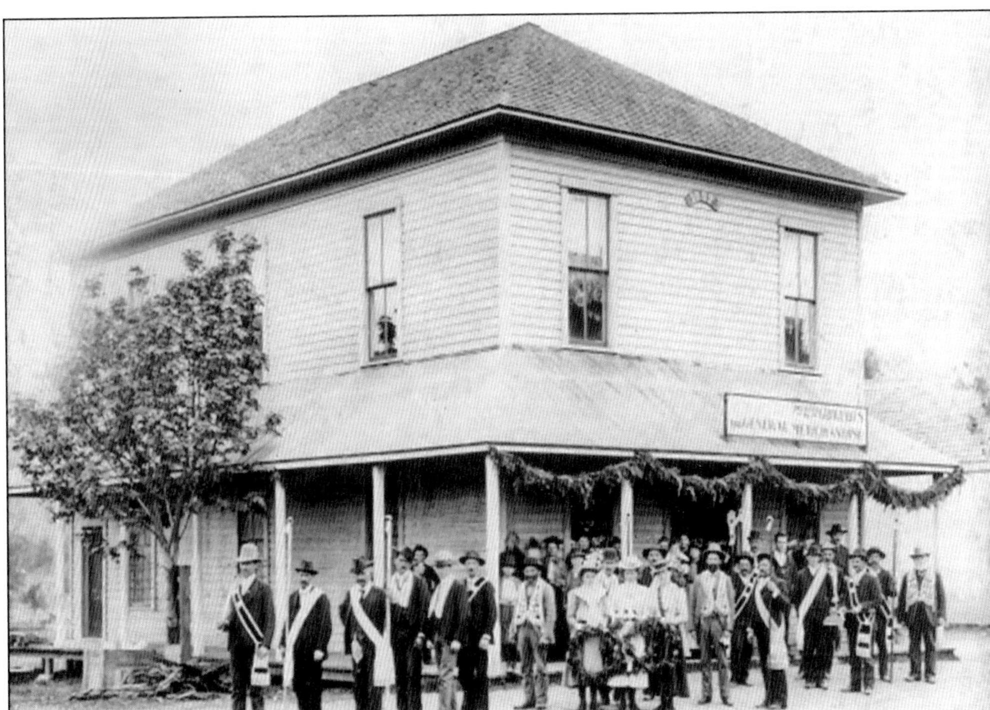

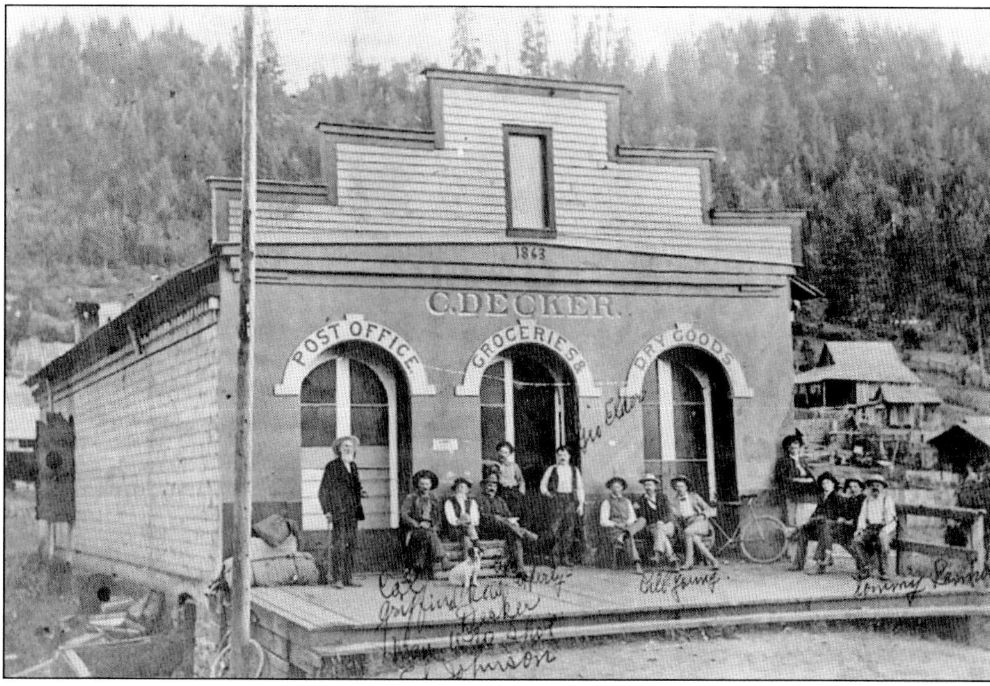

Charles Decker constructed this building in the town of Waldo in 1863. At that time, Waldo was a bustling town. The above photograph was taken in 1888. By 1928, the last residents had left, and the town was abandoned. In 1937, water from hydraulic giants brought in from the mining fields in the hopes of extracting any gold still present in the bedrock where the town once stood destroyed what was left of this building, a nearby hotel, and an old structure that had been wallpapered with newspapers from the East Coast detailing the events of the Civil War.

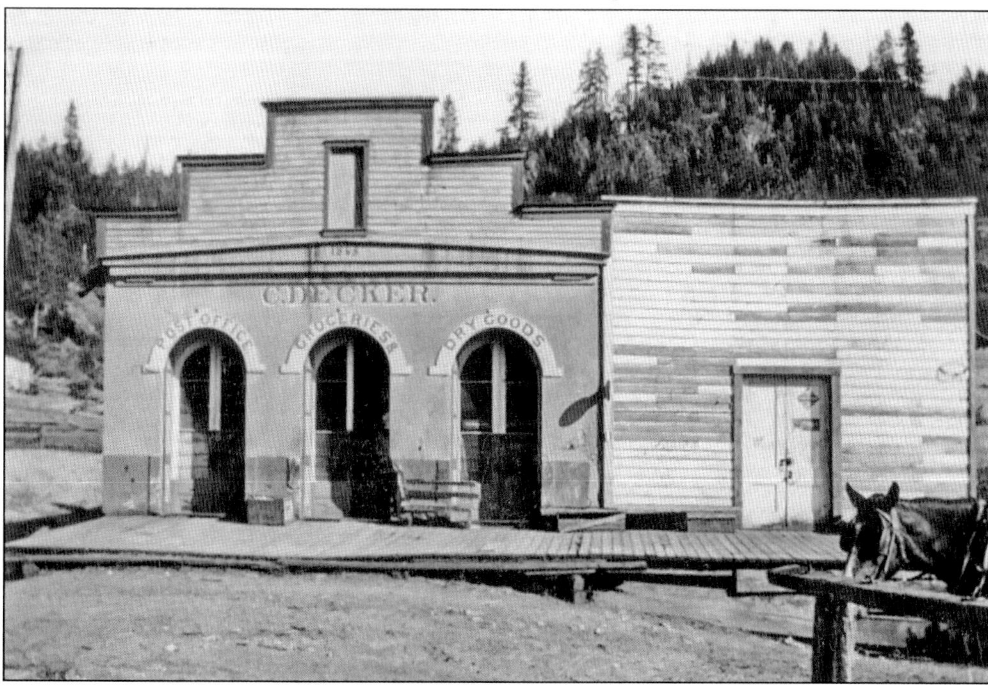

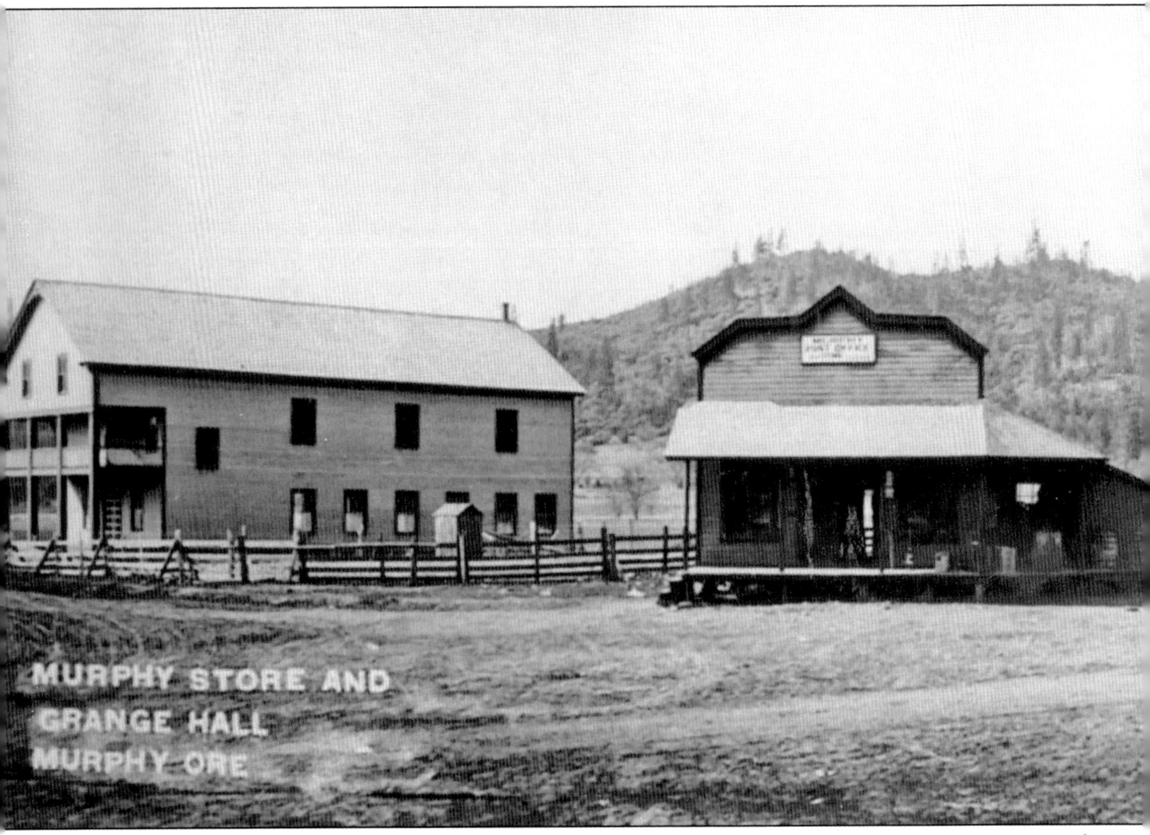

The Murphy Store and Grange hall are pictured here. In 1916, the *Rogue River Courier* reported, "The entire neighborhood gathered at the grange hall Saturday evening to enjoy a fine program of music, songs, and readings after which the lunch boxes were auctioned off by Lon Carson, who made a first class auctioneer. Thirty-two dollars were realized from the auction which goes for a tennis court for the use of the young folks. Mr. Thompson, the new county advisor, gave an interesting talk at the box social and advised us not to forget our very best crop, that of boys and girls, while attending to all the other crops. Mr. Blanchard's reading of the village debating society was very much enjoyed."

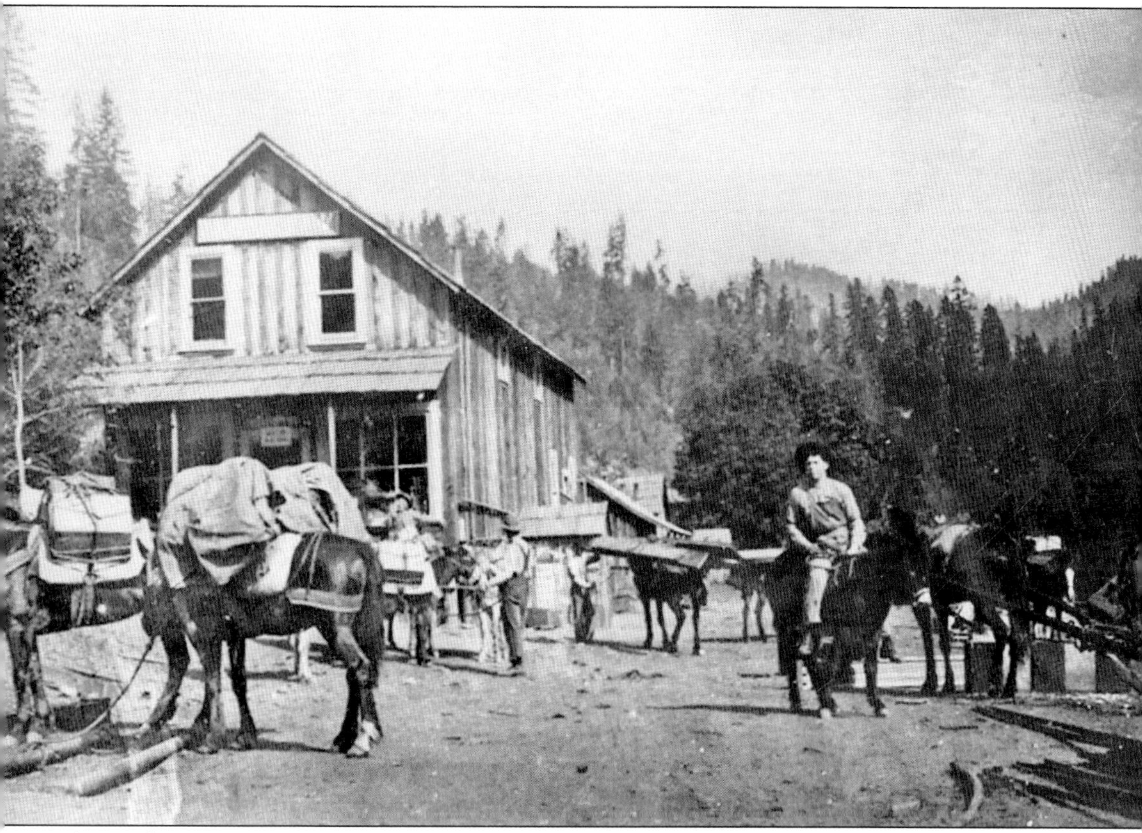

This pack train is getting ready to leave C.L. Barlow's store in Galice and head to the mines. Miners were willing to pay top dollar for items that were not available at the mines. The stores in nearby towns were able to provide the necessities that the miners needed, and pack mules transported the items.

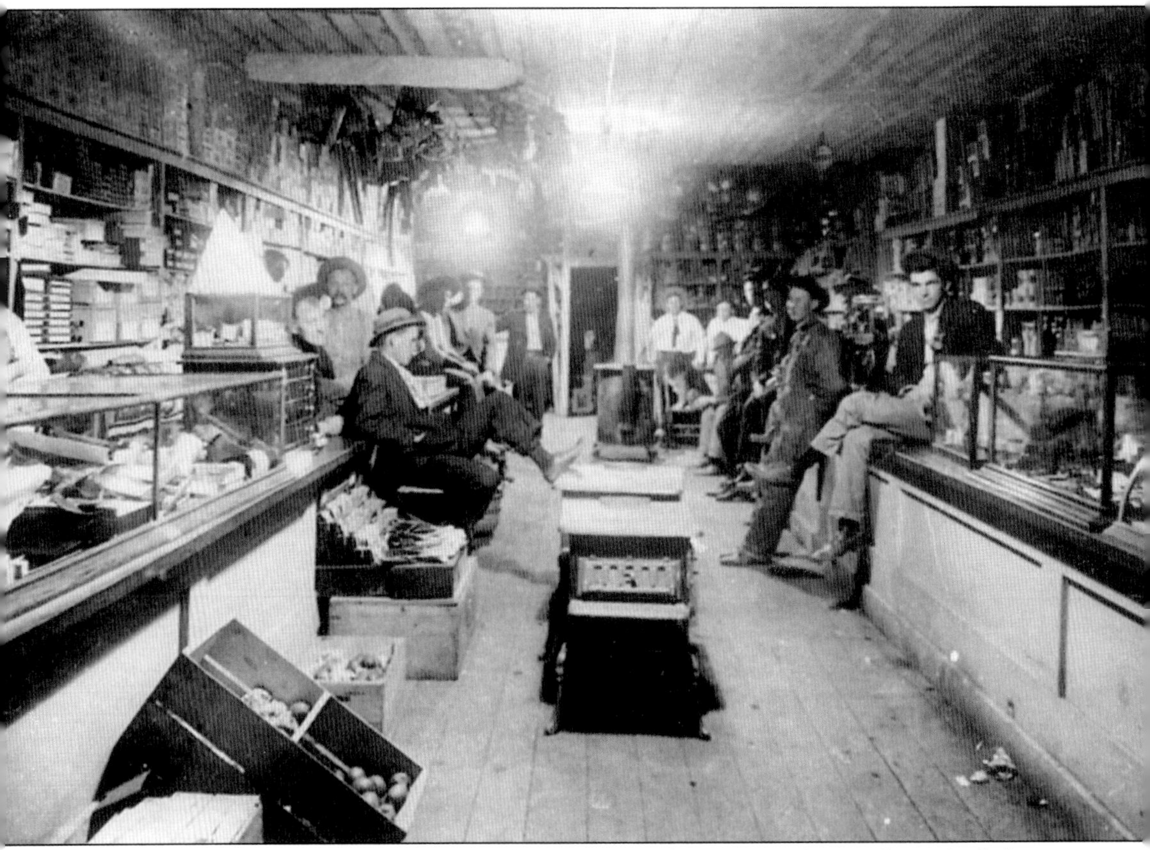

Men enjoy some camaraderie inside the store in Galice. In 1905, a road was built between Galice and Leland; the Almeda Mining Company was the main financial contributor for the road, with other nearby mines paying a lesser amount. The road was built with no more than a six-percent grade at any point so that a team of horses could carry a ton and a half of timber without any problems.

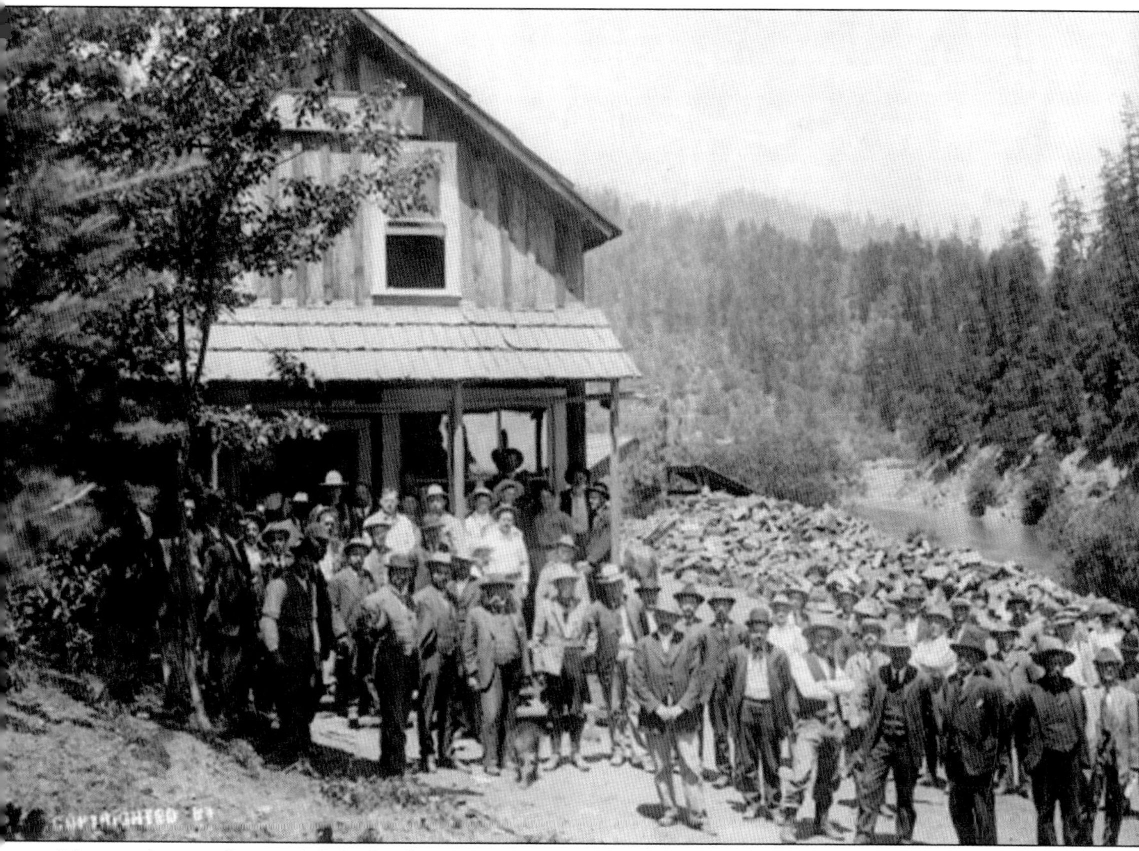

Men gather in front of C.L. Barlow's store in Galice. Barlow's store served as the mail and passenger stage. C.L. Barlow was the Galice postmaster, and his brother Glen operated another store in Galice.

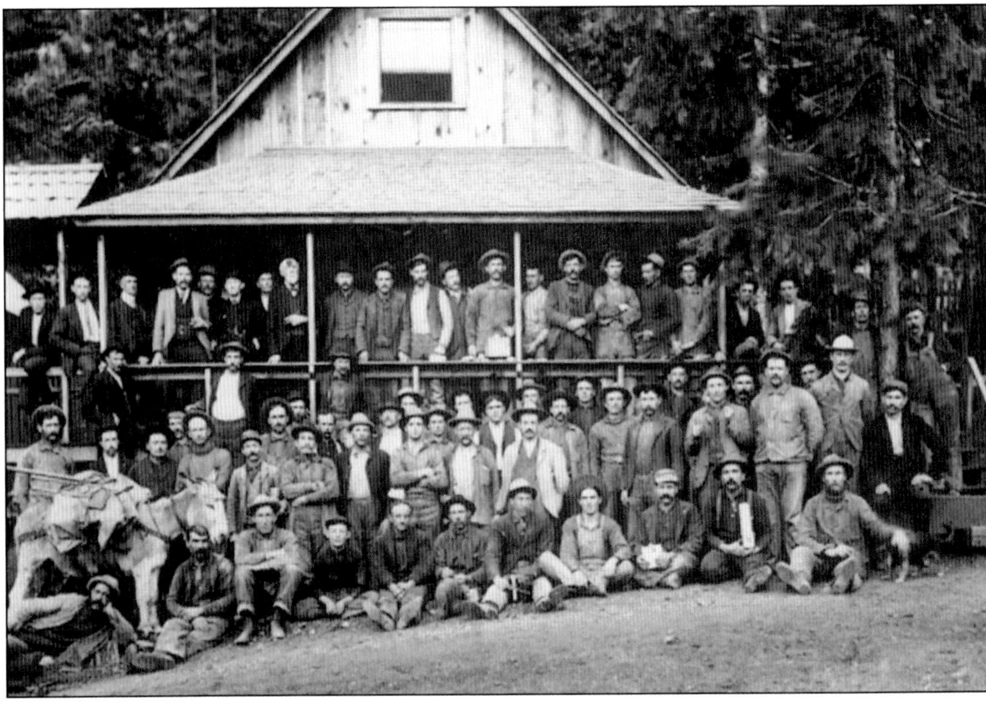

These images show an early-day group of men with a pack mule (above) and a later-day group with an automobile (below). The group with the automobile was part of the Grants Pass Commercial Club, which contained members who made the journey from Grants Pass to the town of Holland by automobile.

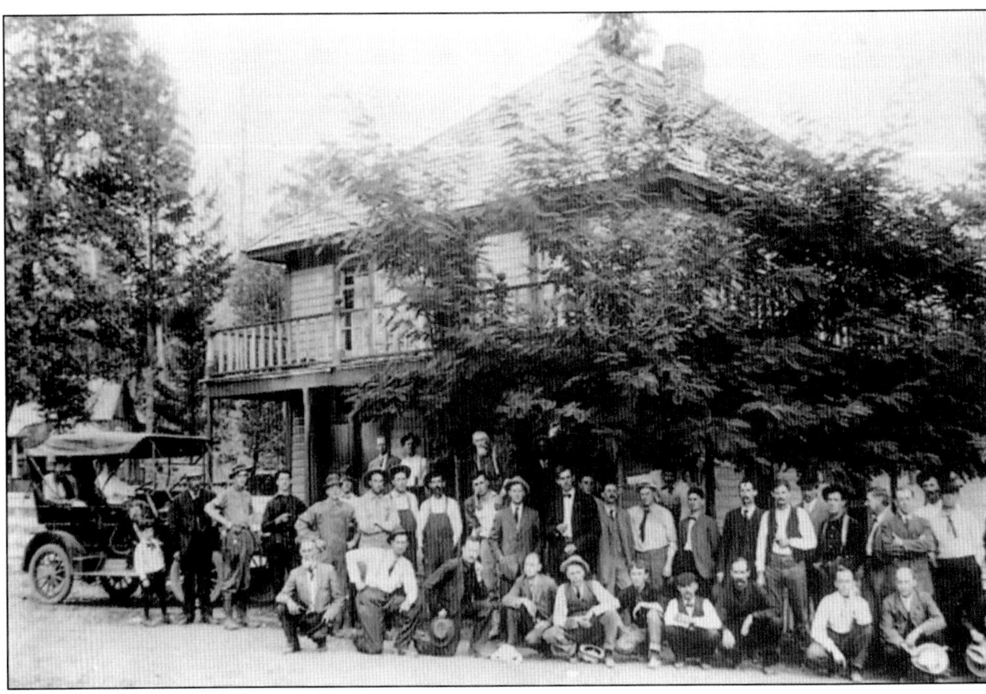

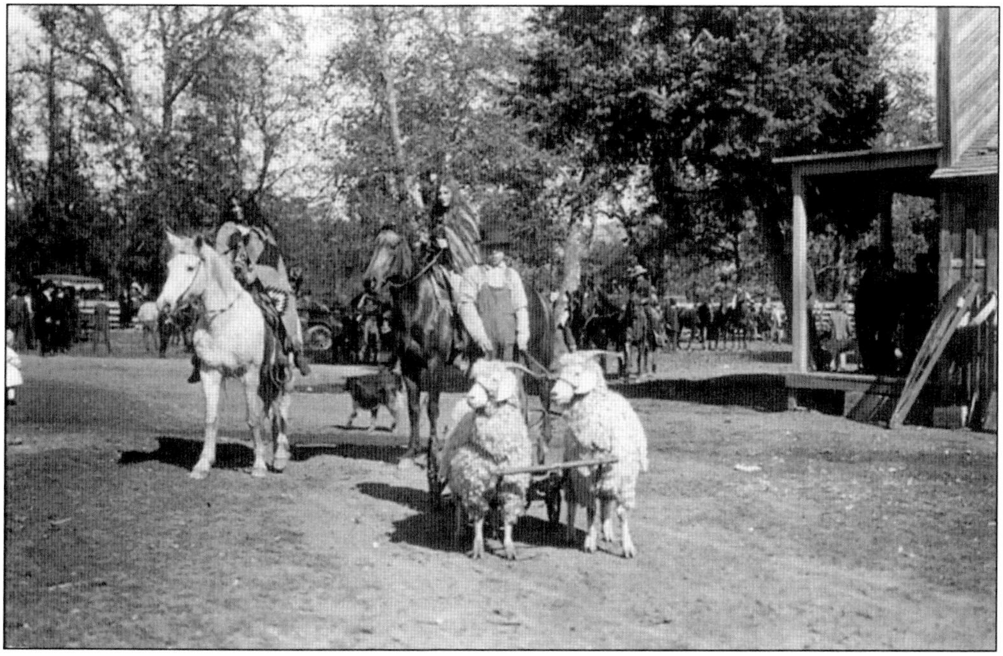

After attending the Holland Round Up in 1913, C.A. Winetrout wrote in a letter to the editor of the *Rogue River Courier*, "Their hospitality was poured as freely as water on this pie-eating, bronco-busting occasion and I would especially compliment the good ladies who prepared the feast. There were over 600 feet of tables simply groaning with big fat pies, delicious salads, baked beans of the real Bostonian stripe, and great heaps of cake like mother used to make. If I weren't a married man, I'd surely go to Holland to find a wife for the ladies out there are simply wizards at the culinary arts. The big stock parade in the morning exhibited as fine a lot of yearling colts, two-year olds and fine heavy Percheron stock as shown anywhere. From four o'clock until six o'clock the races proved most exciting and developed some fast track horses."

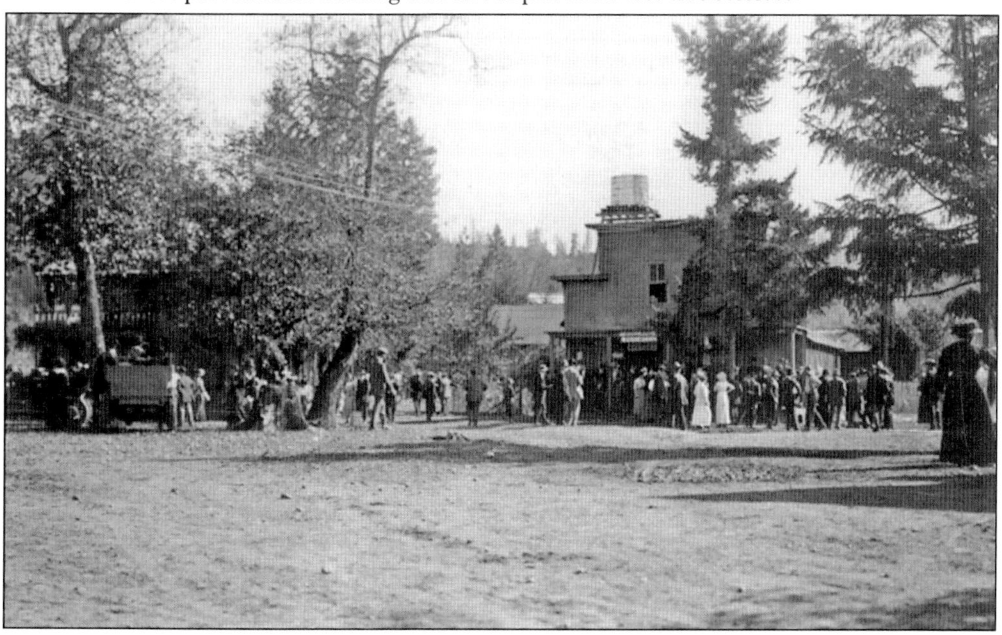

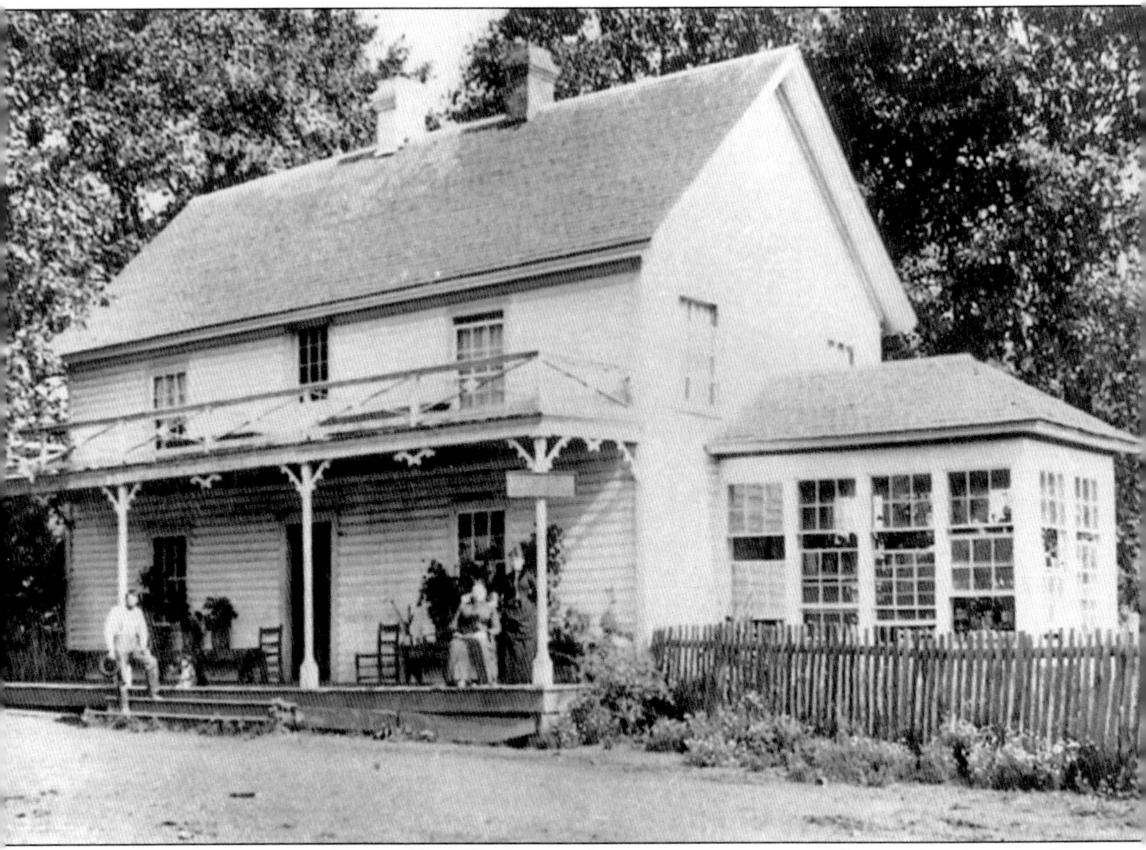

This is the Jones Hotel in Wilderville. It served as a stage stop, post office, and gathering place for the locals. Pictured are, in no particular order, Columbus F. Lovelace, Hanna D. Jones, and Hanna's daughter Edwina Jones. Edwina and Columbus later married, and the hotel became known as the Lovelace Hotel.

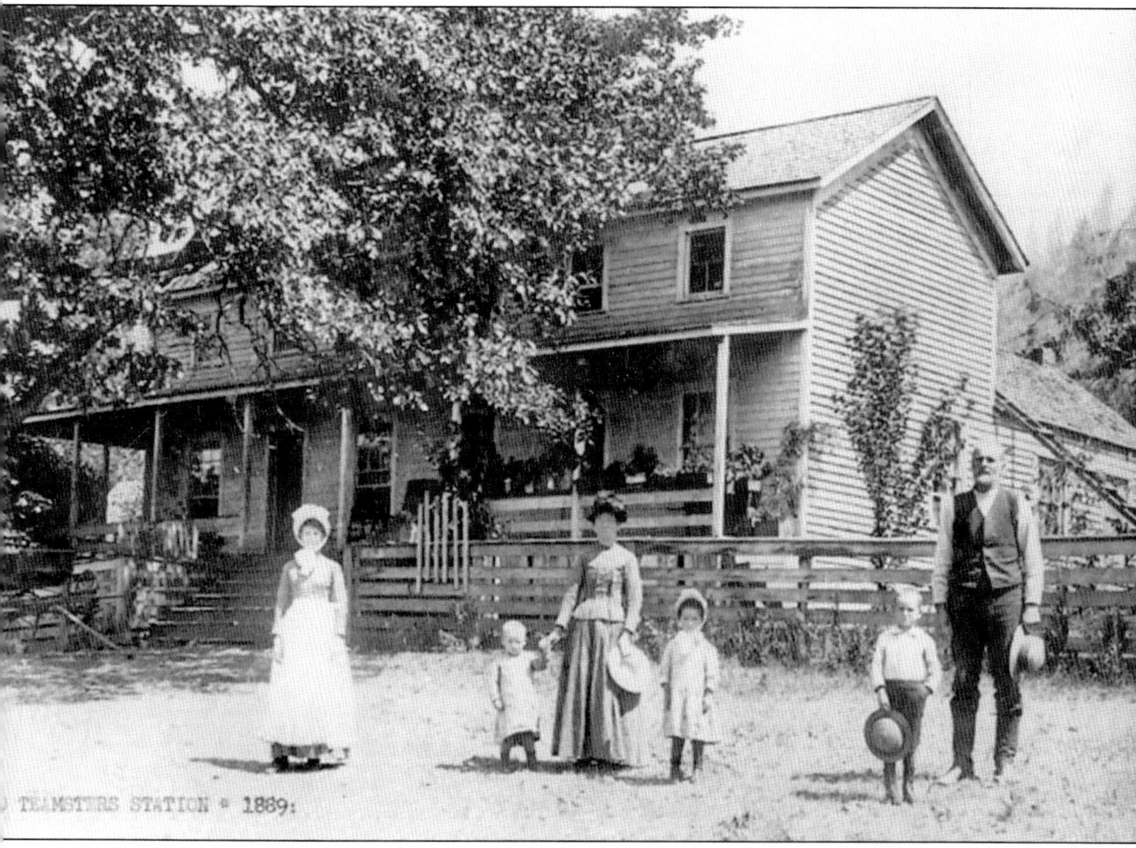

A Teamsters Station is pictured here in 1889. This served as a place for stagecoach passengers to get out and rest and for the stagecoach driver to switch out his horses for ones that were well-rested. The driver and passengers could enjoy a hot meal at a local hotel and stay overnight if they were not pressed for time.

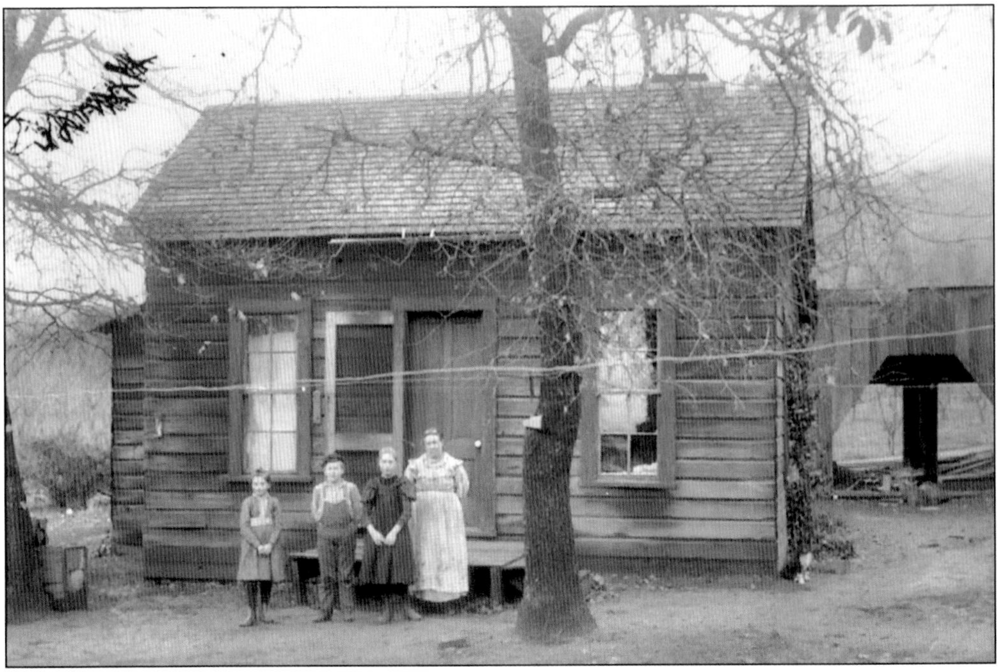

As soon as the pioneers reached Oregon, they had to build shelters and plant crops before winter began. Most of the cabins were rudimentary, and those who had left behind nice homes were disappointed to learn they would be living with dirt floors and only a piece of canvas for a window covering. As time went by and the settlers began to accrue prosperity, they were able to add to their cabins or build a new house on their land. They added windows and floors for comfort.

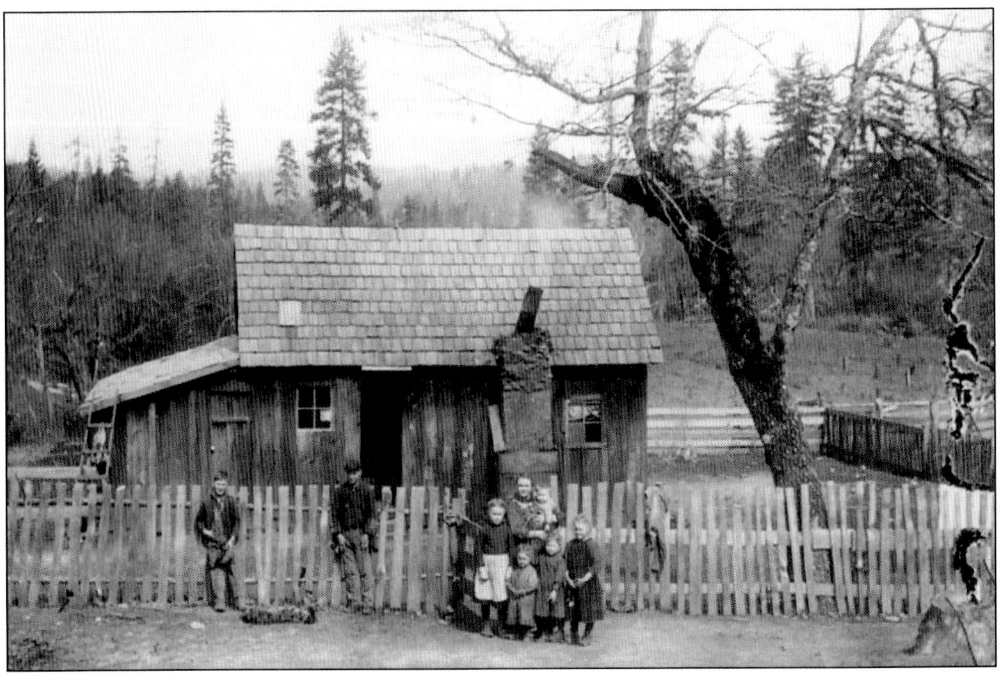

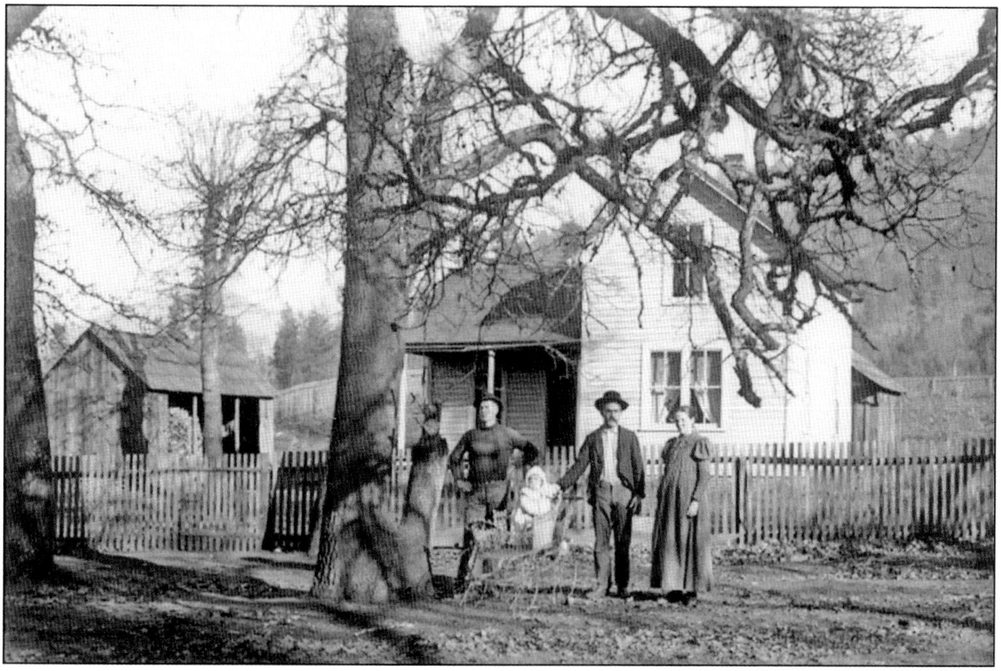

In 1900, properties similar to these were advertised for sale in Josephine County. One advertisement from the *Rogue River Courier* reads: "80 acres on Williams Creek, three miles from post office, 20 miles from Grants Pass. Half under cultivation, four acre orchard, good water rights, two barns, comfortable house, good outbuildings, plenty of berries. 25 acre standing timber, good for lumber. New saw mill nearby. Will exchange for town property or sell for $1200."

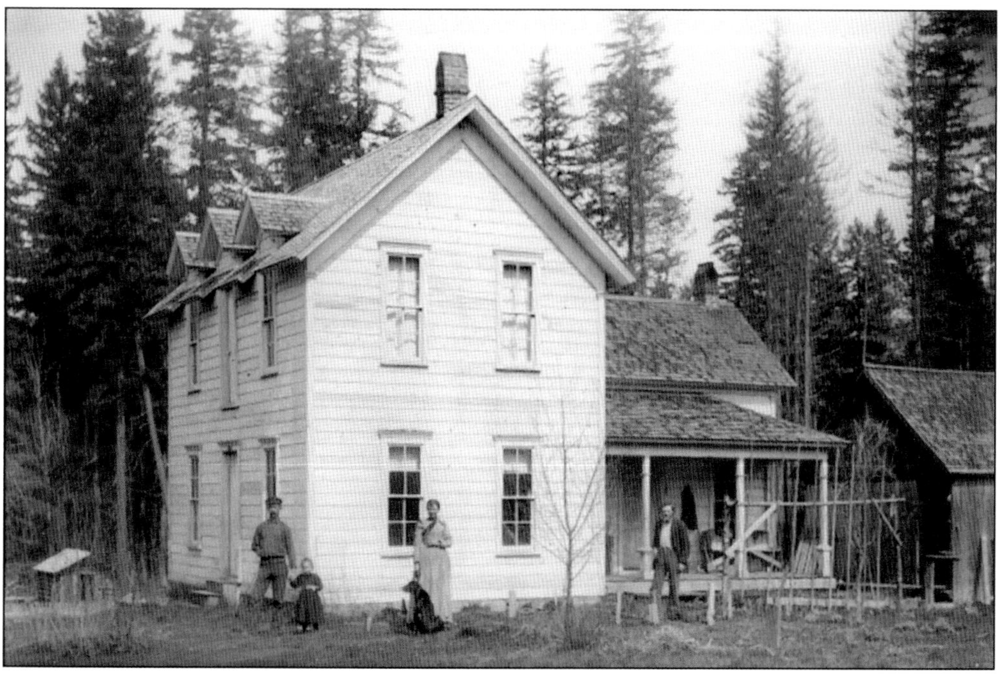

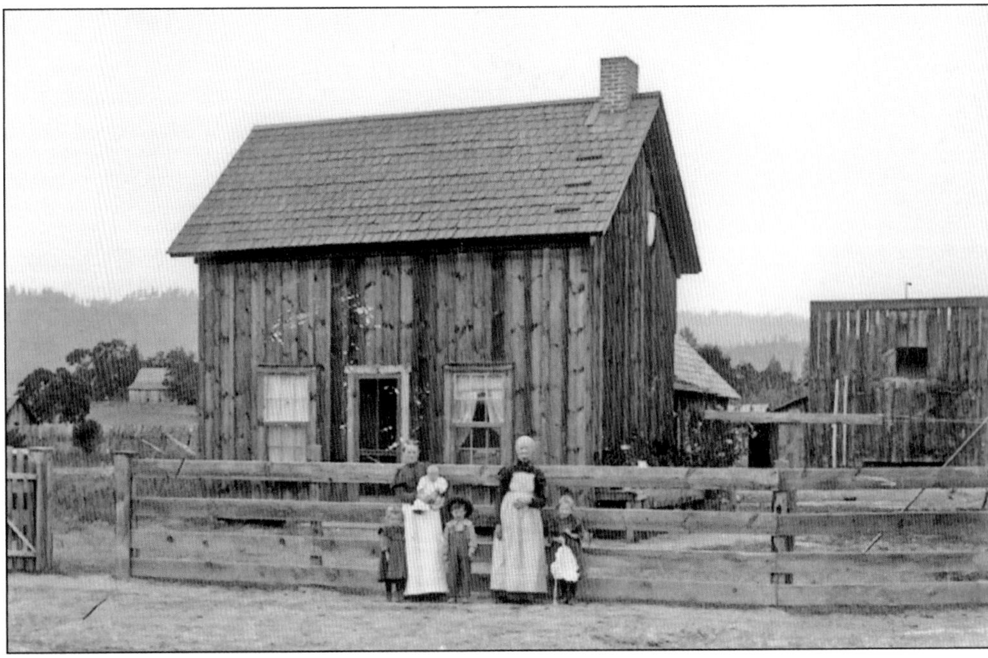

A 1906 advertisement in the *Rogue River Courier* reads: "For sale: 88 acres river bottom land, four-and-a half miles down Rogue River from Grants Pass on county road known as the Turner Ranch. Two houses, one a five room frame, large barns, hop house, and all outbuildings. Nine acres hop, 10 acres orchard. Winter apples. For sale at $3500."

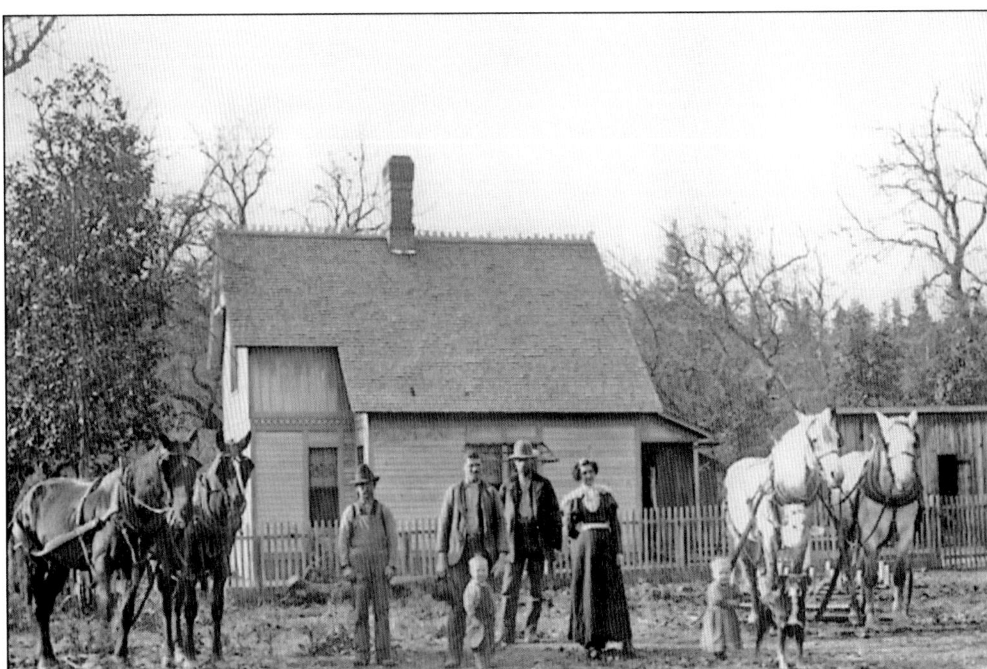

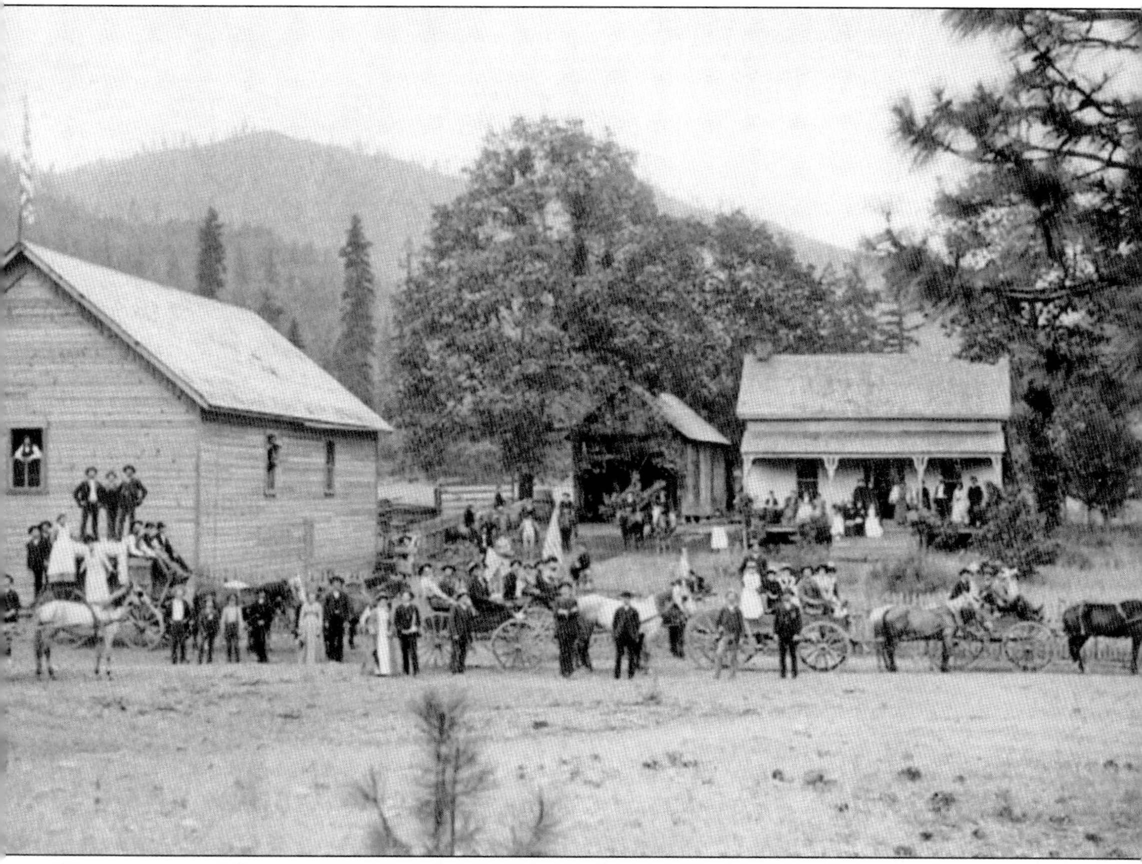

These country folks are getting ready to celebrate the Fourth of July. A.E. Voorhies, publisher of the *Rogue River Courier*, summed up his thoughts on the area's Fourth of July celebrations in 1907, writing, "We all celebrate to our own peculiar temperaments. The farmer with wife and children come into town and get sore footed wandering over the hard pavement, and the city man goes into the country where the ants get into his picnic grub and he gets beautifully stung with poison oak. It is anything for a change."

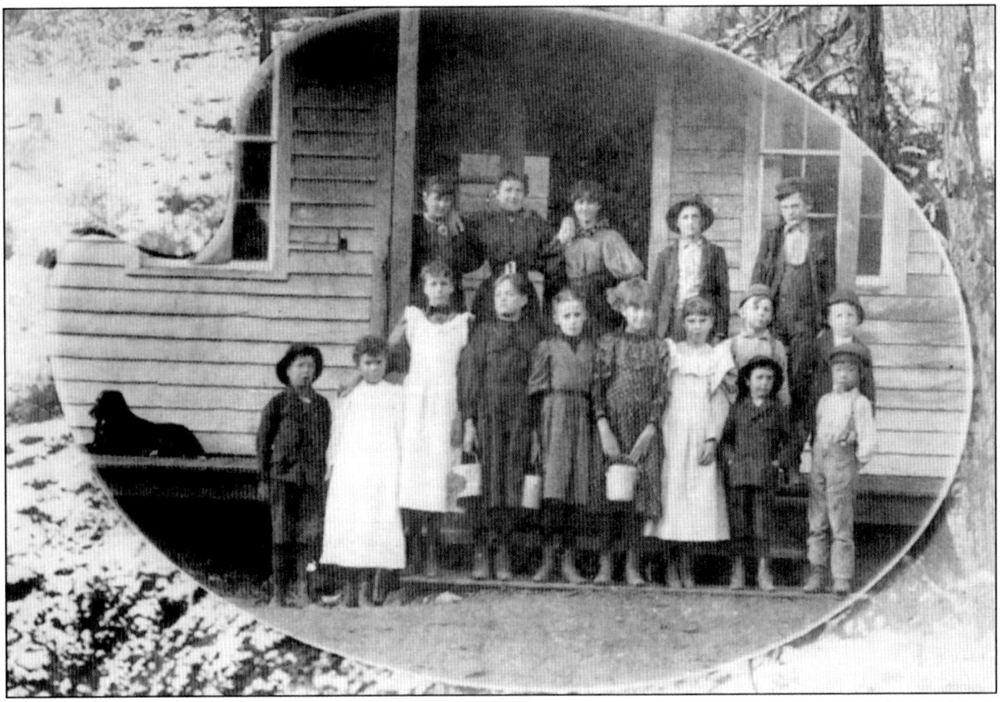

In 1886, there were 23 organized school districts in Josephine County, with 558 male students and 536 female students. In 1886, the average monthly wage for a male teacher was $39.75 per month, and the average monthly wage for a female teacher was $24.50.

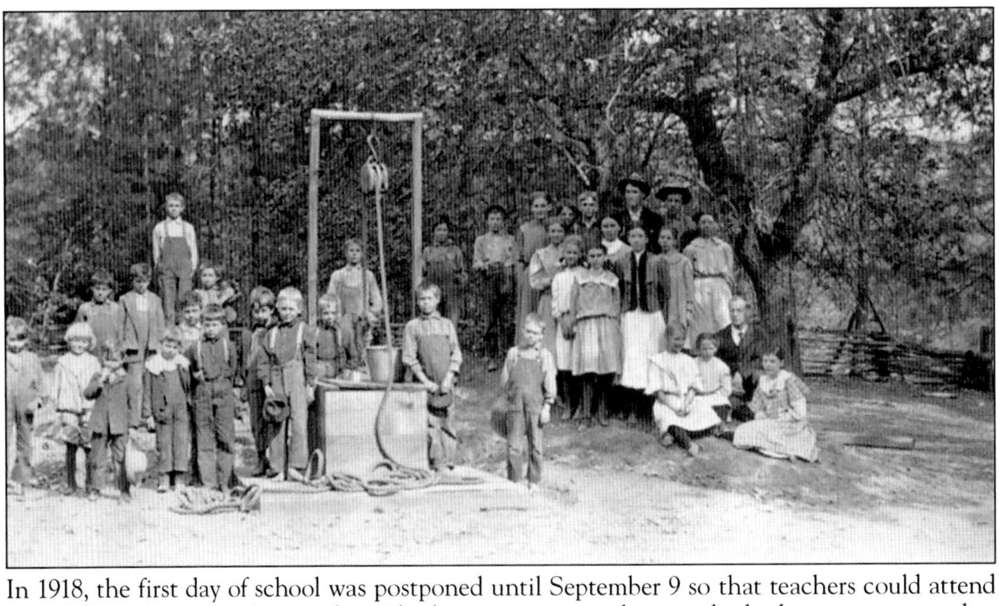

In 1918, the first day of school was postponed until September 9 so that teachers could attend a workshop that was advertised as "the best instruction that can be had in art, water color, crayon, sketching, clay modeling, and painting. Certainly no up-to-date teacher will lose this chance. Each teacher attending this training school is required by law to pay an enrollment fee of one dollar."

Two

Life in the City

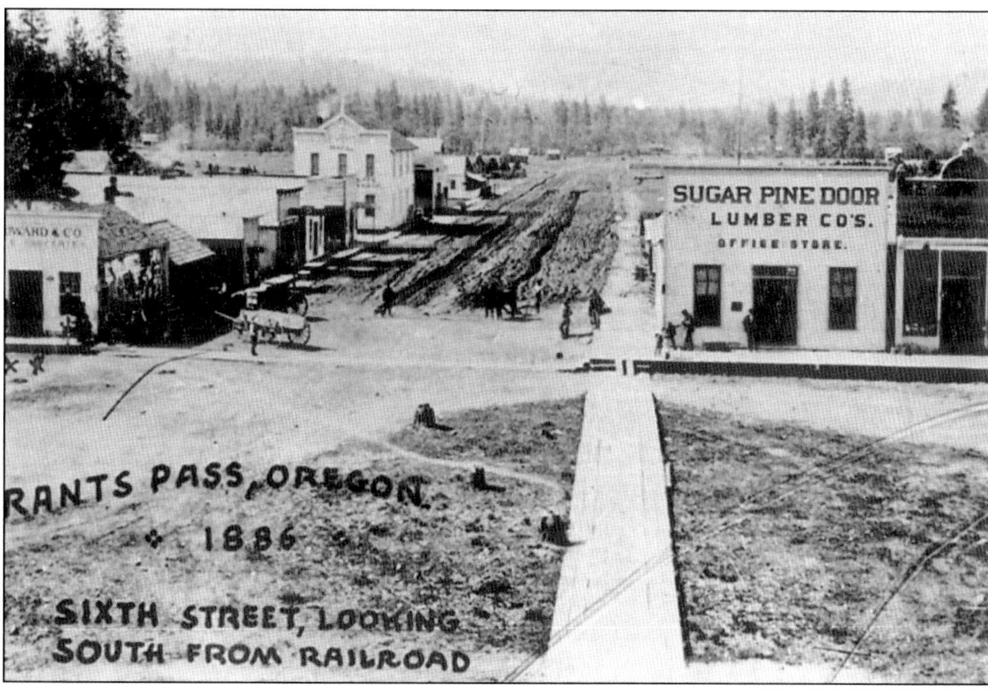

This 1886 photograph shows the following businesses on Sixth Street in Grants Pass: the Sugar Pine Door Lumber Company's office store, John W. Howard General Merchandise, O.H. Starr's Tin Shop, Hale's Undertaking, Sherer's Hardware, and Dr. W.F. Kremer's Drug Store. Tree stumps remain in the foreground. The streets had recently been plowed, and wooden sidewalks were placed in front of the businesses.

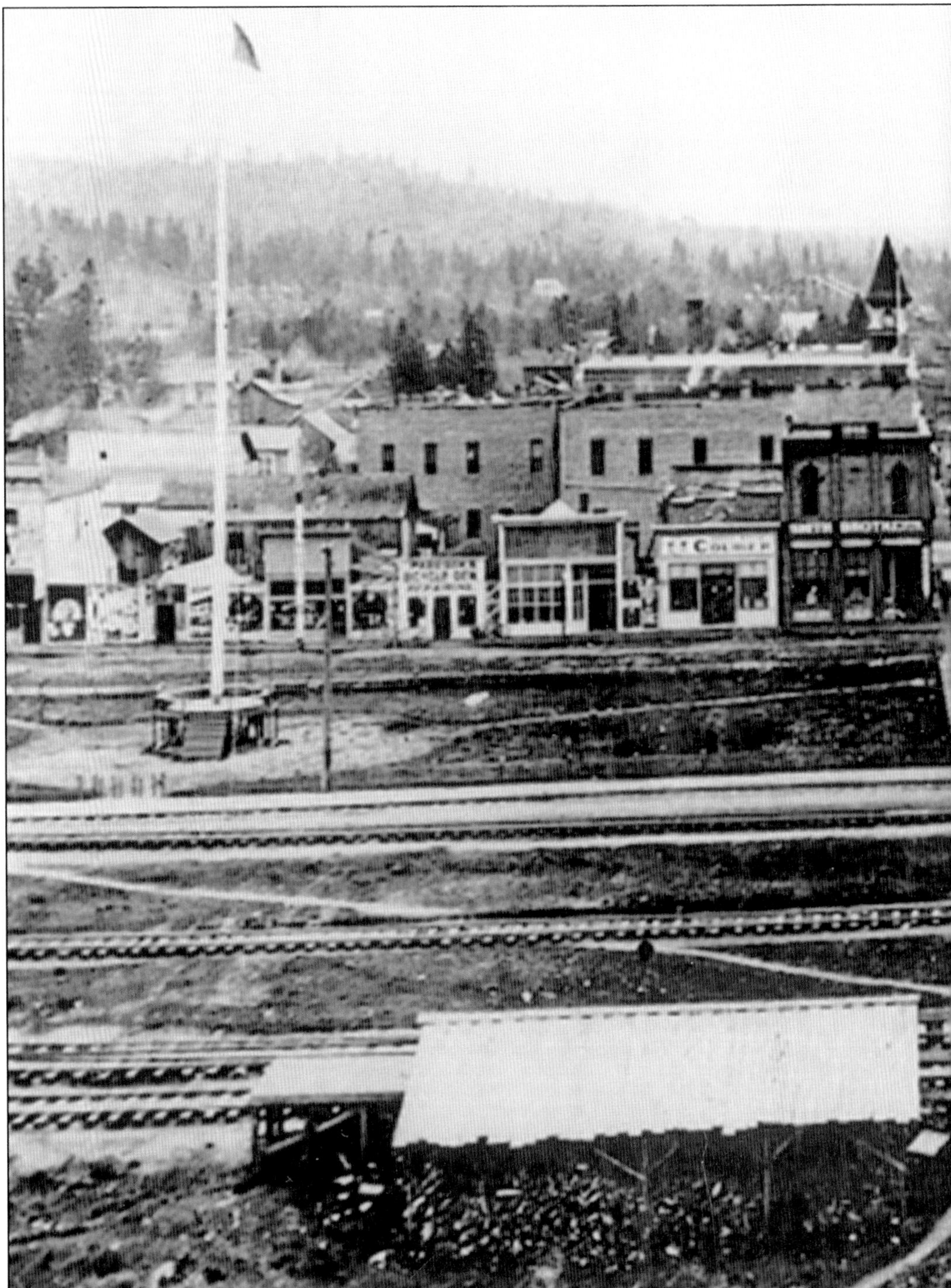

In this photograph, the city of Grants Pass is starting to take shape. The California & Oregon Railroad depot is in the foreground at right, with the railroad park across the street (where the flagpole stands). Just days after the city of Grants Pass was incorporated on March 7, 1887, the

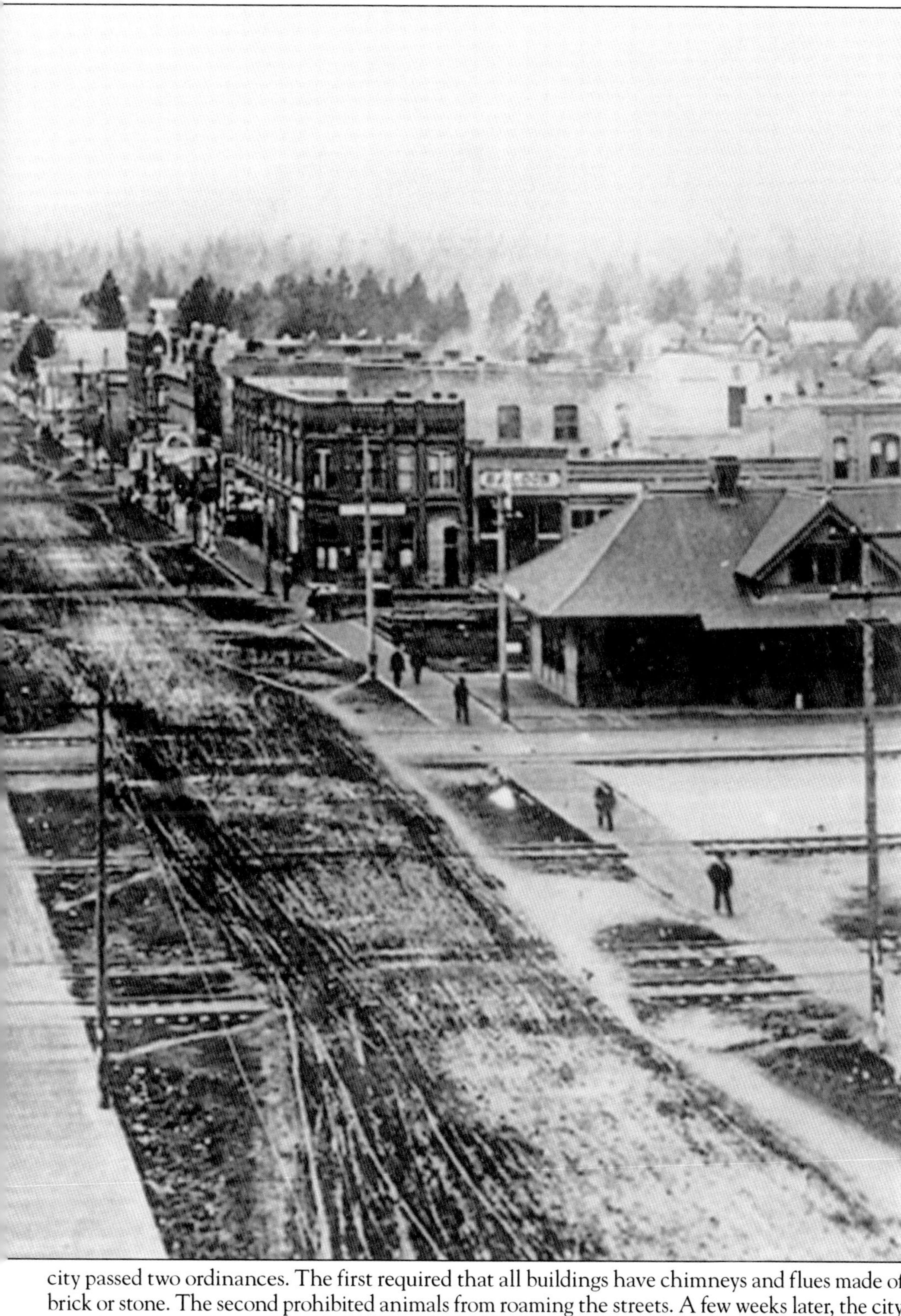

city passed two ordinances. The first required that all buildings have chimneys and flues made of brick or stone. The second prohibited animals from roaming the streets. A few weeks later, the city passed another ordinance stating that no businesses or occupations could be open on Sundays.

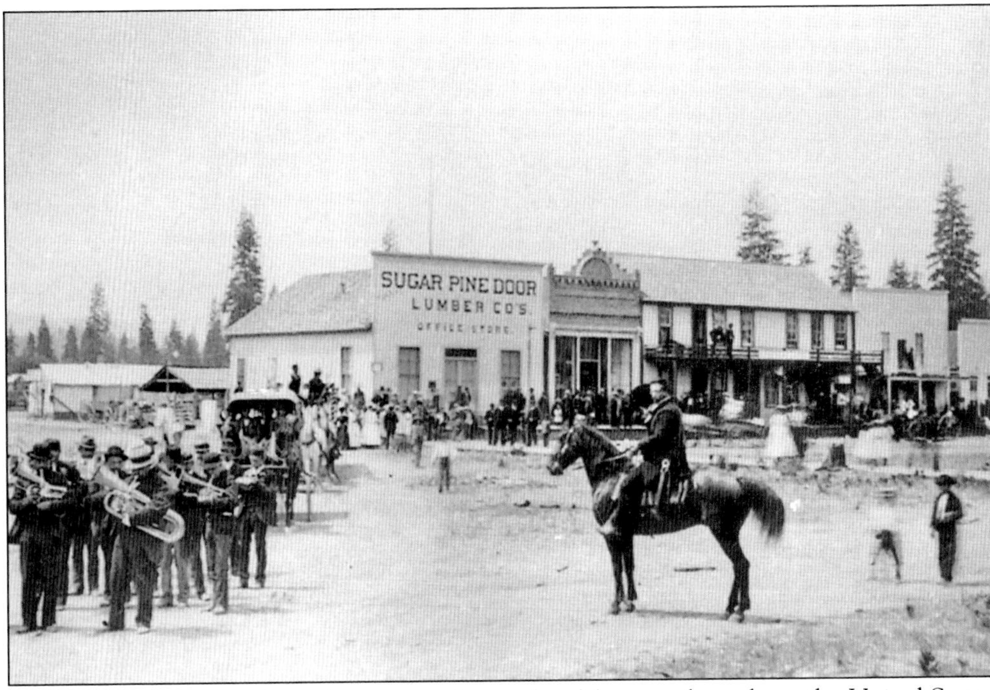

The Fourth of July has always been cause for much celebration throughout the United States, including in the newly formed city of Grants Pass.

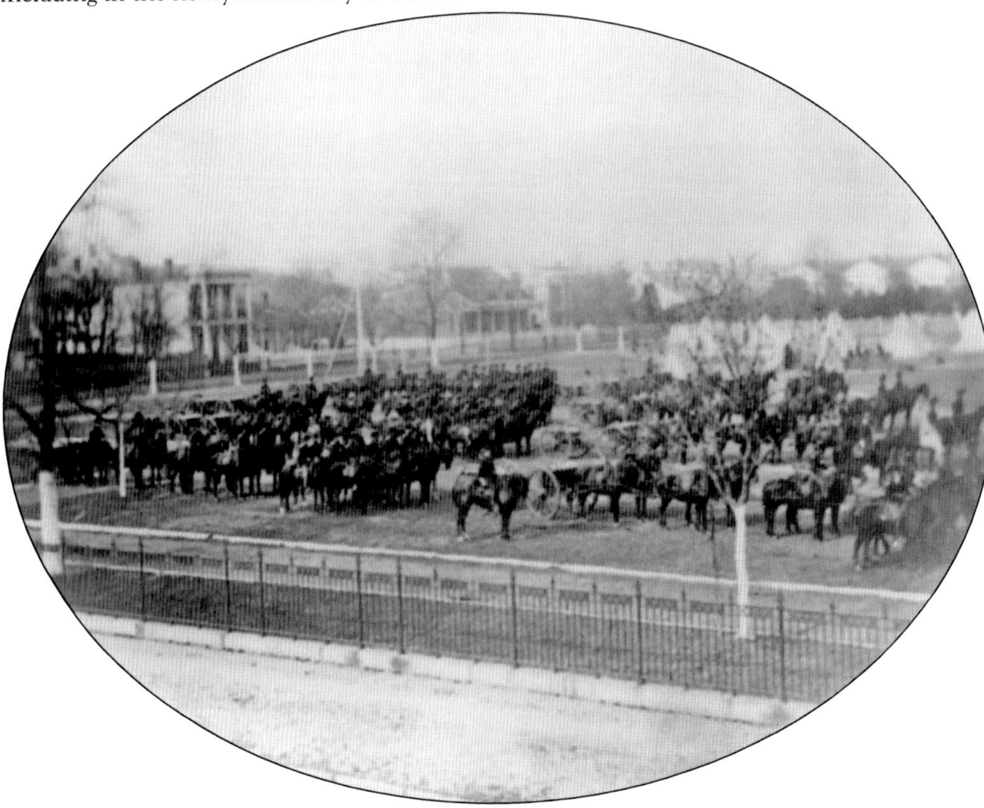

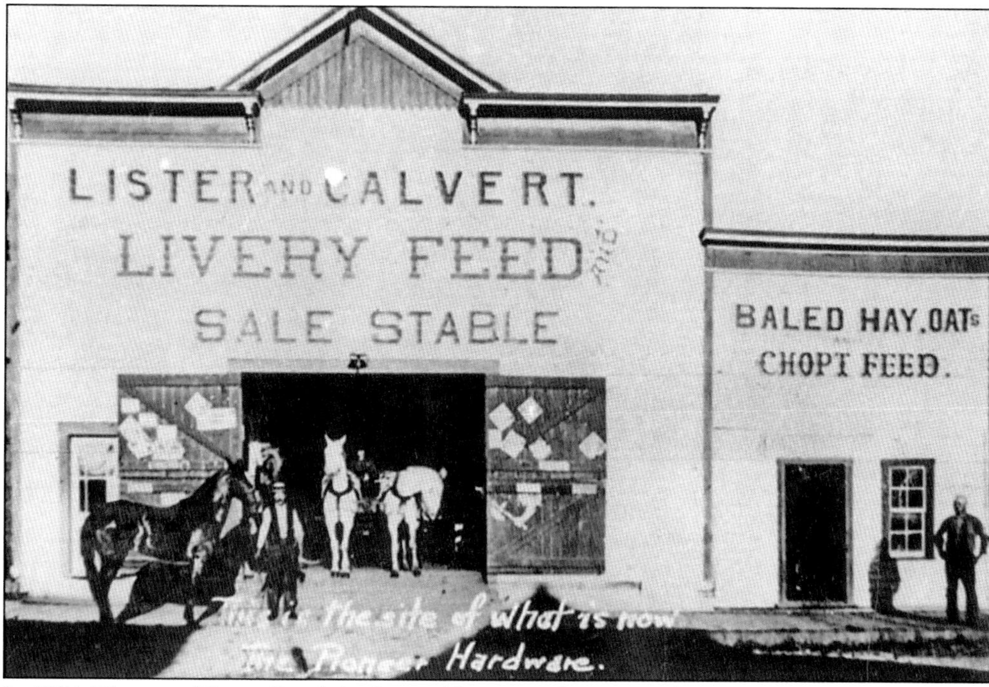

In 1884, Harry and Louis Smith built a stable on Sixth Street. They enlarged the structure over the next few years and added a blacksmith shop. In the early days, all local stagecoaches were serviced at this business. The Smiths also made rigs available for rental so that people could go out to the country. Harry eventually bought out his brother's interest in the business and brought in a man by the name of Ed Lister. In 1889, Harry sold his interest in the business to Lee Calvert, and it became known as Lister and Calvert. They operated the business until 1903, when Calvert moved to Klamath County to raise stock. The building sat vacant until 1910, when it was torn down to make room for a two-story brick building.

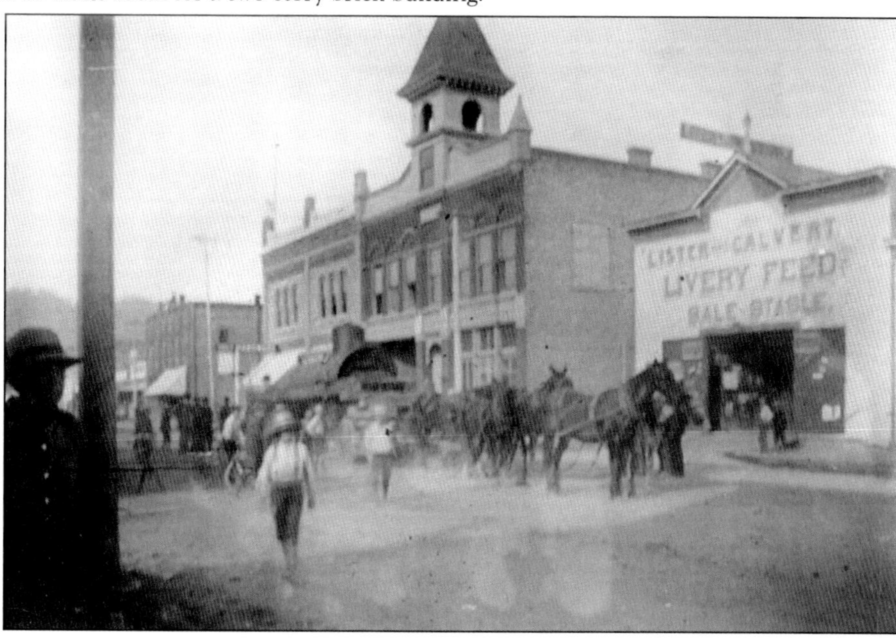

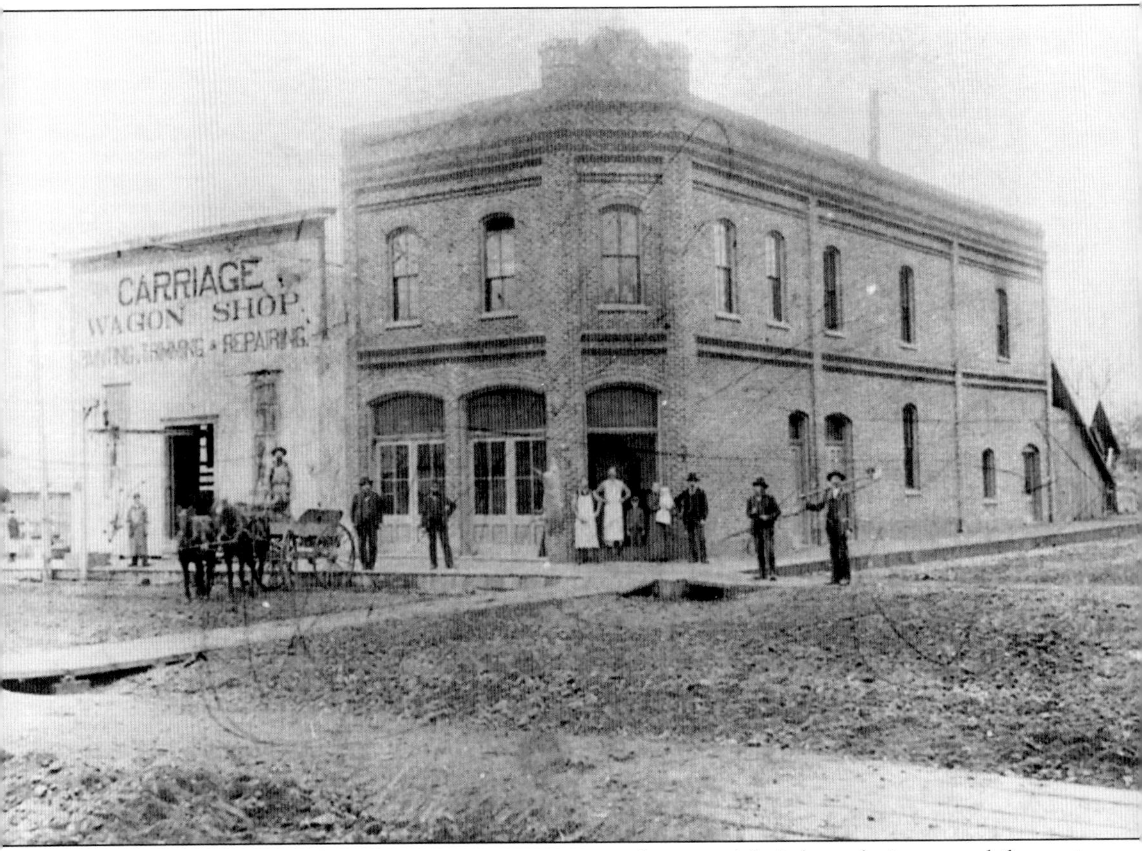

Carriage and wagon shops were an important part of pioneer life. Like today's automobile repair shops, carriage and wagon shops took care of problems.

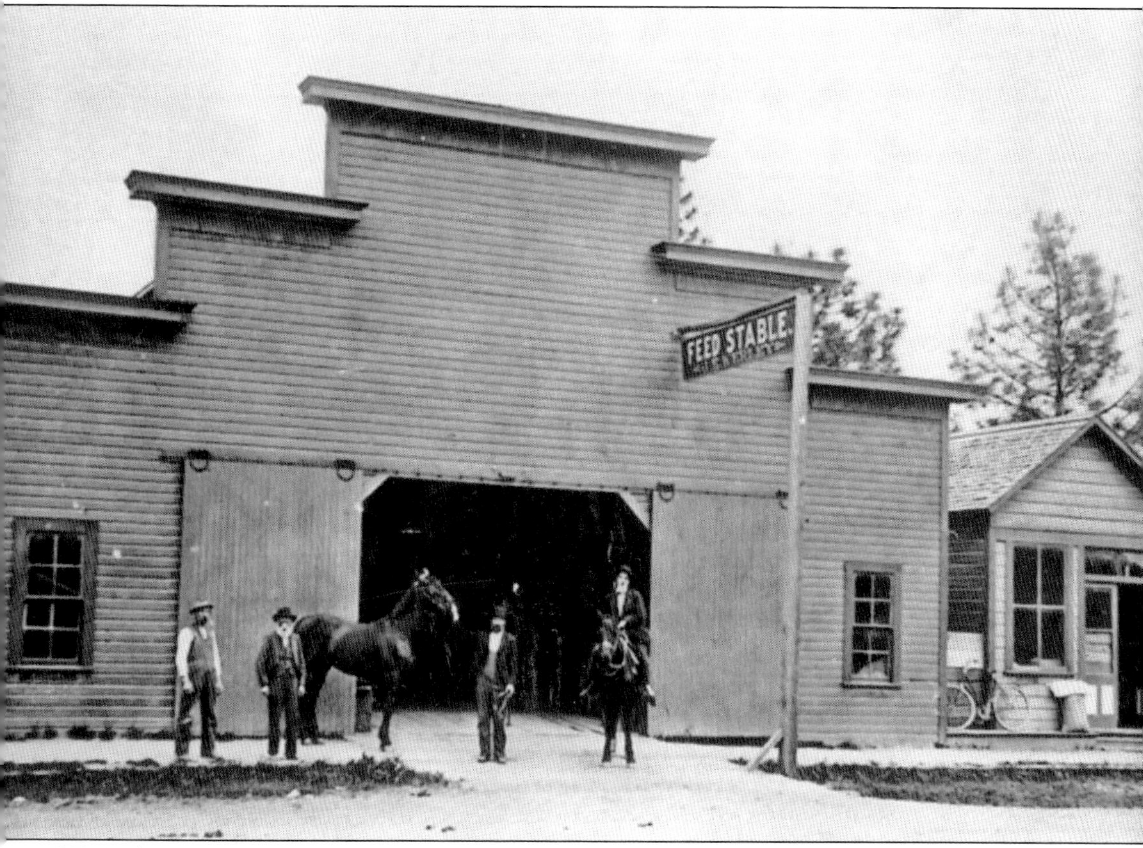

J.E. Kerley is pictured in front of his stables on Sixth Street. Kerley advertised in the *Rogue River Courier*, "Room under cover for 150 horses and 40 wagons. Box stalls. Corral for loose stock. Only the best hay, clean grain, and alfalfa fed. Rolled barley and other grain. No diseased horses allowed. Pure running water and trough cleaned every day."

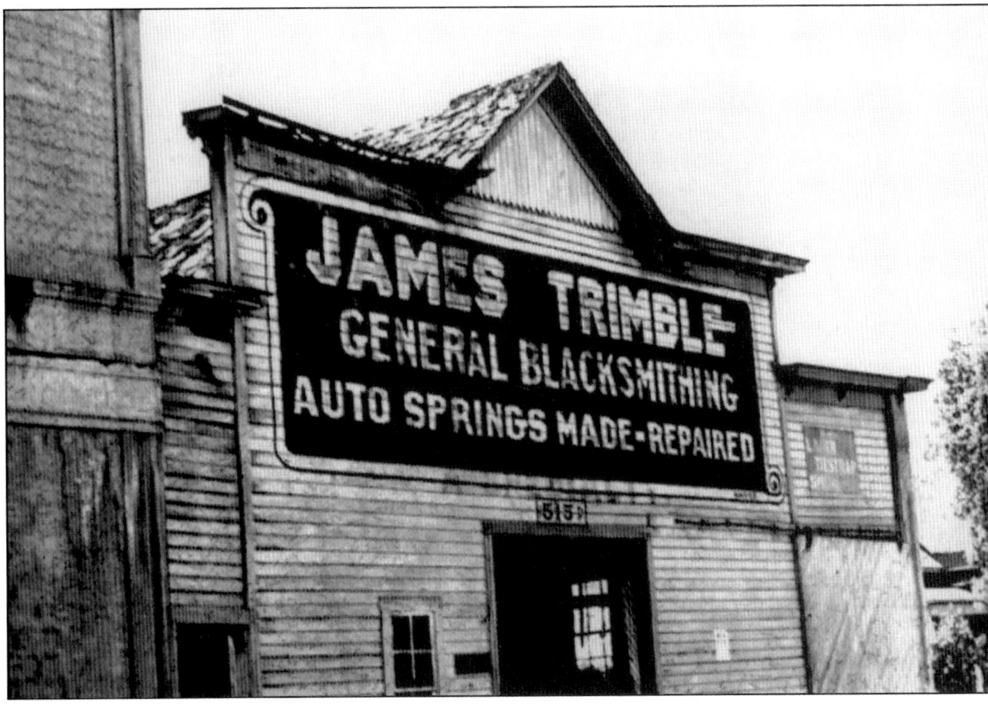

James Trimble's shop provided horseshoeing, blacksmithing, and wagon repairs. In later years, the shop became known as Trimble and Cook, which boasted of using the finest hickory wood available for wagon repairs. In 1904, the shop added a cold tire setter and advertised, "Have your tires shrunk cold. No danger of marring the paint on the wheels. No delay. The entire job requires but 30 minutes. We handle all sizes up to 4 and 7/8ths. Come and see our new machine work."

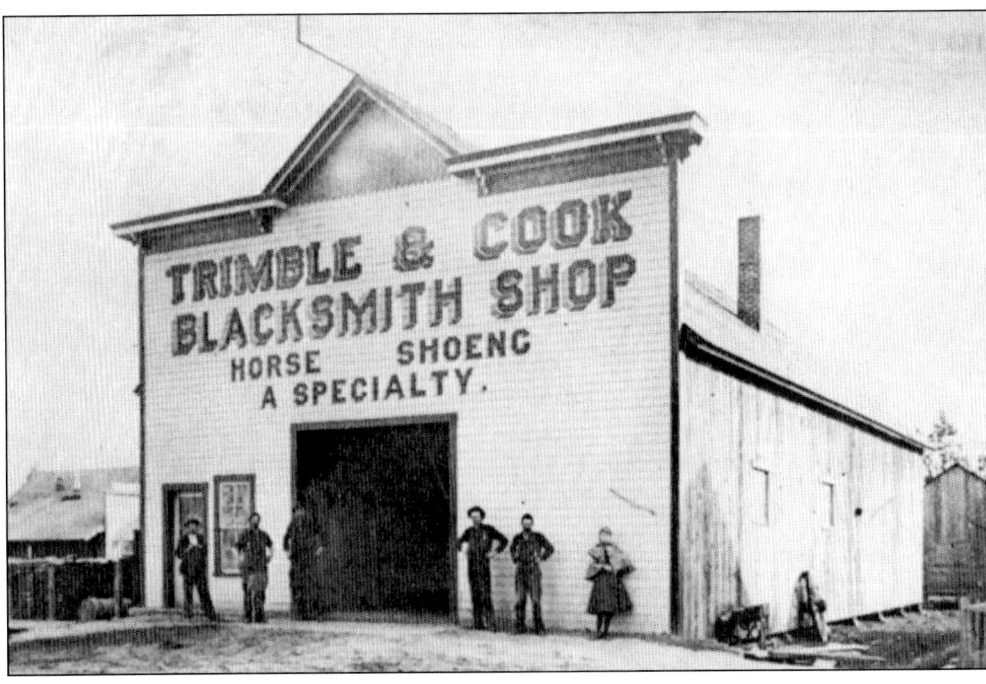

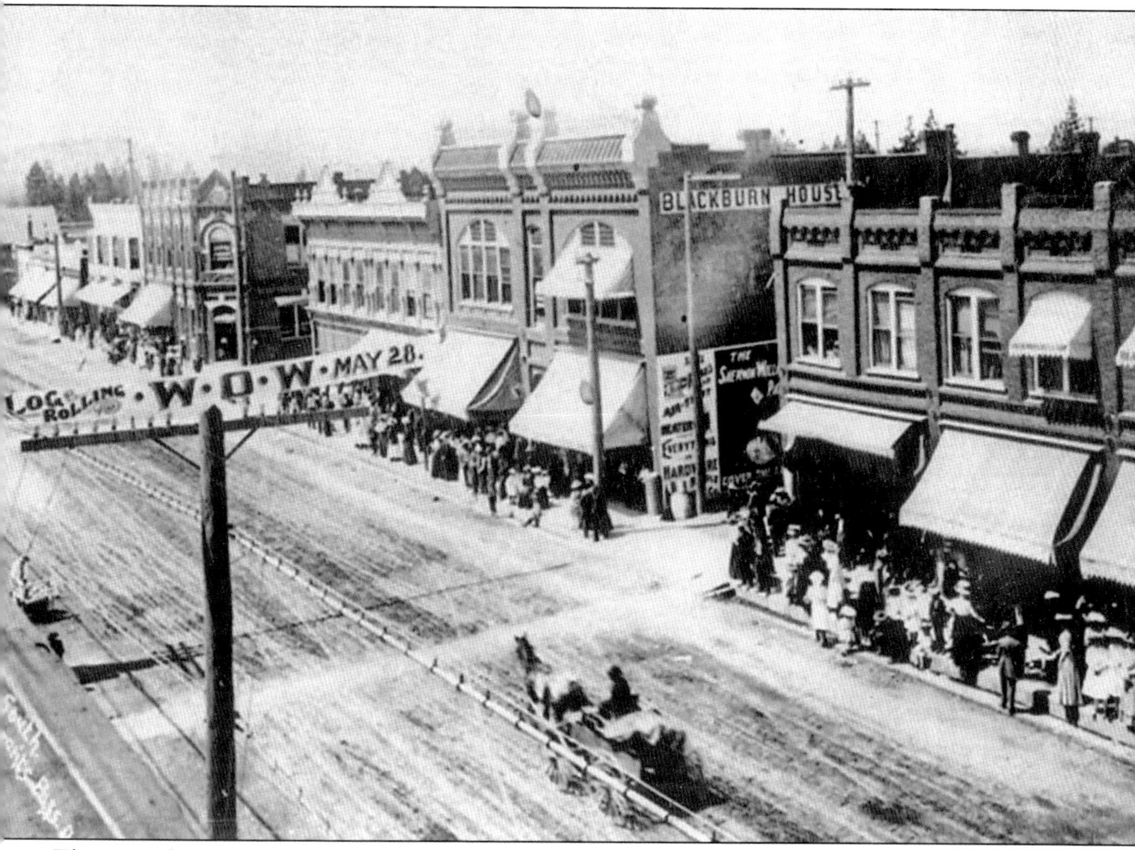

This sign advertises a log-rolling competition hosted by Woodmen of the World (WOW). Previously, Grants Pass had won the hosting duties by default after Ashland decided they could not win the tug-of-war contest. The competition event spanned multiple days and featured games, speeches, and dedications. In addition to hanging banners such as the one shown here, WOW also advertised the event by asking the public, "Are you on for the big log rolling May 28 of the Double You, Oh! Double You?"

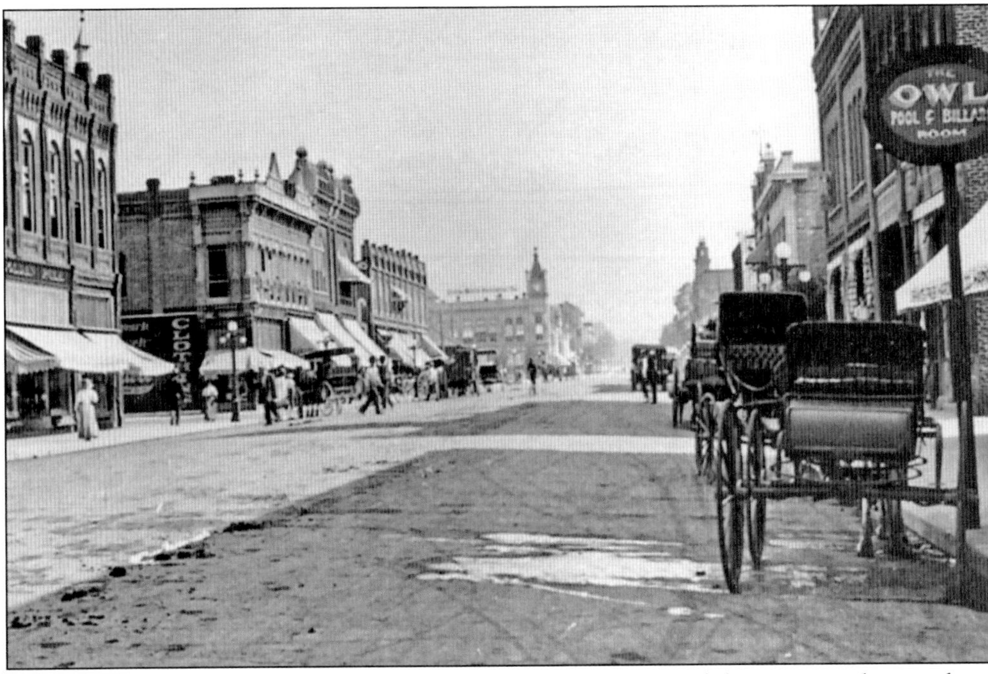

The downtown streets in Grants Pass were not paved until 1910. Until that time, residents endured thick mud in the winter and dry, dusty streets in the summer. A sprinkler wagon led by a team of horses watered down the streets in the summer. When these photographs were taken, the wooden sidewalks had been replaced and an electric lighting system had been installed. Residents were very proud of the lights, referring to them in the *Rogue River Courier* as "the crowning achievement of the municipality this year. . . . At night it presents a dazzling appearance."

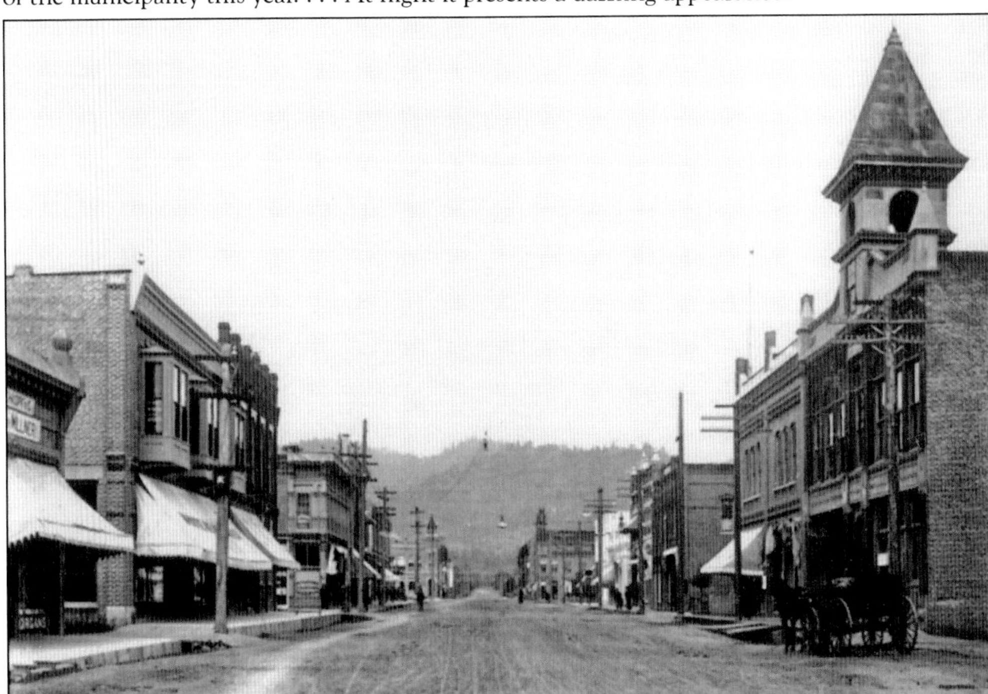

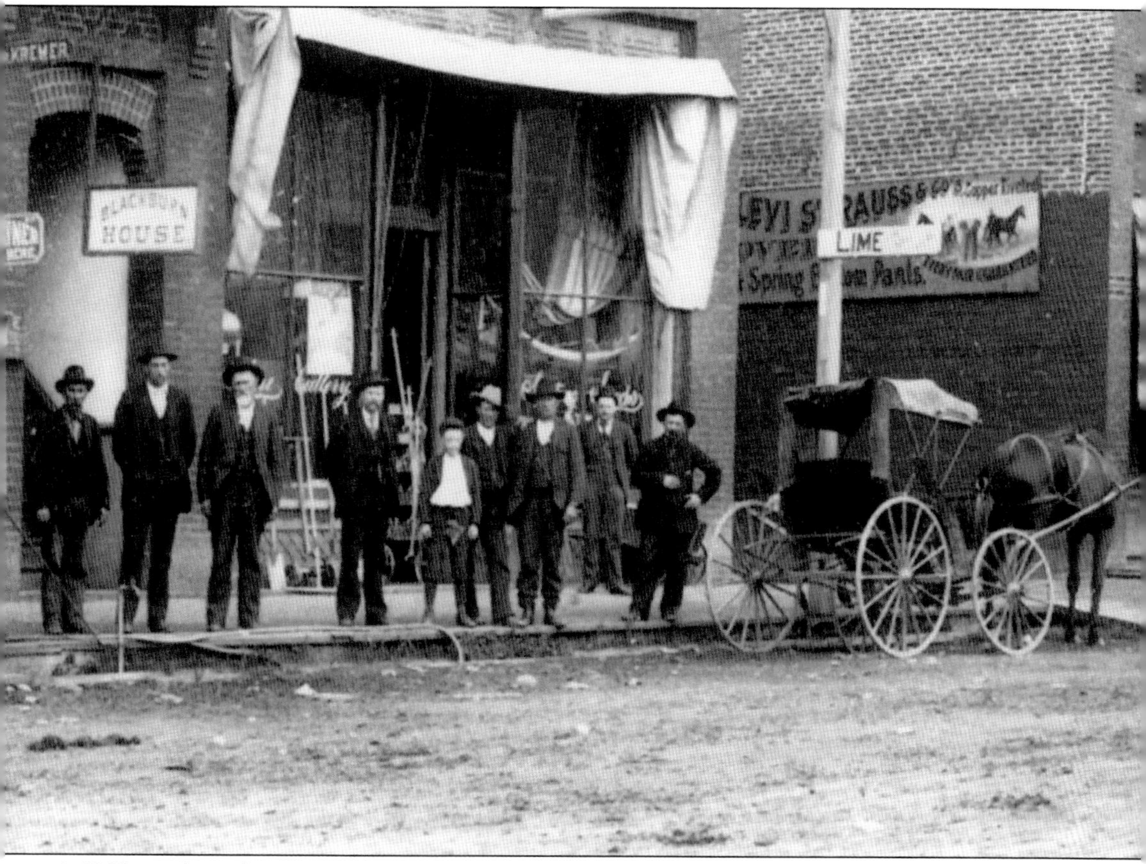

A 1905 article in the *Rogue River Courier* stated, "The free and easy way that some of the residents of Grants Pass have of using the streets and sidewalks for garbage dumps, for old shoes, chicken feathers, old cans and boxes, should be unpopular by heavy fines, as should also the habit that some of the business men have of sweeping the refuse from their stores and offices into the street."

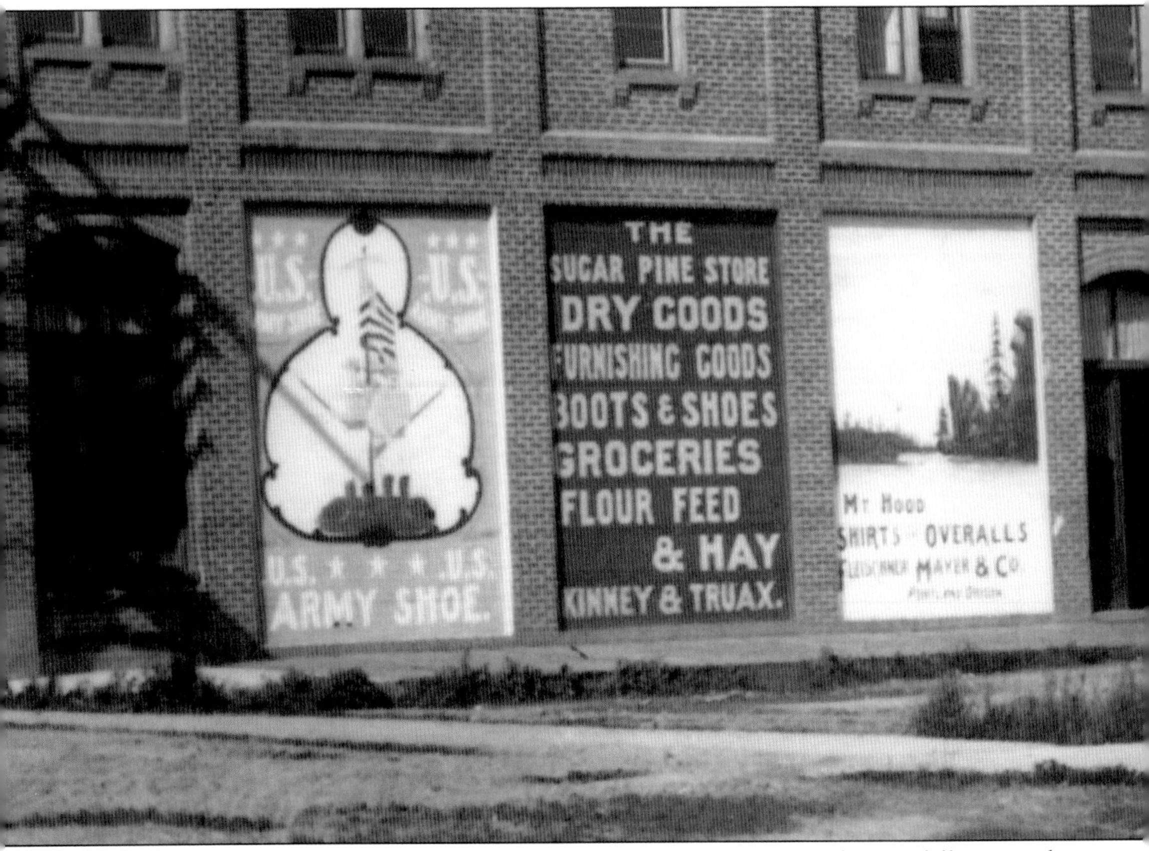

These graphics on the side of the Grants Pass Opera House were used to advertise different products or businesses. Hotels would use the graphics to list their prices and any amenities they had, such as electricity and hot and cold running water. The people who painted the graphics were known as "wall dogs" and would travel around the country painting advertisements.

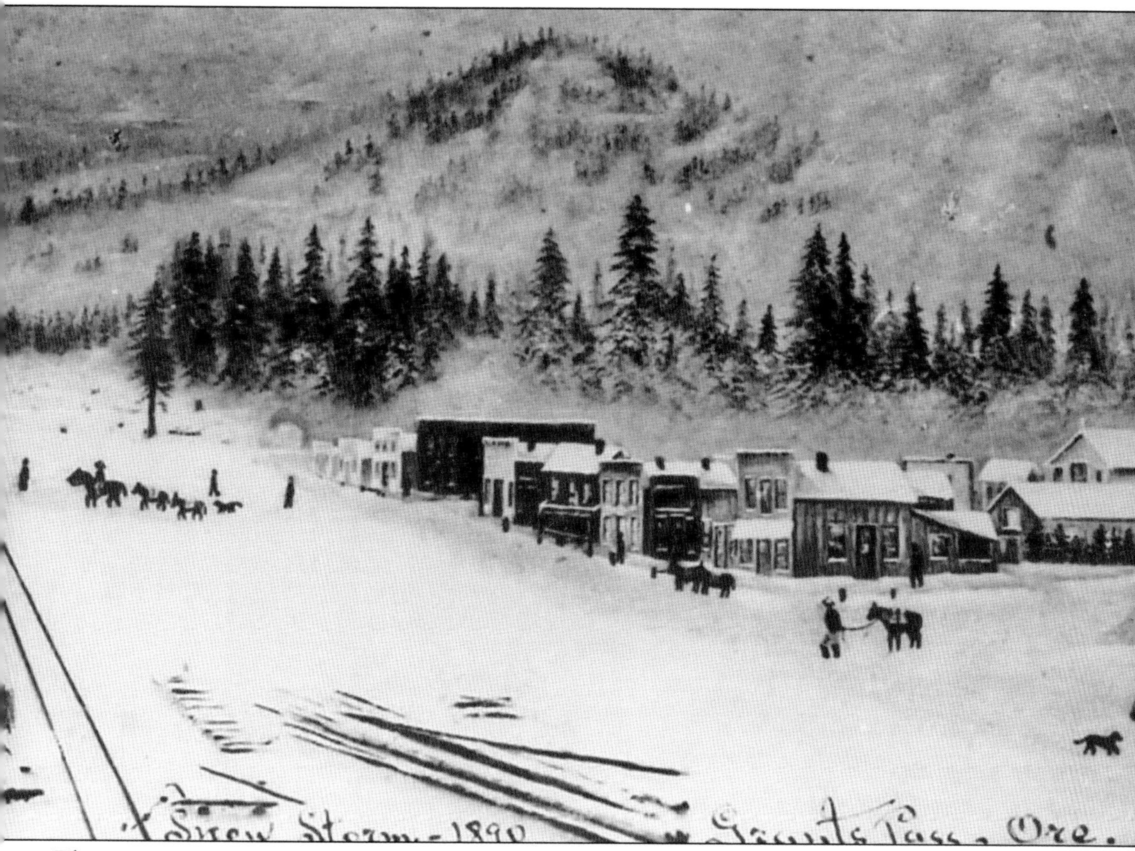

This is an artist's painting of a snowy scene in Grants Pass in 1890. Snow began to fall on Christmas Eve in 1889. No trains could get into or out of the city, which meant no supplies, mail, or newspapers. Travelers were stranded in hotels, families could not leave their homes, and food was scarce. Parts of Josephine County received four feet of snow in the nonstop weeks of snowfall. Once the snow stopped, the ensuing flooding caused destruction.

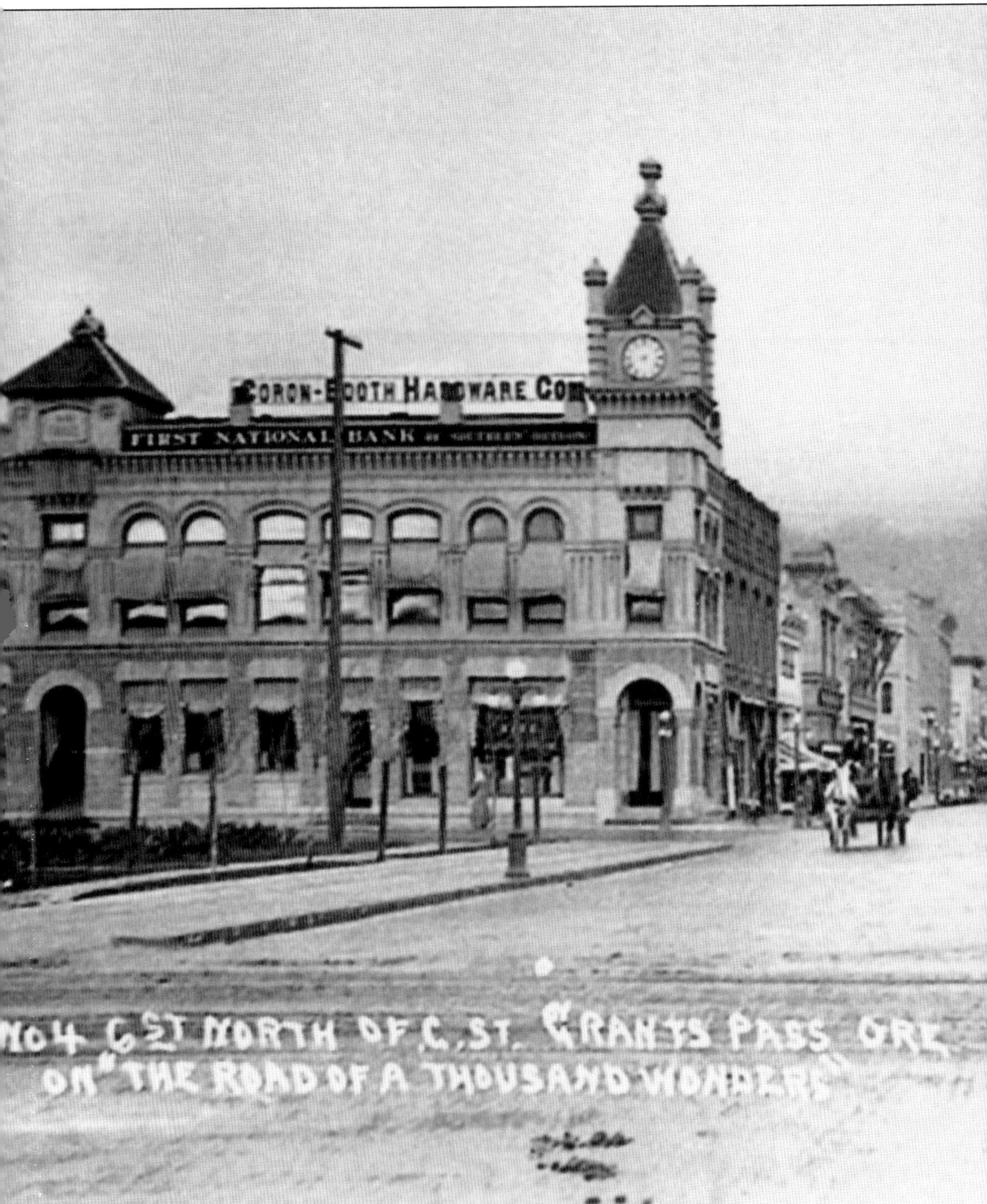

"The Road of a Thousand Wonders," printed on the bottom of this postcard, refers to U.S. Route 101 (aka the Pacific Coast Highway). In 1917, M.F. Duryea, former secretary of the Ashland Commercial Club, wrote about Route 101 in the *Rogue River Courier*: "It is indeed a 'road of a thousand wonders!' Not only does this highway traverse a country rich in scenic beauty, but leading from it are roads of the most magnificent scenic attractions of the United States. The

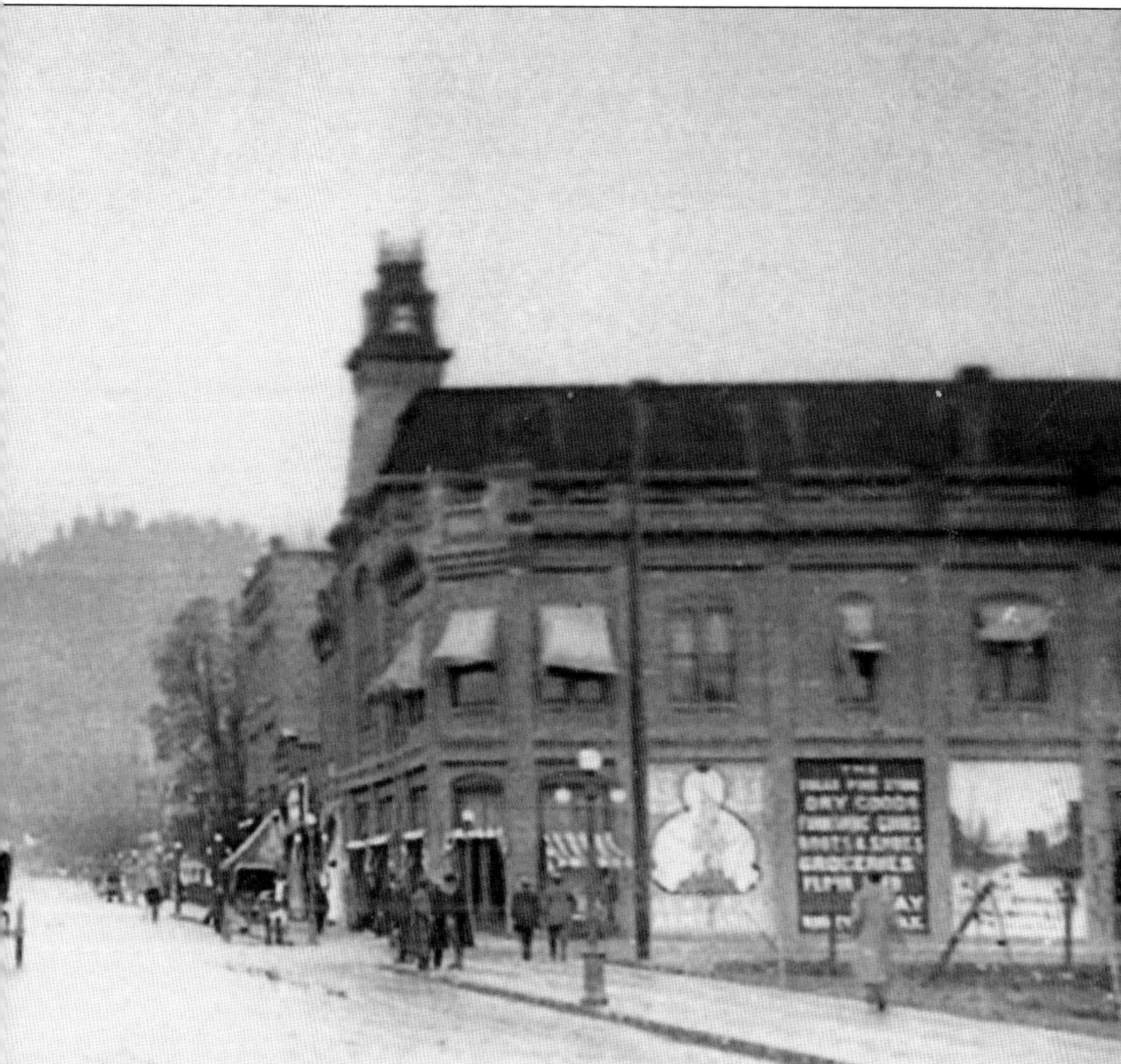

touring motorist will find much to interest him as he journeys over this main artery of travel up and down the western part of the United States, for it will lead him through fruitful valleys and thriving towns, along peaceful rivers and mountain torrents, through shadowy forests and over mountain tops and close to snow-clad peaks."

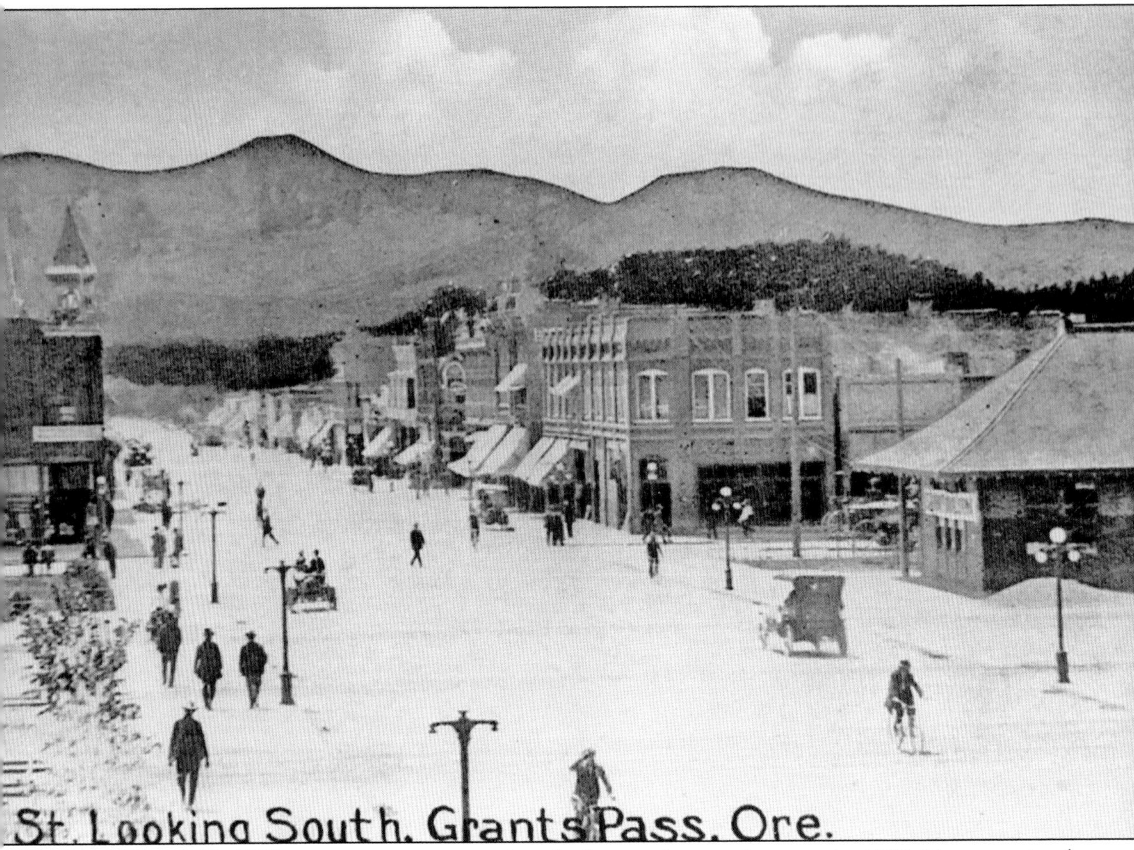

Pioneer F.A. Wilbur was very impressed with the newly paved streets in 1910. He wrote in the *Rogue River Courier*, "I came to Grants Pass when the village was in its infancy and I have seen it grow gradually. In all that time I failed to see any artificial boom. It was a steady growth. The residents of this town need not envy the seemingly booming condition of the neighboring towns. Such inflated prosperity is not lasting."

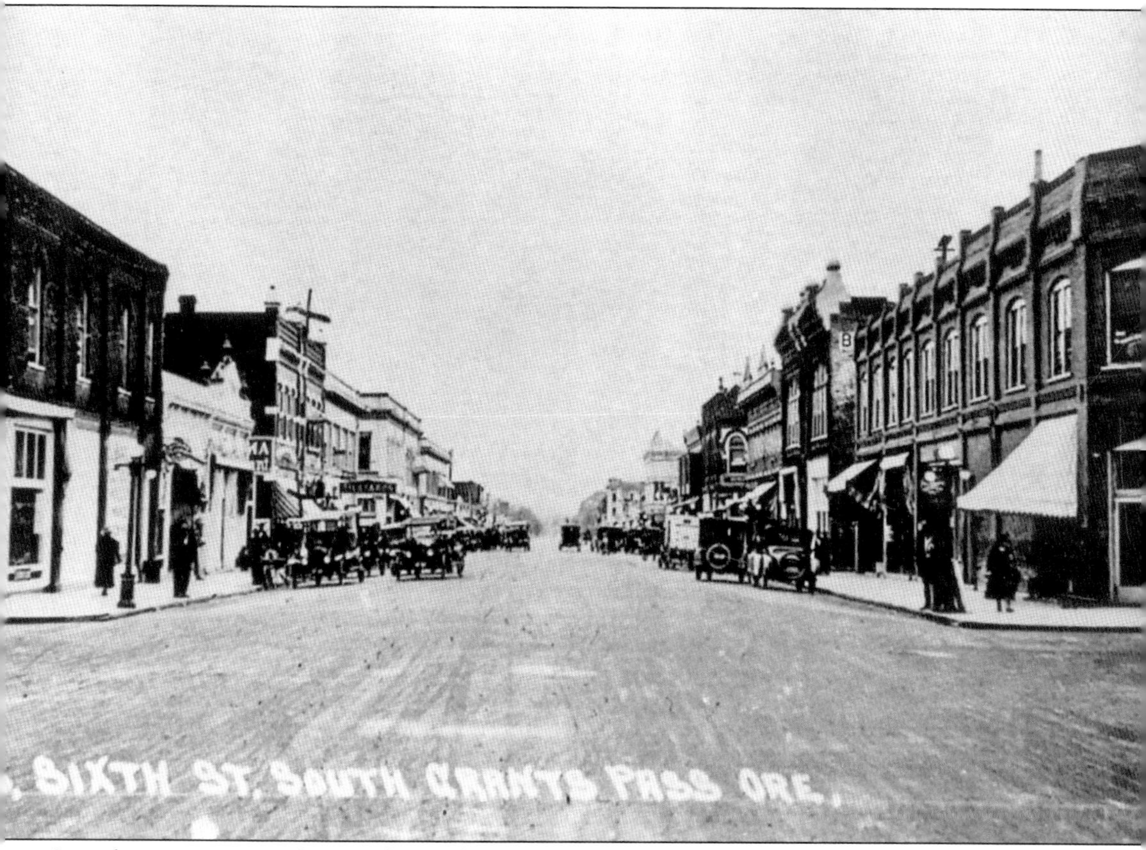

In order to receive an Oregon driver's license, one had to be at least 16 years of age, have five days of experience driving, and pay 25¢. In the beginning, there were no stop signs, lanes, or traffic laws. In 1904, there were only two automobiles in the city of Grants Pass, but by 1911, there were more than 100.

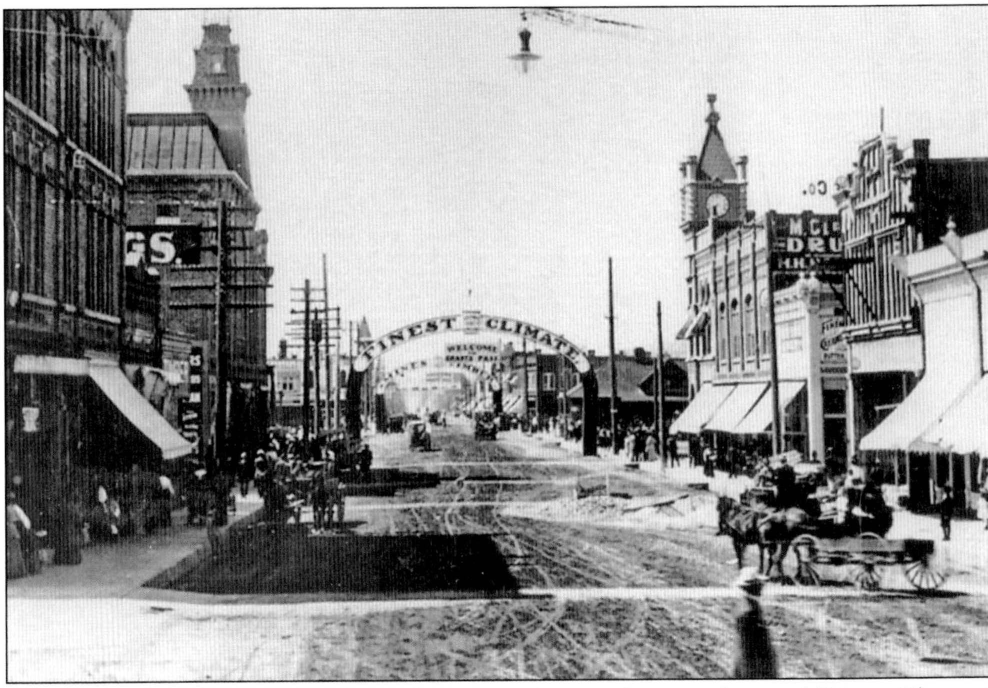

A predecessor to the "It's The Climate" sign was this wooden sign that read "Finest Climate." Beyond this sign was another wooden sign that read "Mines Timber." The last sign advertised Woodmen of the World.

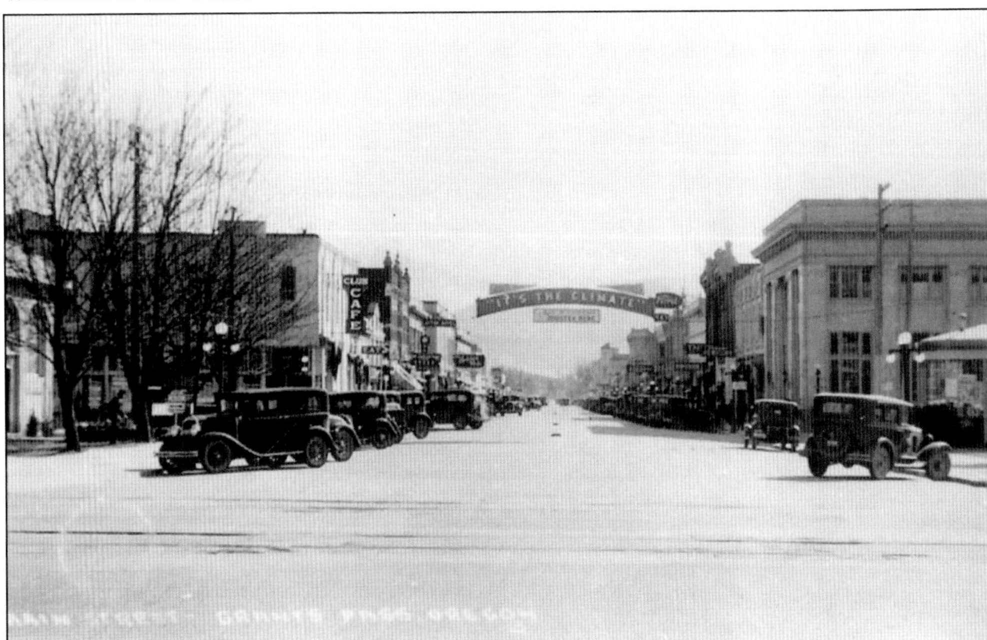

In 1919, Grants Pass began advertising with the slogan, "It's The Climate—We're Telling The World Come And Enjoy It." The original "It's The Climate" sign was hung on July 20, 1920. Two smaller signs on top of the main sign were adorned with the words "Grants Pass." Below the main sign was a smaller sign that read "Out Of State Cars Register Here."

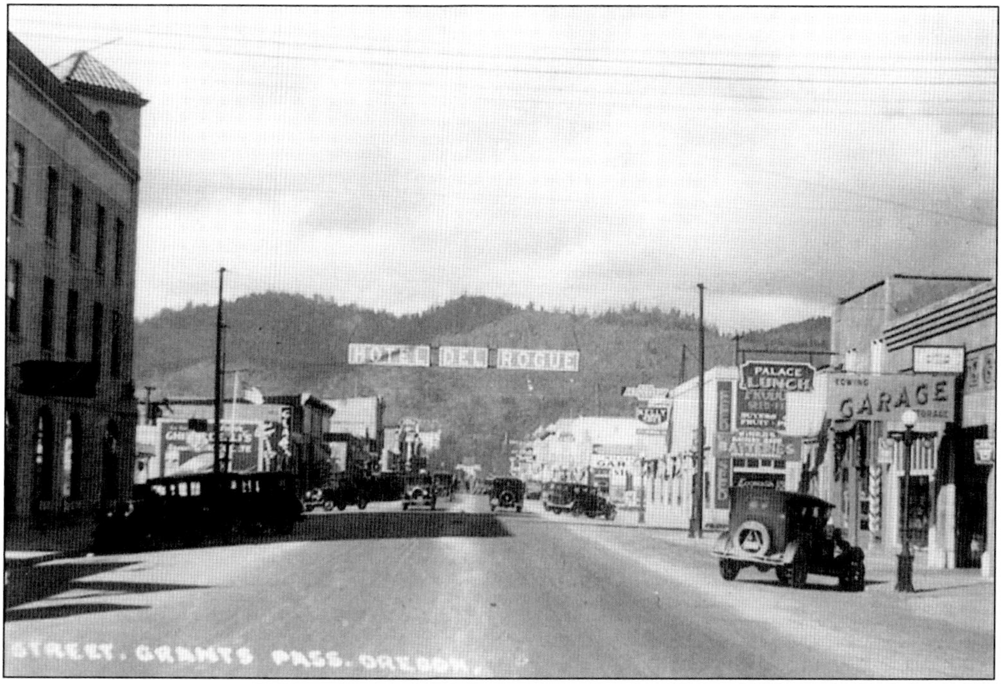

The sign hanging over Sixth Street in the above image advertises the Hotel Del Rogue. Once automobiles gained popularity in the United States, hotels had to compete with autocamps. Grants Pass had an autocamp (pictured below) with a bathhouse. The *Rogue River Courier* reported, "Tourists are making good use of the auto park, many of them taking advantage of the bathhouse privileges. Almost every night the park is well besprinkled with tourists from almost every part of the country."

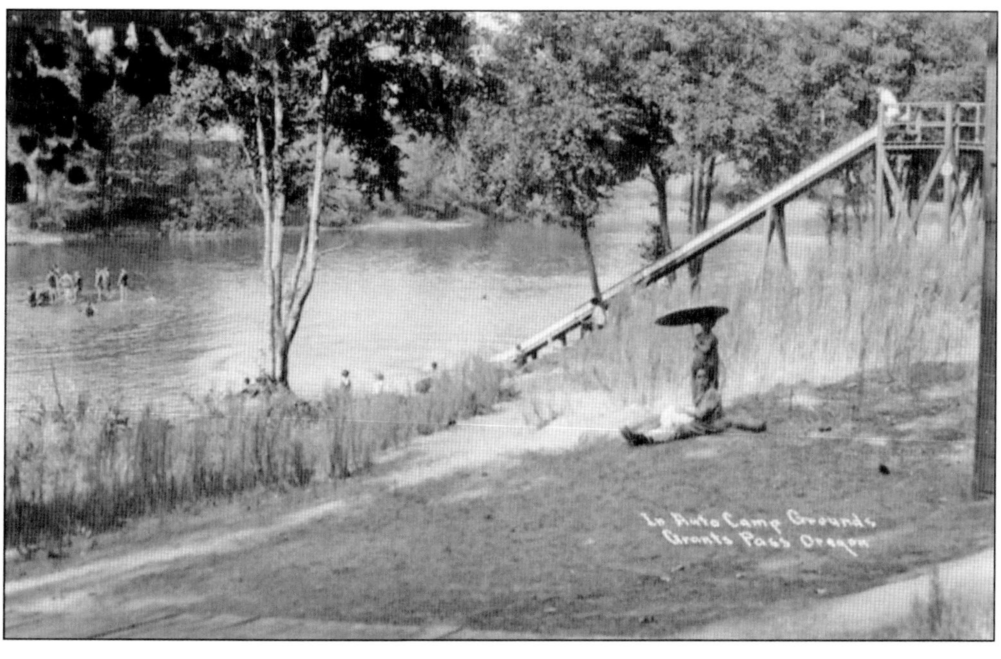

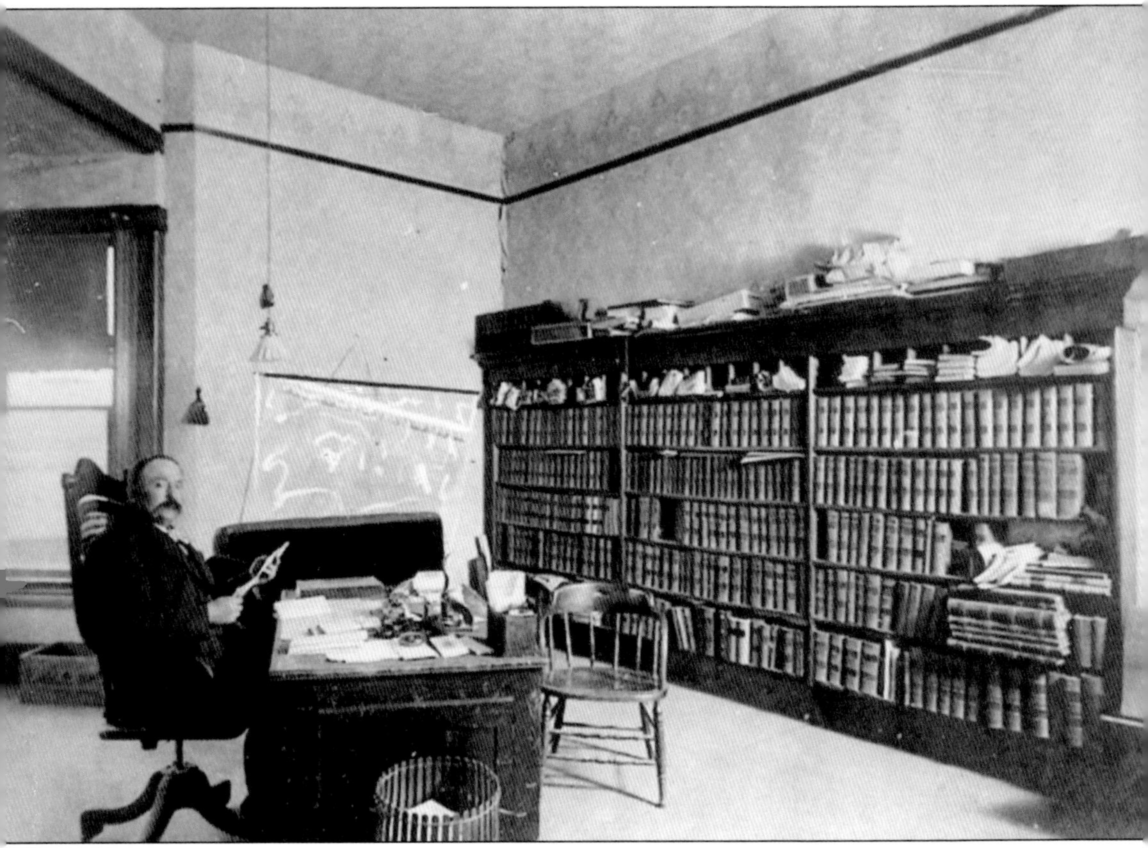

Amos Voorhies is pictured here in his office at the *Grants Pass Daily Courier.* The *Rogue River Courier,* predecessor of the *Grants Pass Daily Courier,* published its first edition on April 3, 1885, and Voorhies began his career as publisher of the newspaper on July 1, 1897. He remained publisher of the newspaper until his death in 1960, when his son (Amos Earle Voorhies) and grandson (John) took over as copublishers. In 1905, a subscription to the newspaper cost $1.50 per year or 5¢ per day. By 1919, that fee had increased to $6 per year, with an average circulation of 2,000 papers. Voorhies also operated a music shop and a photography studio within the newspaper's building.

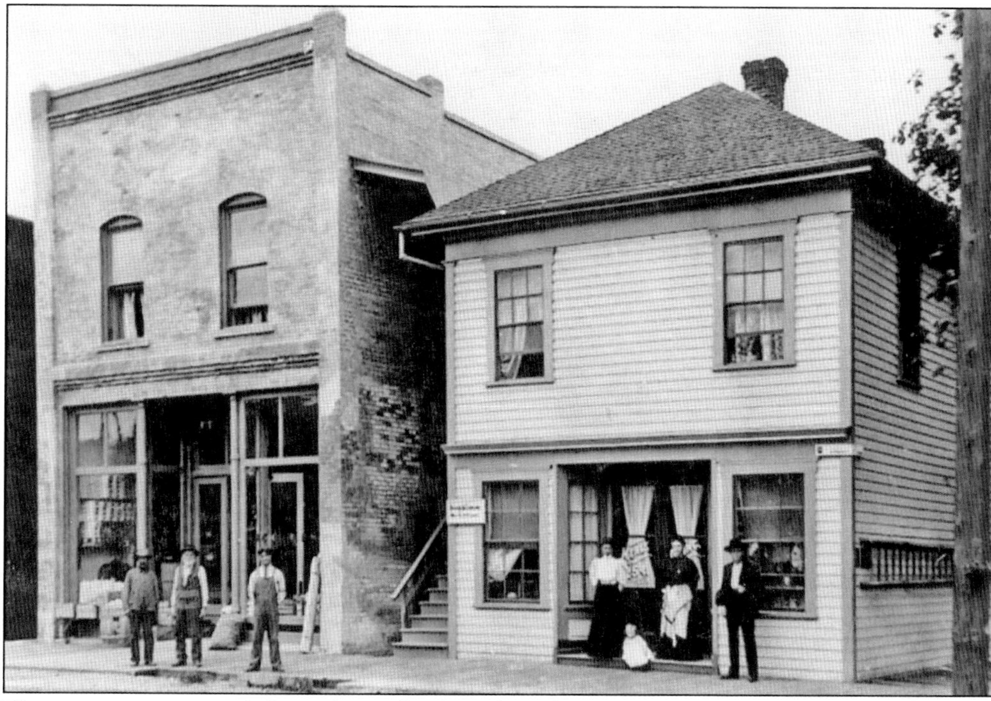

The restaurant pictured above, located at Fourth and G Streets, is advertising meals for 25¢.

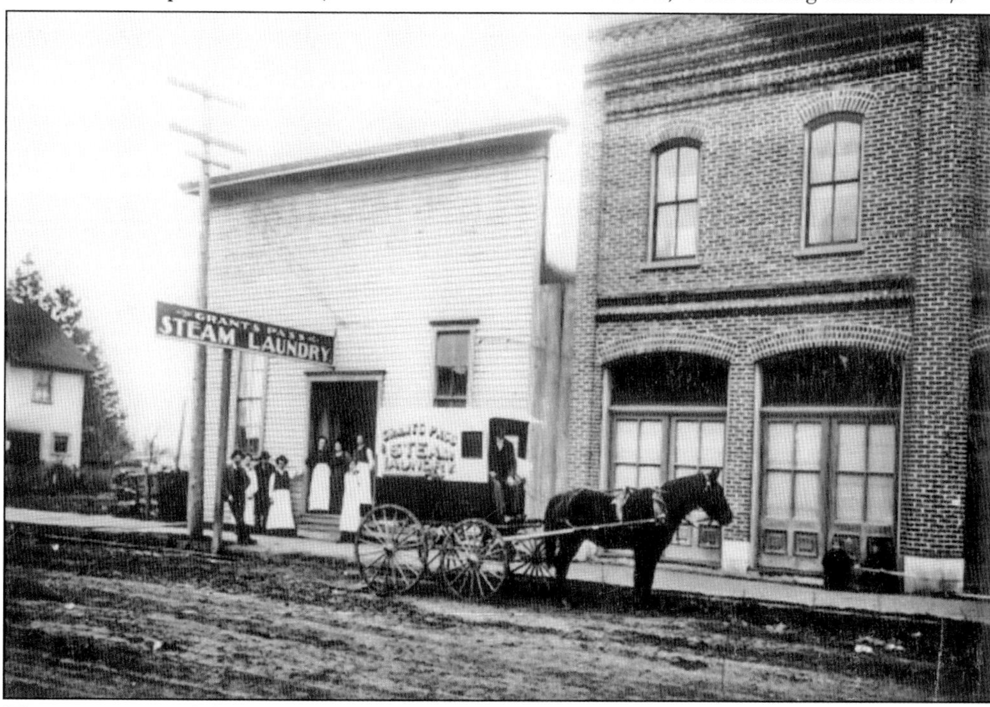

The proprietors of the Grants Pass Steam Laundry, George G. Peil and F.A. Peil, advertised in the *Rogue River Courier*, "Send your family washing to the Steam Laundry. All rough dry work twenty-five cents per dozen. Your clothes called for and delivered and all flat work that goes through the mangle washer ironed at twenty-five cents per dozen. Phone 373."

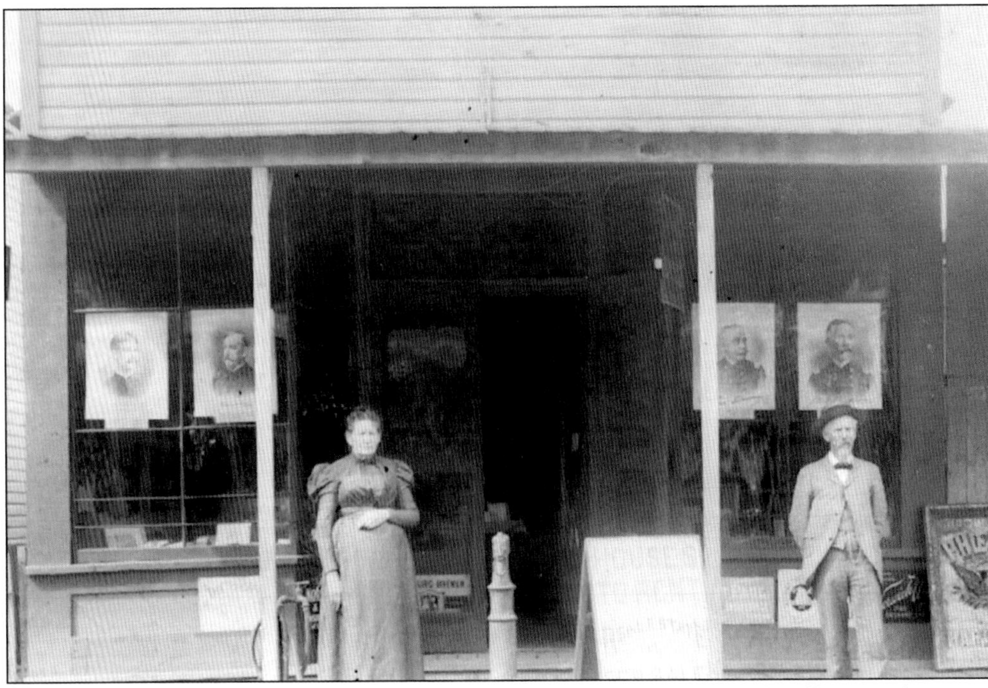

In the above photograph, an unidentified couple is standing next to a sidewalk sign advertising "Houses To Rent, Real Estate For Sale." In 1917, there were many houses for rent in Grants Pass. One advertisement in the *Rogue River Courier* read, "Six room modern house 305 C Street, opposite school house. $10 month." Another featured a "three room house and fine garden spot on river bank. Four blocks from 6th Street. $4.00 month." For $8 per month, one could rent a six-room house with a sleeping porch at 727 North Fifth Street.

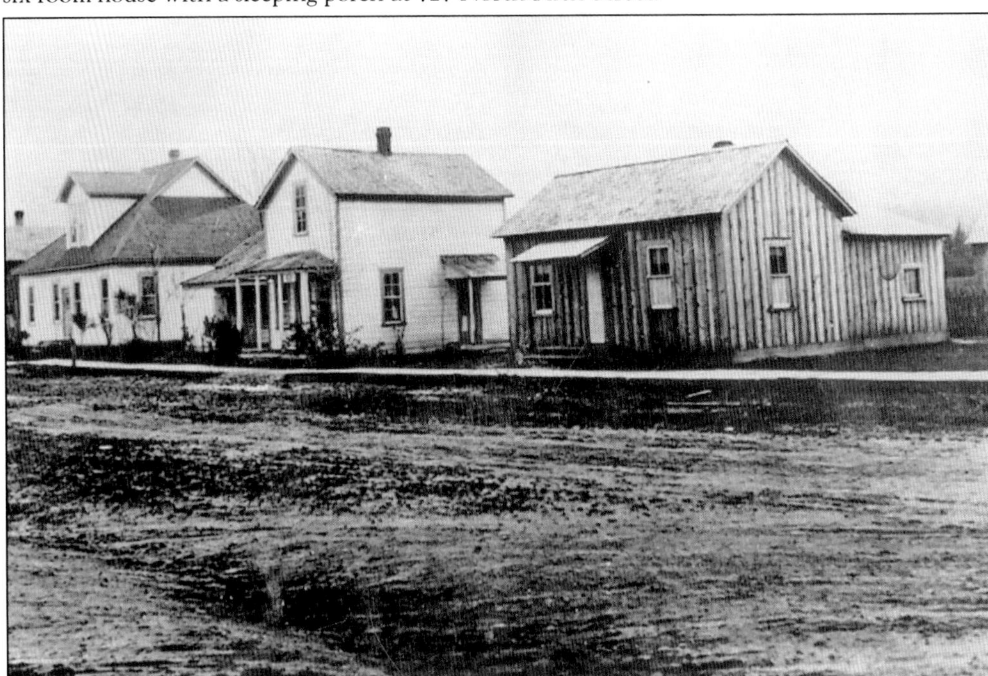

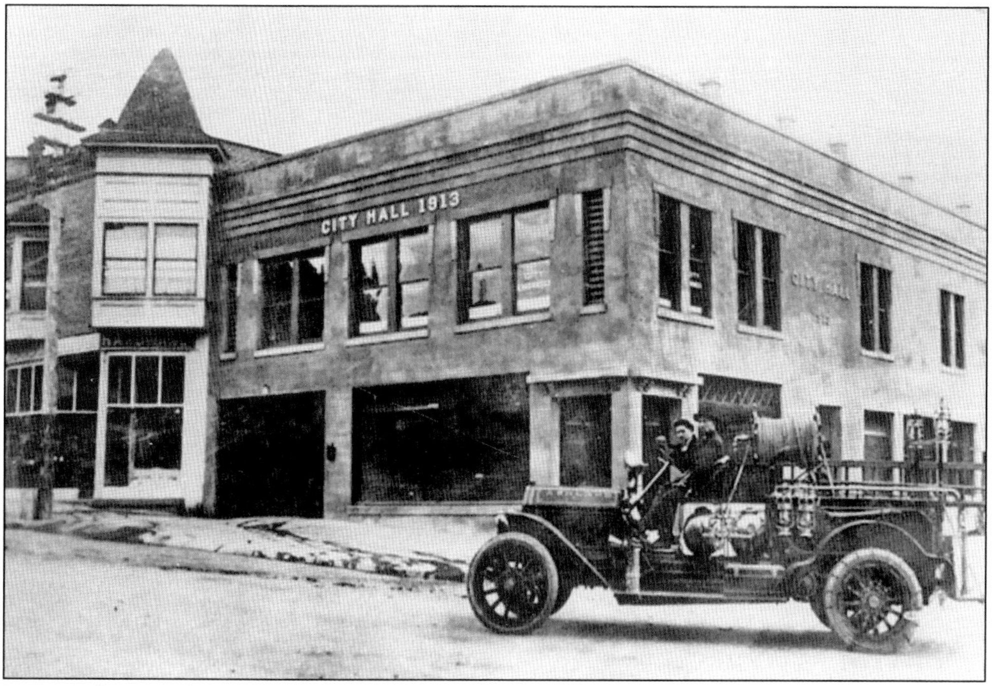

In 1916, the city of Grants Pass had to cut expenses. They began with the fire department, cutting the fire chief's salary from $85 to $80 per month and lowering the fire assistant's wages from $65 to $60 per month. However, they did make the following concession: "Both these men have been on constant duty at the engine house during the 24 hours, but a committee from the council is to attempt a re-adjustment of duties and give the men some hours of relief during each 24 hours, during which time only a single man need be at the station."

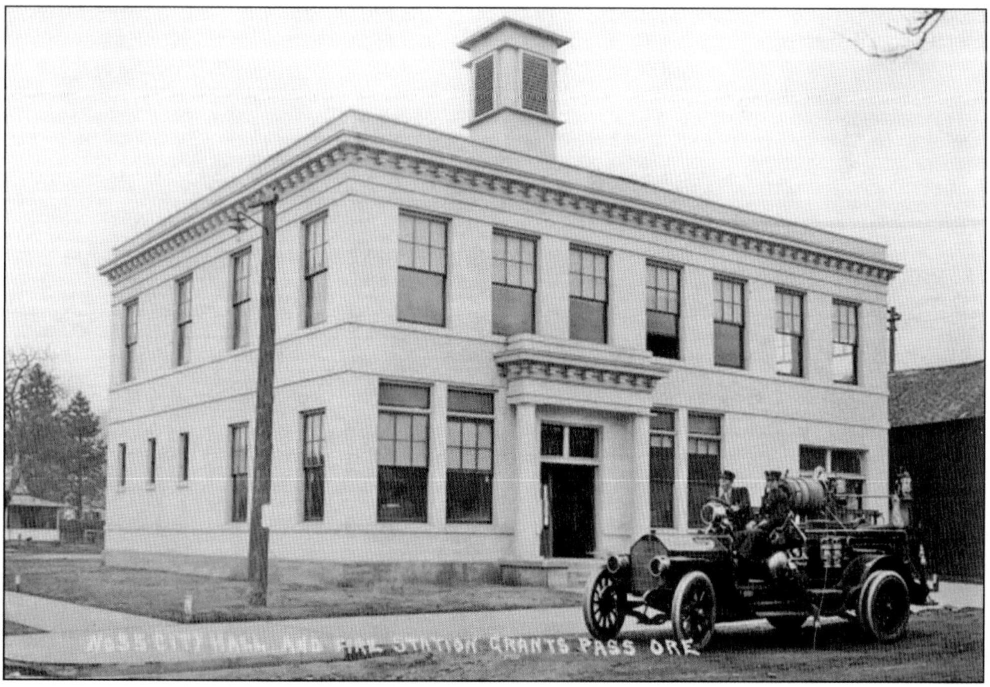

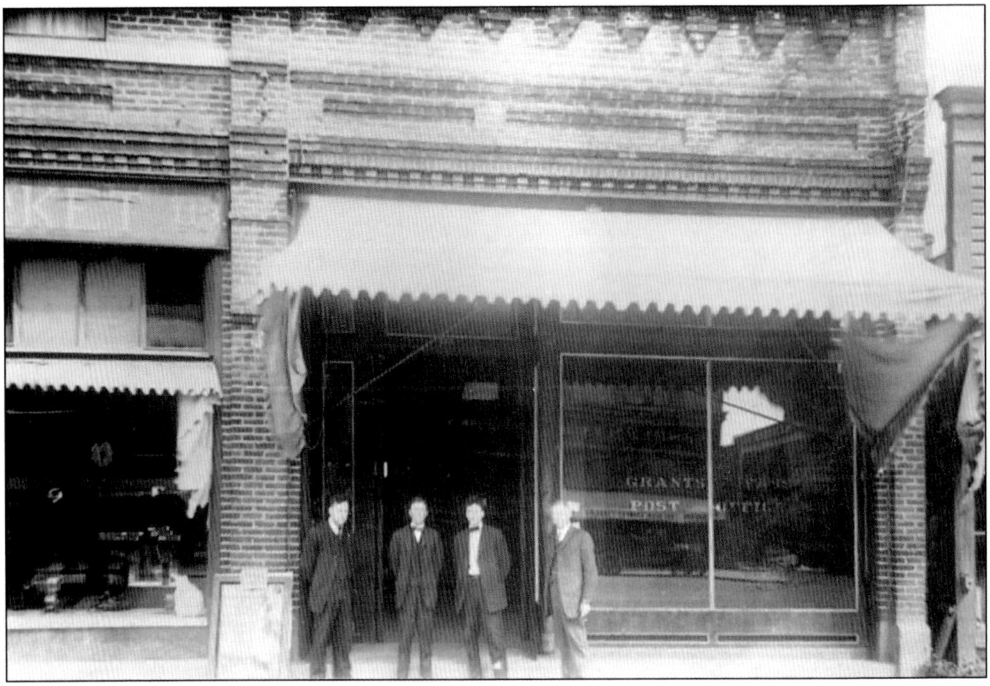

On June 15, 1909, the US Post Office Department declared that Grants Pass, Ashland, Hood River, and McMinnville could begin city delivery service. However, the nearby cities of Medford and Roseburg were deemed too small to warrant such service. In 1910, 11 men made a living by working at the Grants Pass post office, handling 50 bags of mail per day. During the holiday season, that increased to 80 bags per day. When the below photograph was taken on March 2, 1929, the amount of mail had increased, and more routes had been added.

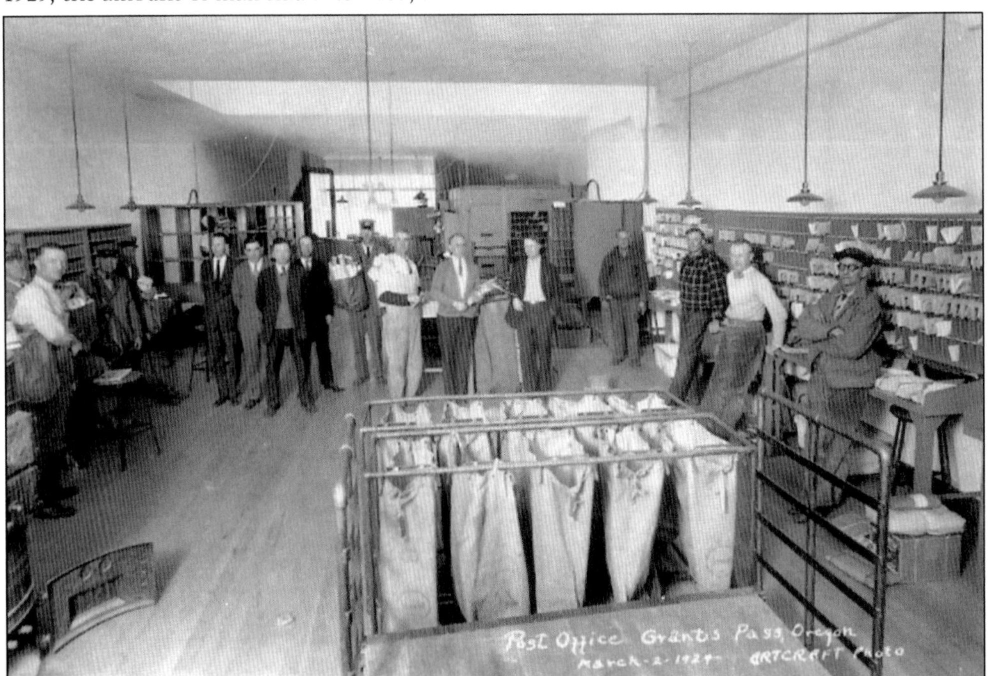

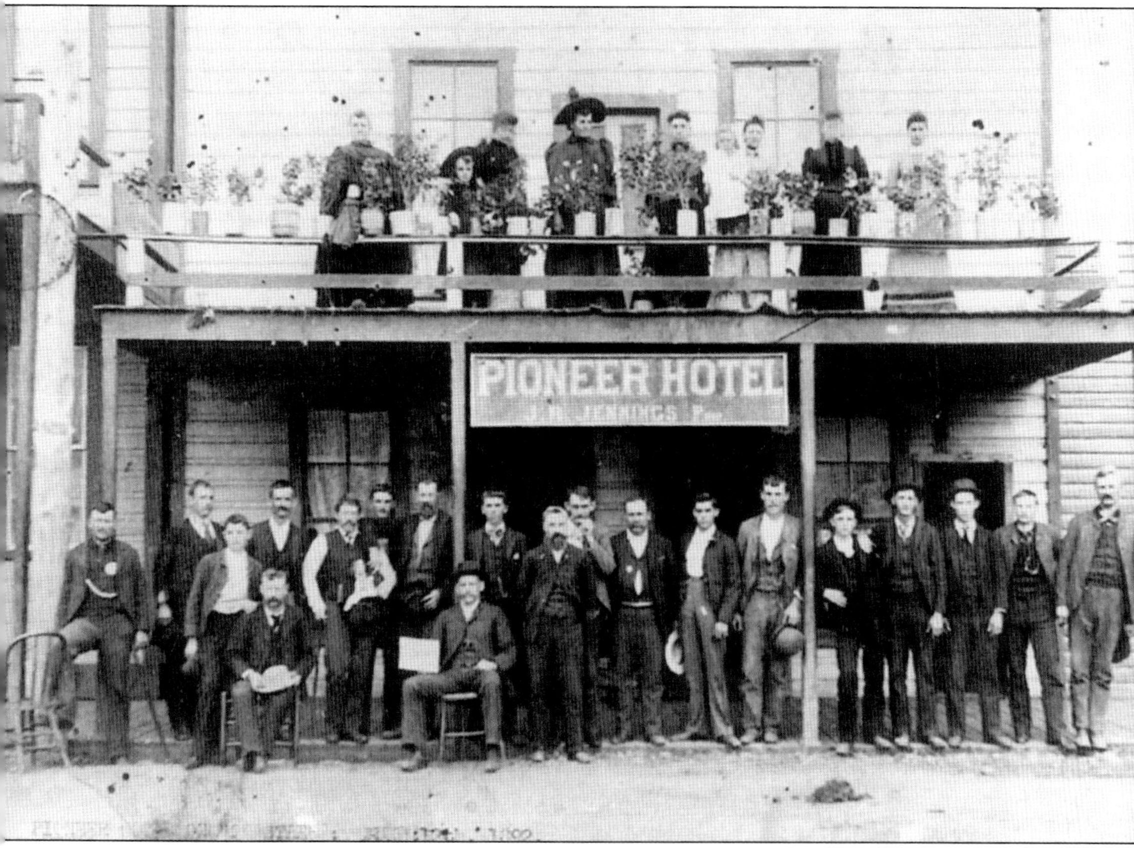

When this photograph was taken in 1892, J.R. Jennings was the proprietor of the Pioneer Hotel. Hattie Floyd took over the business in 1897 and operated the hotel until selling it to Mrs. Lowden in 1917. The *Rogue River Courier* reported: "Mrs. Floyd purchased a residential property from Dr. C.O. Dixon and retired to private life which she is so justly entitled. Mrs. Lowden is from Wilderville but was raised in Kerby. The traveling public will find Mrs. Lowden ready to accommodate their wants and we bespeak for her a fair share of the patronage of the public."

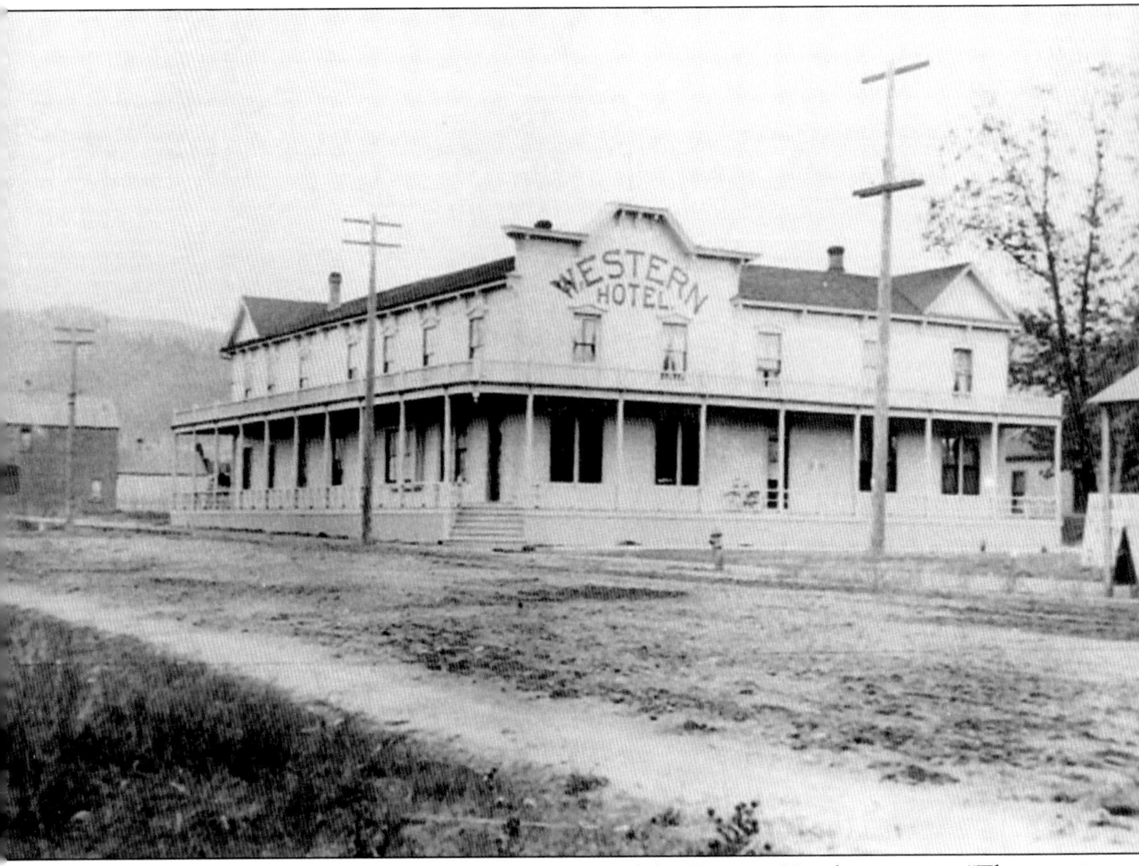

In 1903, the *Rogue River Courier* sang the praises of the Western Hotel in writing: "This city is better than usually supplied with good hotels, but the one we have in mind now is the Western Hotel conducted by Judge J.O. Booth. Judge Booth has conducted this hotel for eight years and is well and favorably known to the traveling public. The Western Hotel has 33 nice, clean rooms, comfortable beds and a table supplied with the best the market affords. Popular prices prevail and it is the headquarters for mining men in this section. It is lighted by electricity and provided with modern conveniences. Mr. Booth gives his personal attention to the details of the business and greets the new arrival with a cordial welcome and speeds the departing guests on the road with pleasant recollections."

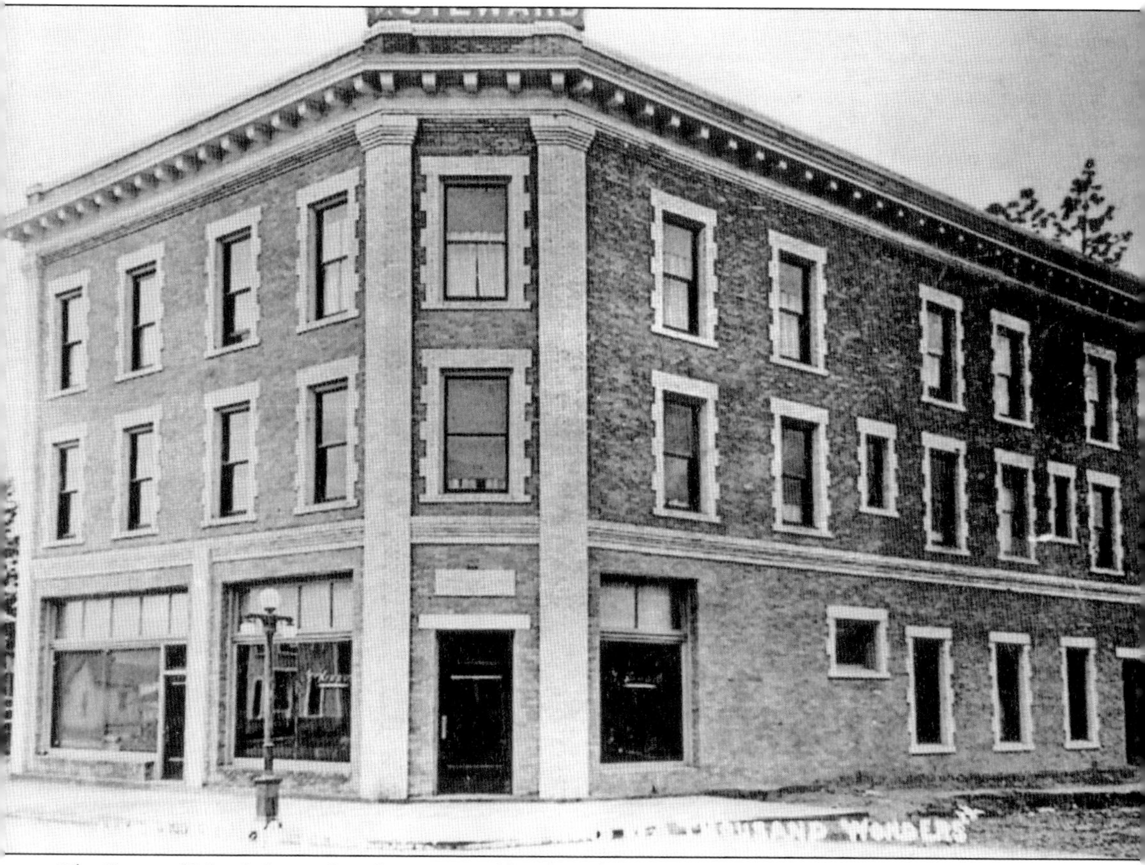

The Steward Hotel, located at the corner of Sixth and K Streets, was built in 1911. It took 200,000 bricks, manufactured in Tolo near Gold Hill, to complete the building. In order to finish the job on time, the brick manufacturer had to produce 2,500 bricks per day. The first hotel guests, John J. Curtis and his daughter Mrs. A.H. Fetters, were received on September 14, 1911.

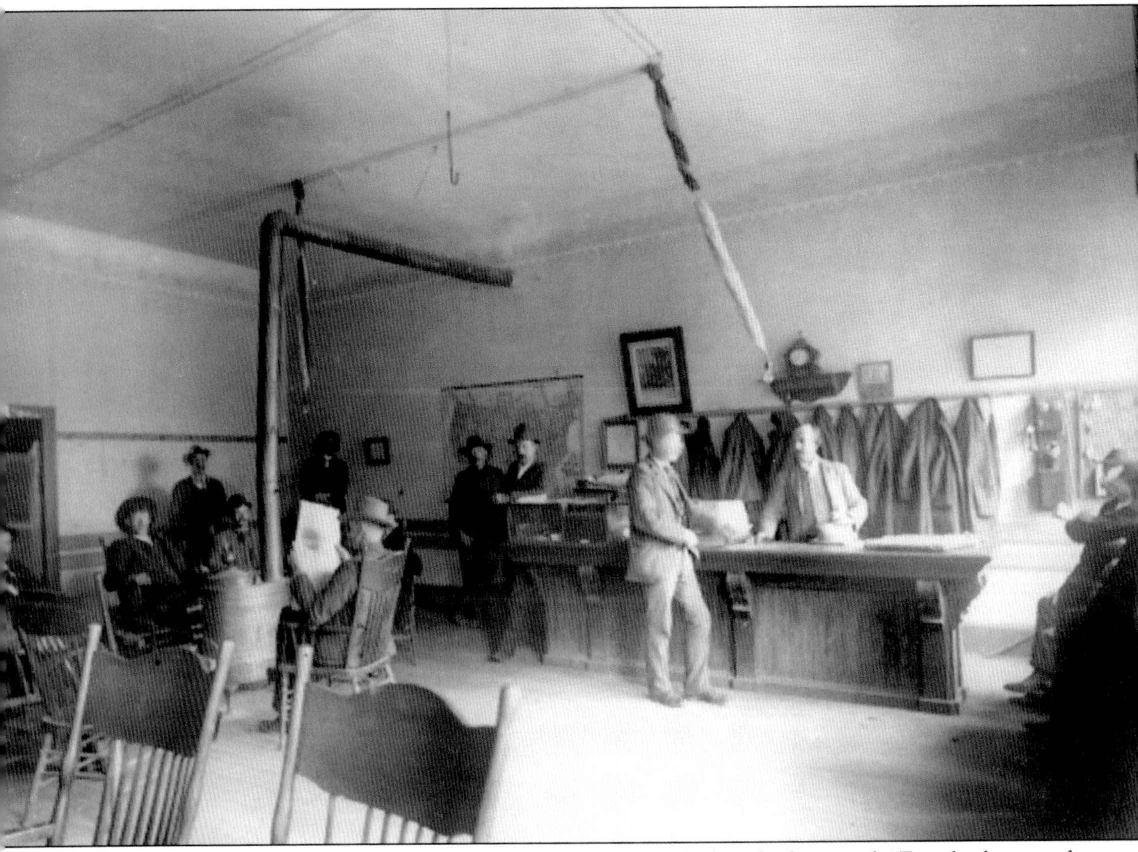

The interior of the Palace Hotel is shown here. In 1915, the hotel advertised, "Eat chicken pie for dinner 25 cents." By 1918, the cost was 40¢ or 50¢ for a Sunday night chicken dinner.

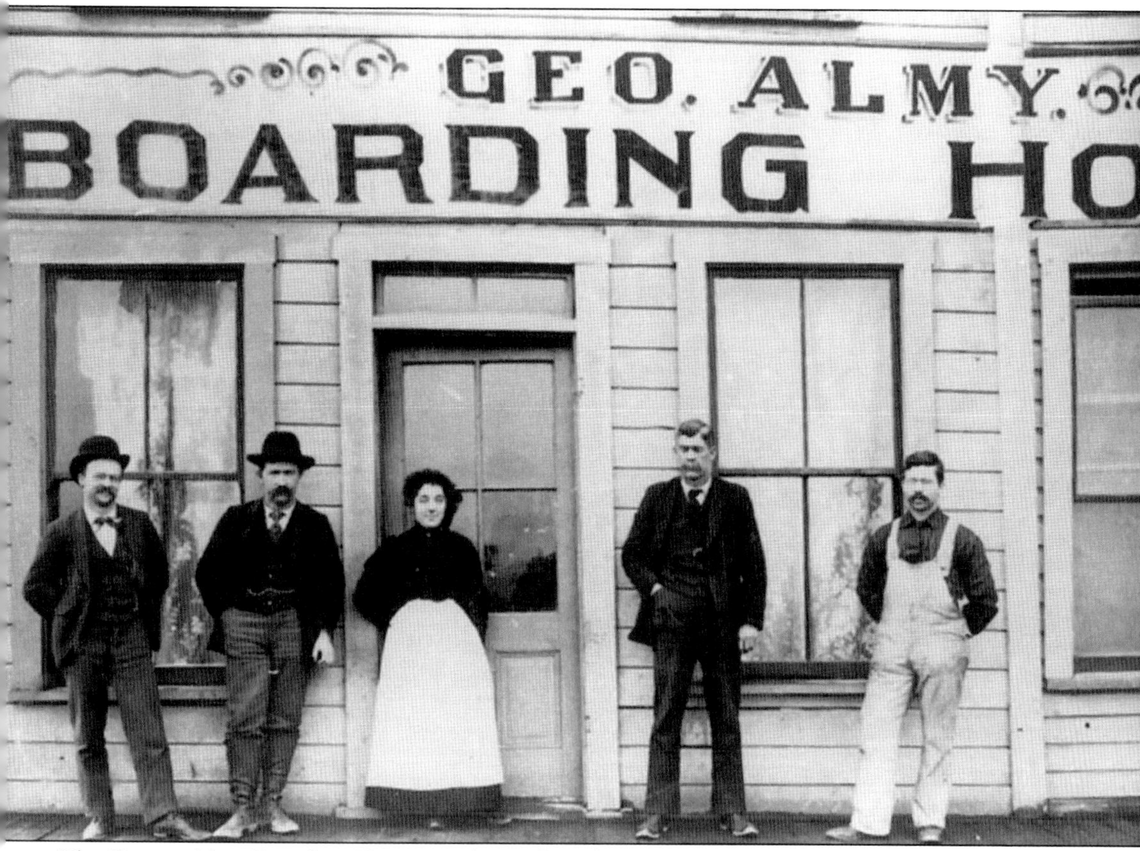

The George Almy Boarding House was located on the corner of Front and Seventh Streets. Mrs. George Almy advertised in the *Rogue River Courier*, "The Almy Restaurant will be open day and night and will serve oysters in any style, brown bread and Boston baked beans for sale at all times. The Almy Boarding House will be conducted as a short-order restaurant, meals at all hours."

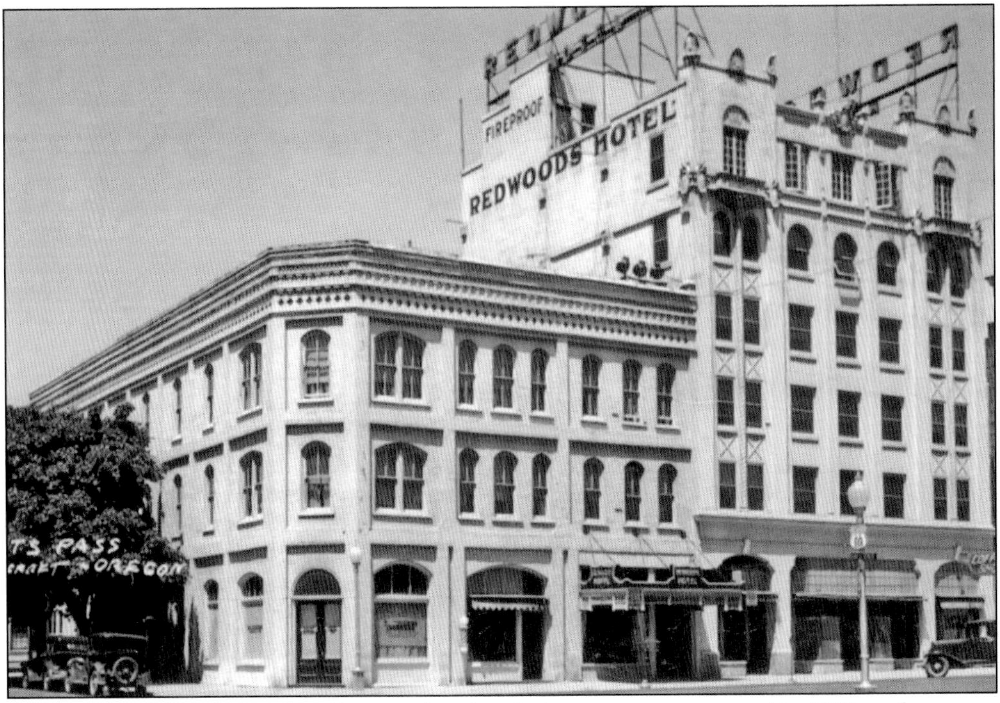

The Josephine Hotel was a first-class, modern hotel when it was constructed in 1893 on the corner of Sixth and E Streets. More than 200 people turned out for a reception at the opening of the hotel, which was said to be the most modern of any hotel between Portland and Sacramento. In 1909, the hotel was sold for $22,000. Two years later, the owners completed an extensive remodeling project at a cost of $20,000. When the 1920s saw an increase in automobile travel on the newly constructed Redwood Highway, the hotel was enlarged and the name changed to Redwoods Hotel. The six-story addition (pictured above) was finished in 1925 and had the word "fireproof" proudly emblazoned on the side. The lobby is pictured below.

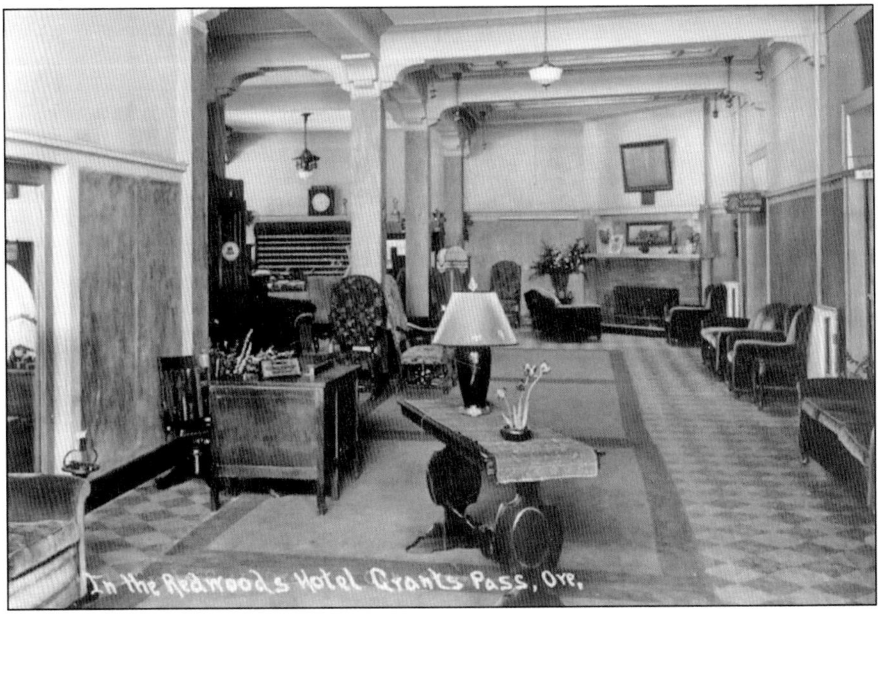

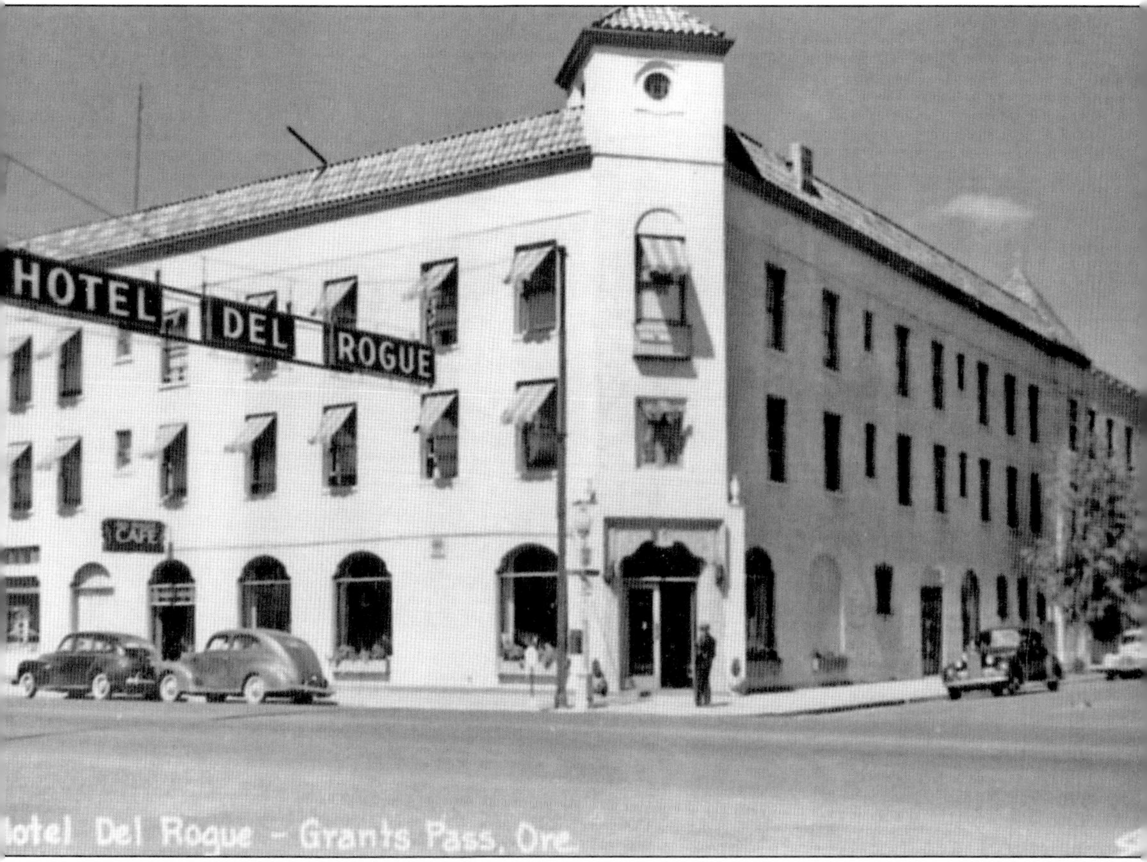

After just three years in existence, the Steward Hotel became the Oxford Hotel. The Oxford prided itself on being "a quiet refined place with hot and cold running water, and steam heat." At the end of the 1920s, the hotel underwent a large transformation at a cost of $175,000. It became known as the Hotel Del Rogue and featured a new Spanish-style exterior.

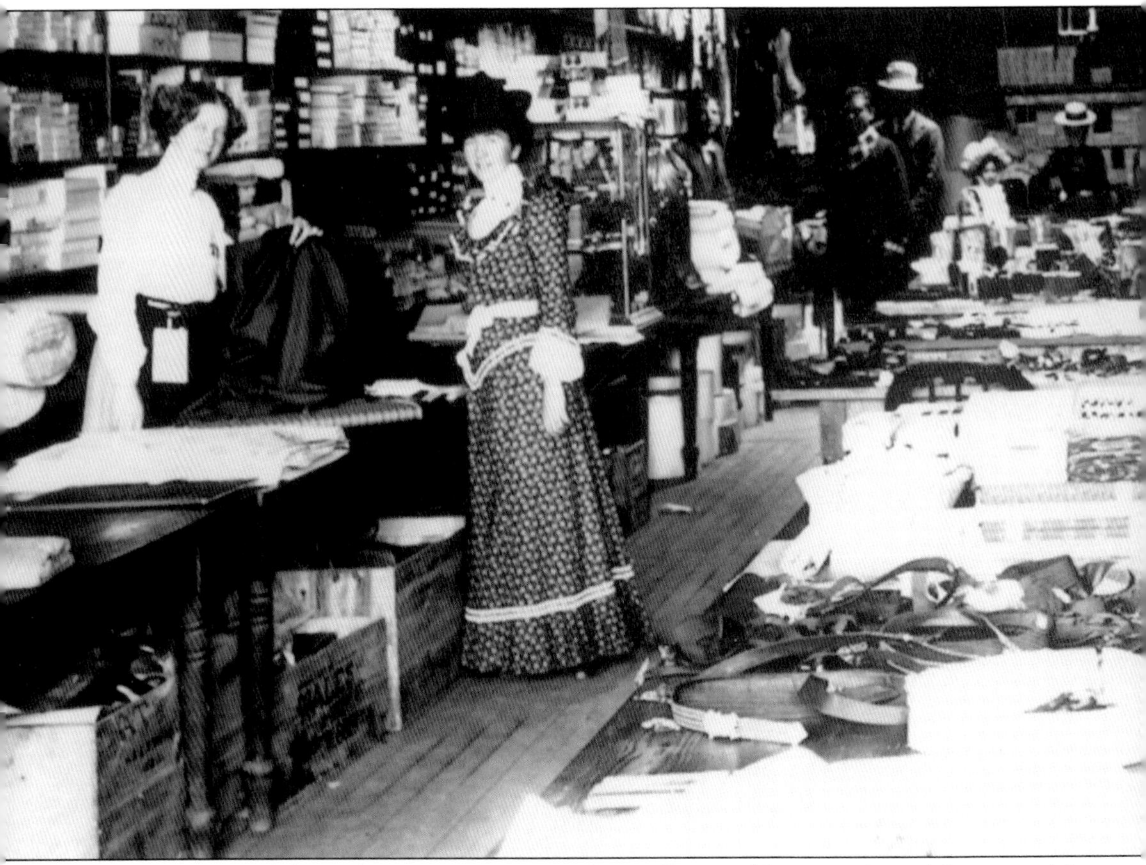

Near the start of the 20th century, women in Grants Pass paid between 4¢ and 7¢ per yard for calico material. Lace cost anywhere from 2¢ to 15¢ per yard, and ribbon cost between 1¢ and 20¢ per yard. Handkerchiefs were two for 5¢, sun bonnets were 25¢, and belts were 75¢.

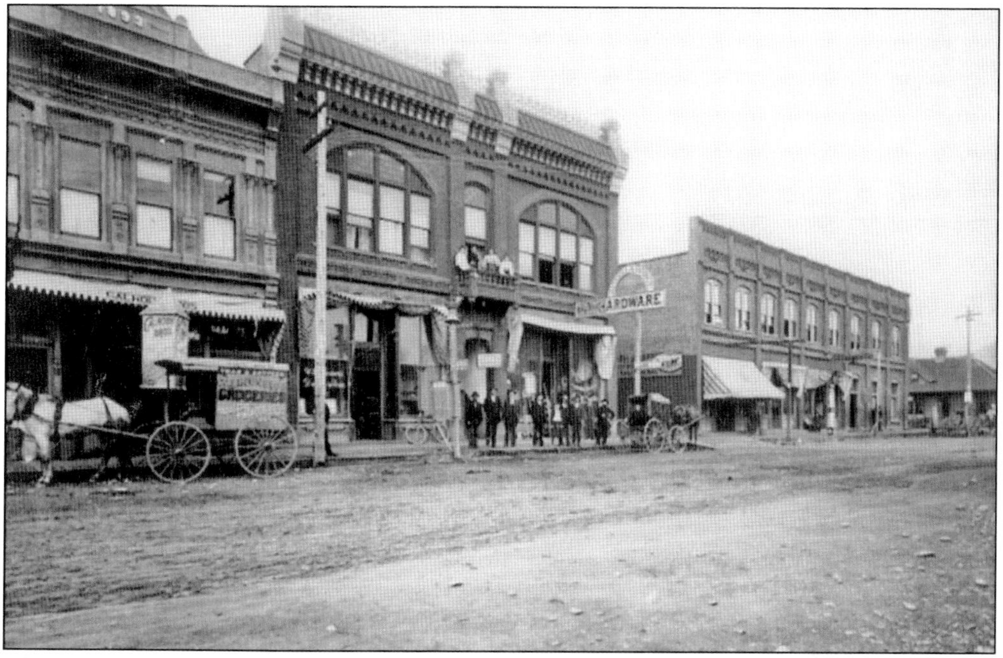

The Calhoun Grocery Company's horse and wagon are pictured above waiting to go on a delivery run. Calhoun Grocery Company advertised: "This is not just our store. We always have what you want to eat for yourself, horse or cow." In 1901, Calhoun Grocery Company advertised three cans of string beans, peas, corn, or tomatoes for 25¢. However, they did advise that "these are not our best brands of canned goods." They also wanted the public to know that "clover, wheat, grass, hay, and a big supply of wheat mill feed, rolled barley, corn, etc. always to be had at the Calhoun Grocery Company."

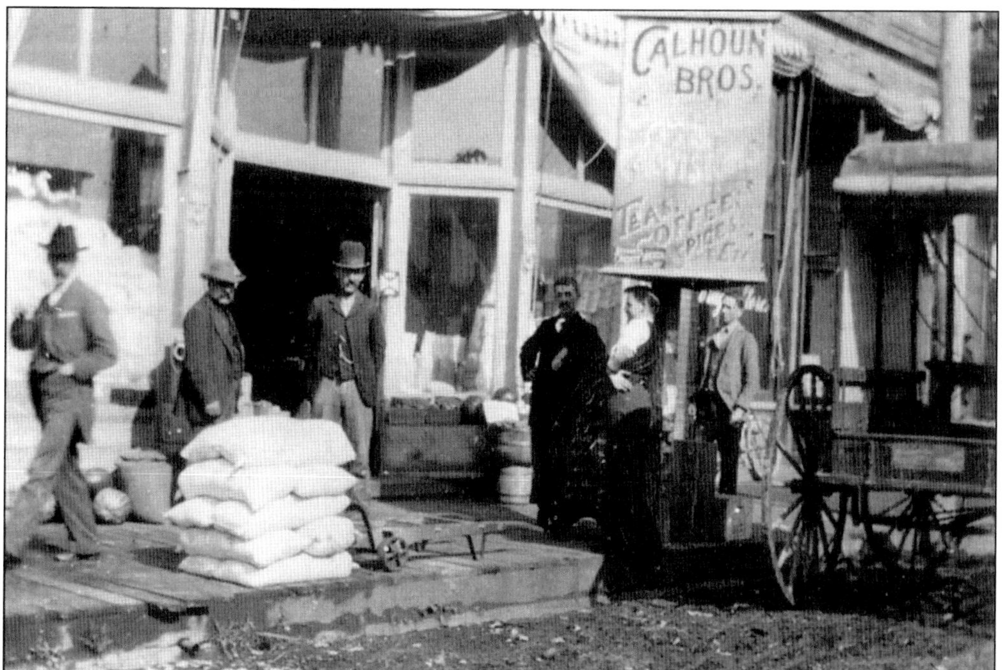

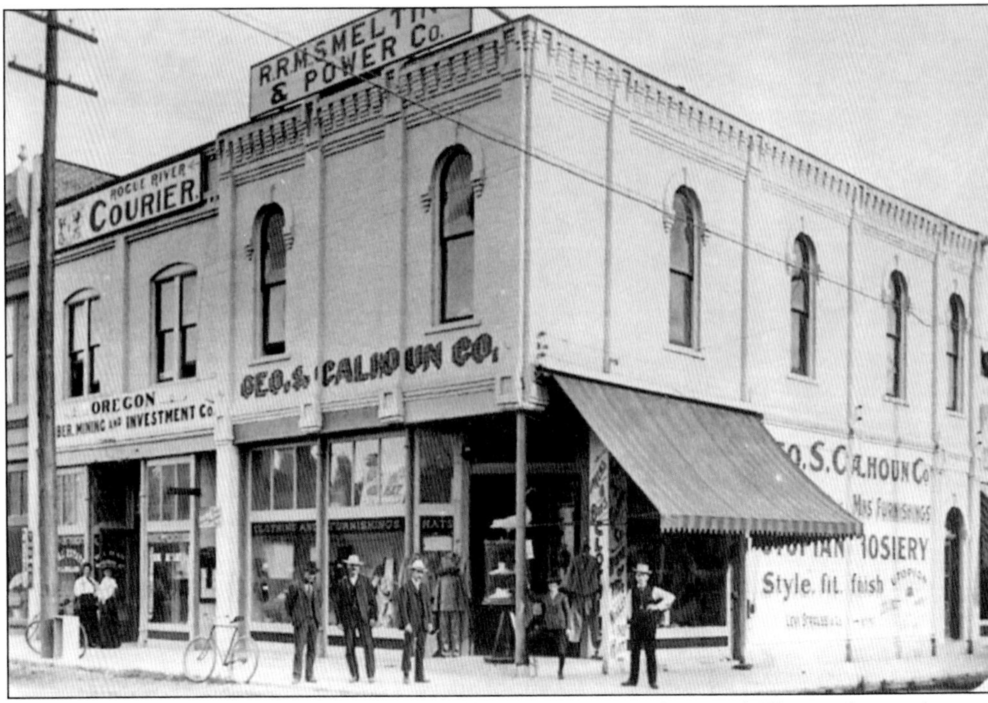

Just before Christmas 1916, the George S. Calhoun Company advertised, "Free turkey with every suit order placed Monday and Tuesday. Made on the Pacific Coast. If we take your measure for a tailored suit, it will be made on the Pacific Coast by western labor. It will be as good as any on earth at the price, $20 upward. Give us your order and keep your money west of the Rocky Mountains where western laborers can get it back. George S. Calhoun 603 G St." In the below photograph, the sign on the outside of the George S. Calhoun Company building reads, "July Stock Reduction Sale: We are not looking for profit, just a part of the cost. Geo S. Calhoun Co."

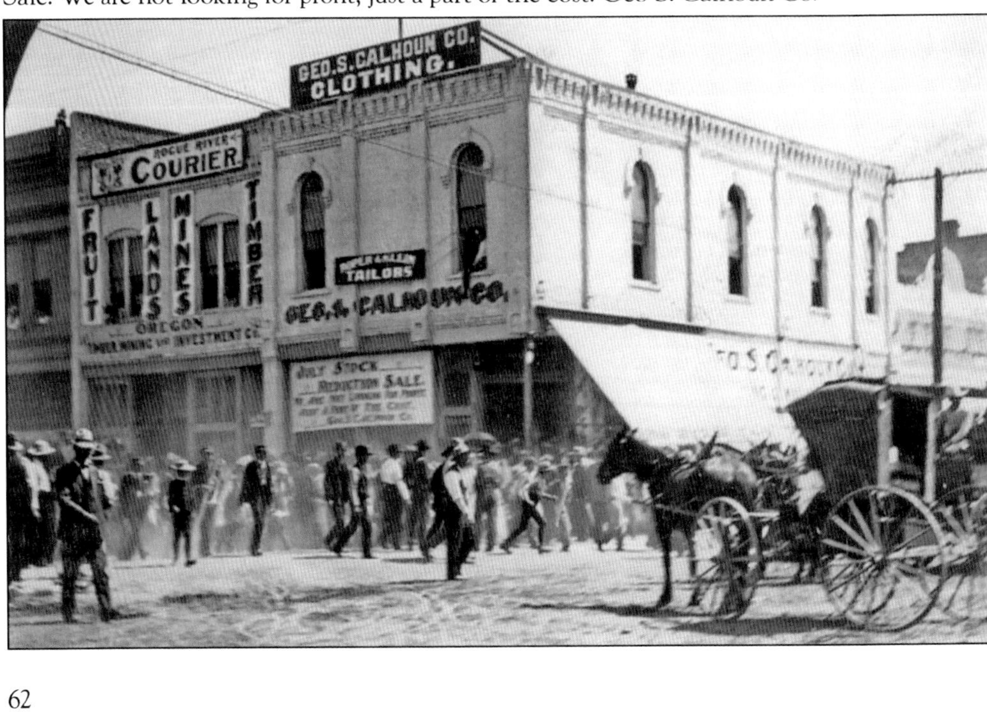

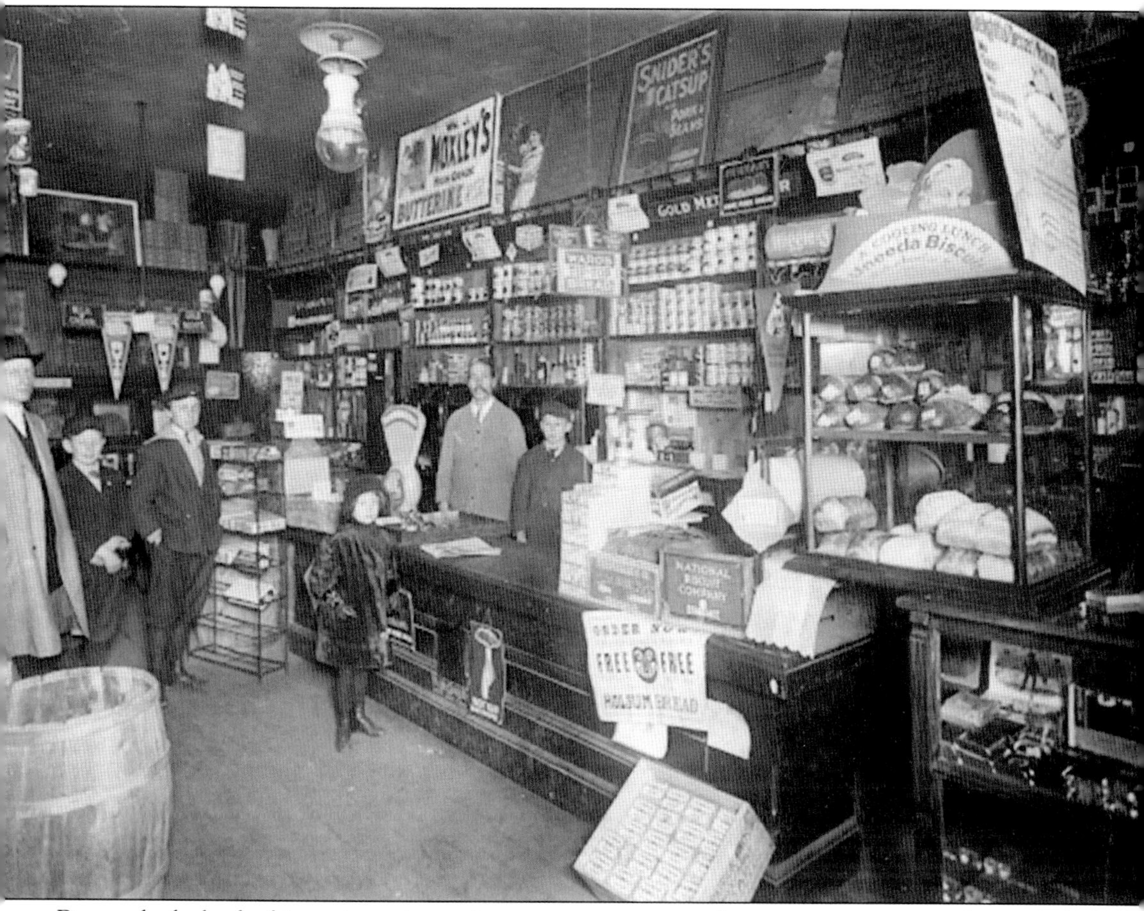

Due to the lack of refrigeration, trips to the grocery store were a frequent occurrence, and ice was delivered weekly to homes in Josephine County. The ice company provided signs for customers to place in the window to indicate if they needed ice that week. If no one was home, the iceman would enter the house and place the ice in the icebox.

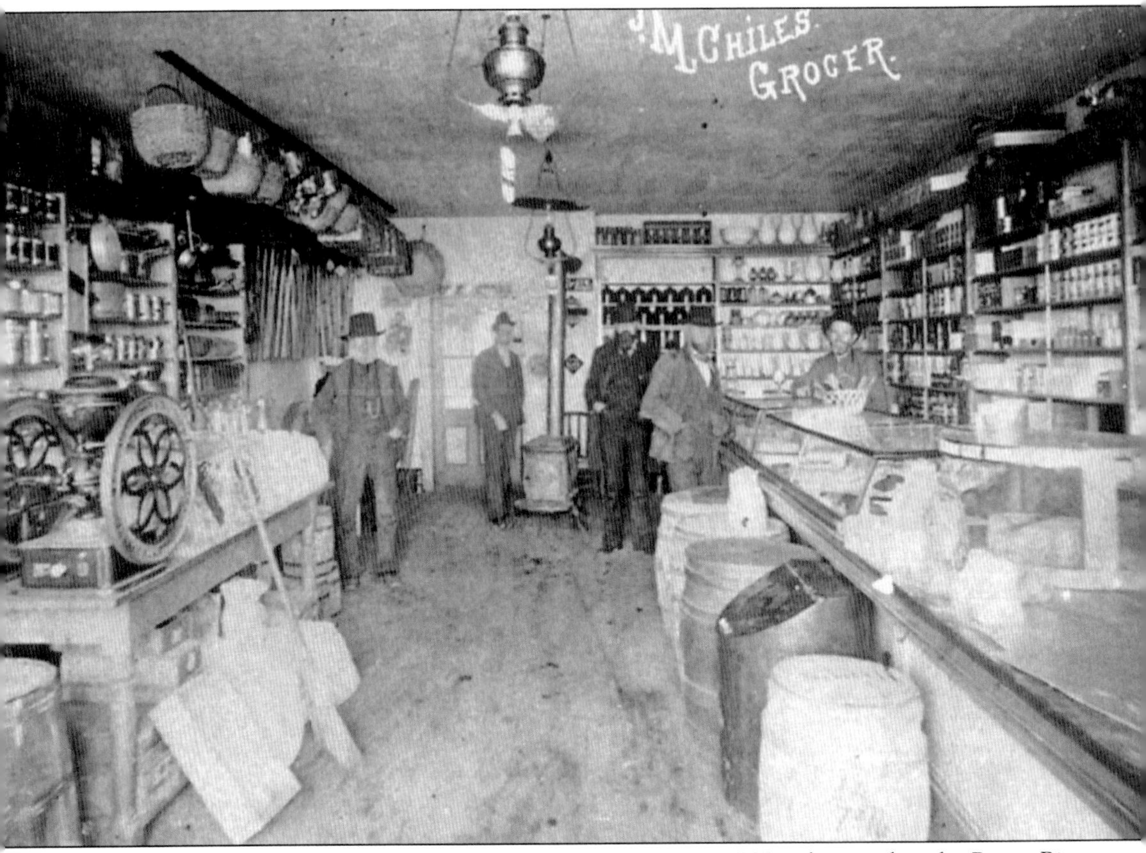

Grocer J.M. Chiles referred to himself as the "Pioneer Grocer." He advertised in the *Rogue River Courier*: "Reliable goods at reliable prices. Not only will you find the staple goods in stock but fancy groceries and shelf goods." He went on to say that he always had the best potatoes on the market and boasted that the farm-cured bacon that he sold was "the finest ever brought to Grants Pass."

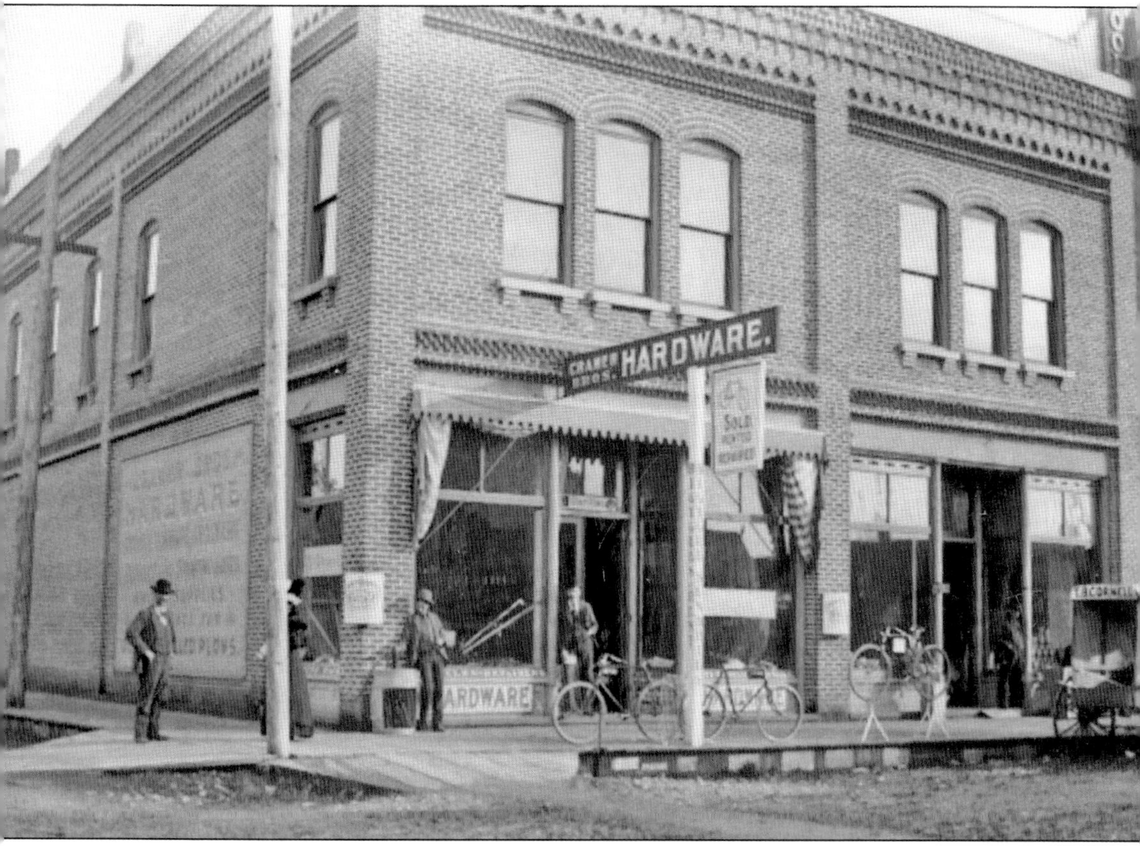

Cramer Brothers Hardware sold just about everything a person could need. A sampling of the items included the following: grass seeds, garden seeds, flower bulbs, poultry supplies, incubators, scratch feed, garden tools, rose bushes, plants, oil heaters, Westinghouse Mazda lamps, lunch boxes with a thermos, carving sets, silverware, nut sets, useful Christmas gifts, pocket knives, jelly jars, camp stoves, fishing tackle, fly swatters, cycle wringers, carpet beaters, house numbers, hammocks, paint guaranteed for five years, camping outfits, tents, fountain pens, hoses, floor varnish, prospector's outfits, sewer pipes, wagon covers, plows, meat grinders, stone jars, rifles (made by Winchester, Marlin, and Savage), birdcages, Garland stoves and ranges, antirust tinware, glassware, decorated crockery, and sterling silver pieces. The store also sold, rented, and repaired bicycles in its "bicycle hospital."

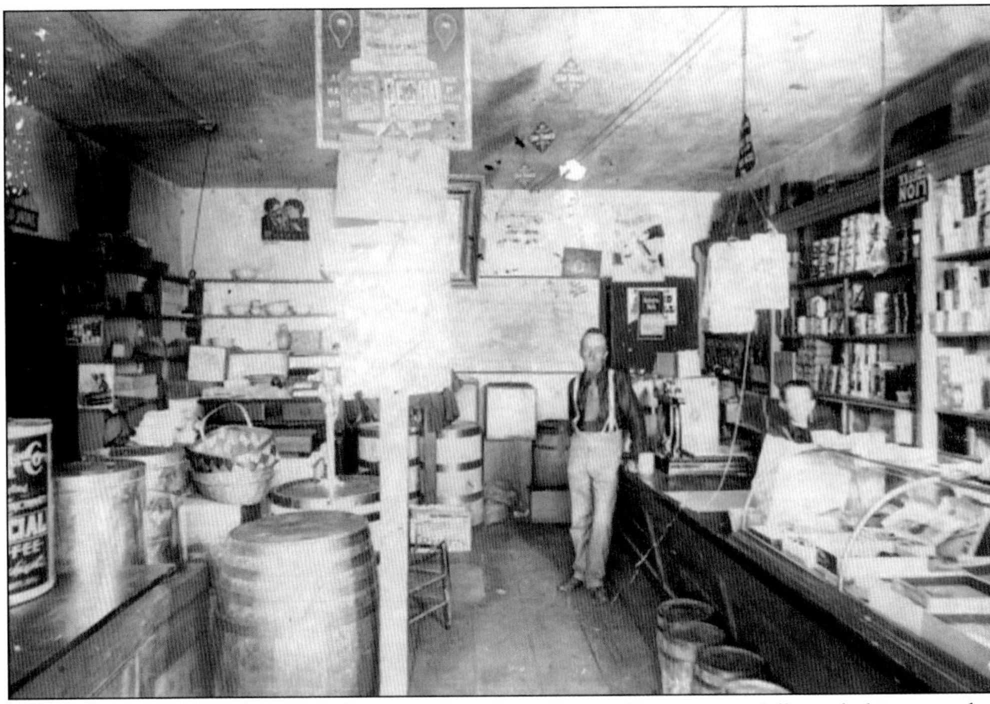

At the end of the 19th century, the cost of goods in Grants Pass were as follows: baking powder, 20¢; Heinz mustard, 50¢; Shredded Wheat biscuits, 15¢; apple vinegar, 10¢; raspberries, 50¢ per dozen; gooseberries, $1 per dozen; rhubarb roots, $1 per dozen; horseradish roots, $1 per dozen; a broom, 25¢; seven bars of soap, 25¢; six cups with saucers or six dinner plates, 50¢; a coffeepot, 8¢; an eggbeater, 10¢; a block of matches, 1¢; and lamp wicks, 6¢ per dozen.

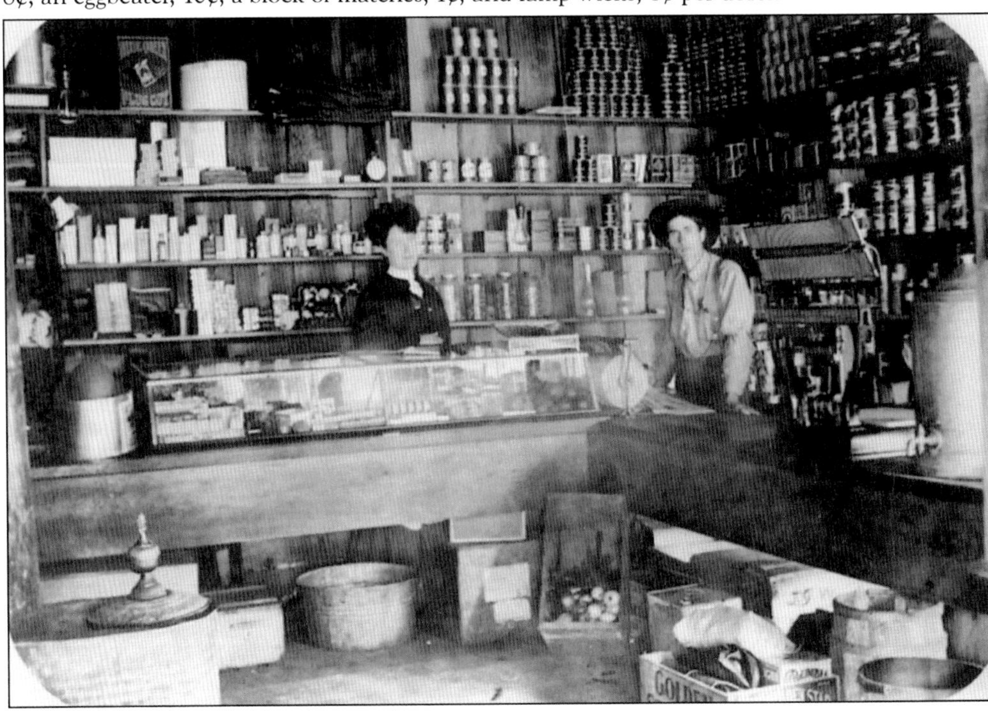

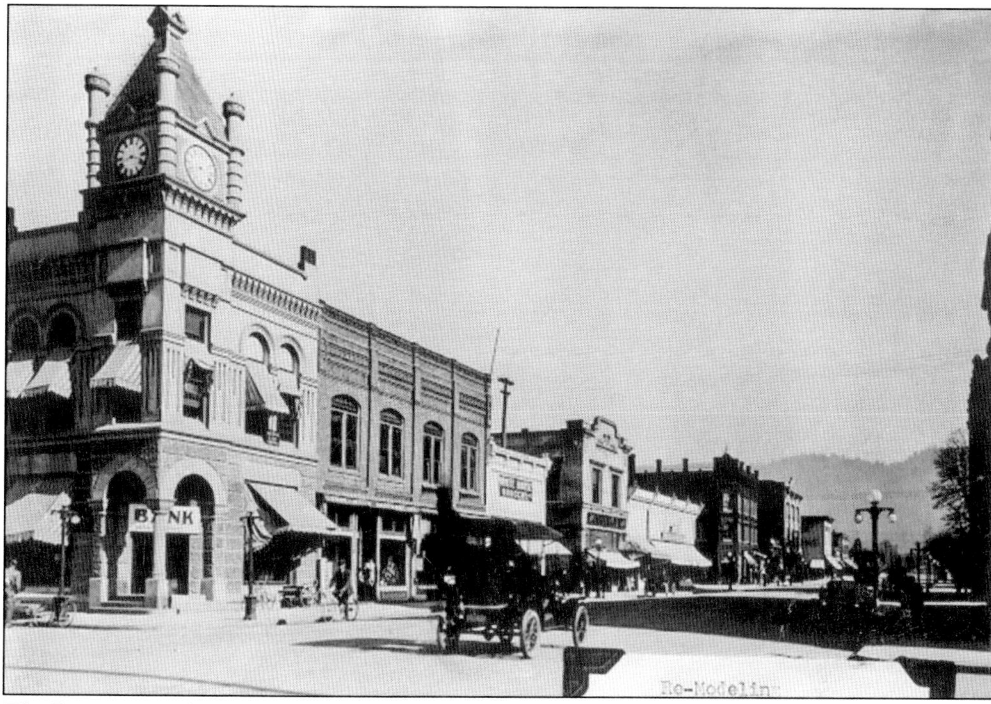

The First National Bank (pictured above and below) had an advertisement in the *Grants Pass Daily Courier* that read: "Extravagance Not Efficiency: A great writer describes the efficient extravagance of the American people. But he is wrong. Extravagance can never be efficient, except in waste. And waste makes want. But savings insures comfort, and comfort is the highest goal. You can take care of your own comfort while you are making money. But if you waste your money, the time will come when you can't have comfort. The bank wants to cooperate with you in saving for future comfort." They also warned, "Bank or Pocket: When your money is in the bank it is safe. It is never frittered away. There are no holes in this bank. When your money is in your pocket it is not safe. You fritter it away in dribs without knowing it. Your pockets are full of holes."

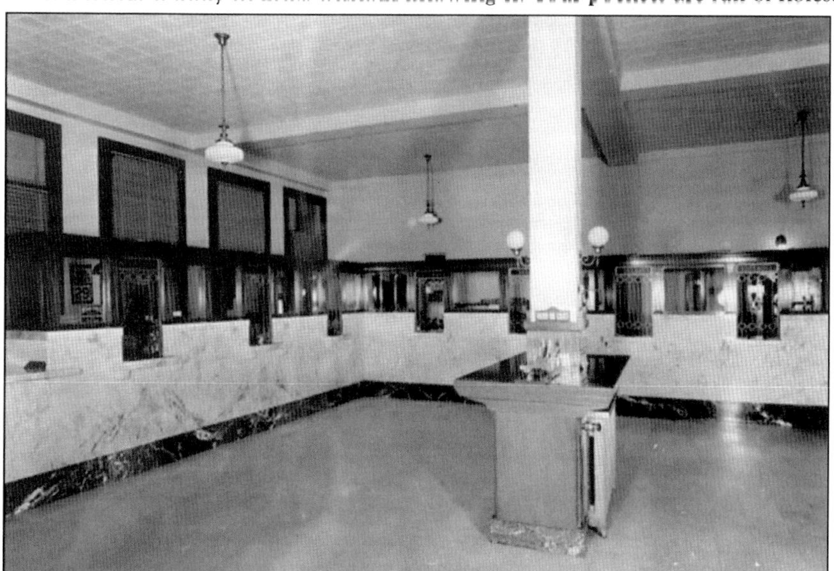

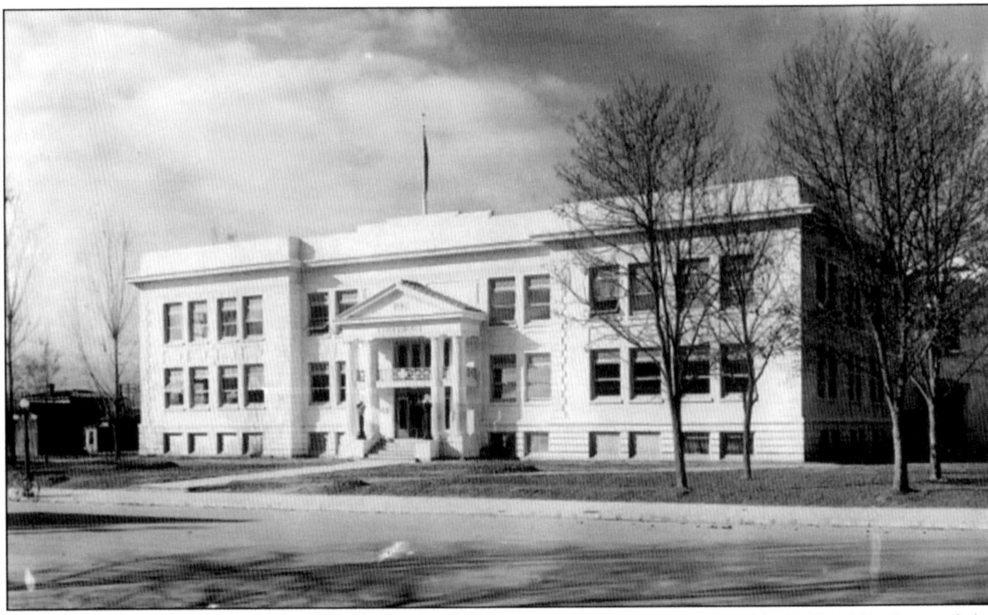

The Grants Pass courthouse pictured was constructed in 1919 at a cost of $109,744.75. One of the first murder trials that took place in the new courthouse was that of Clarence Johnson. Johnson was arrested in Nome, Alaska, and returned to Grants Pass to stand trial for the murder of Eunice Freeman. Johnson was acquainted with Freeman, who was 60 years old and worked for the Woman's Christian Temperance Union. Johnson told the police that he was afraid Freeman was going to report him to the authorities and he would be returned to San Quentin prison. He confessed to police that he killed Freeman with a lead pipe after an argument about another woman. Johnson told the police that he tried to kill the other woman, but he failed. He then fled to Alaska.

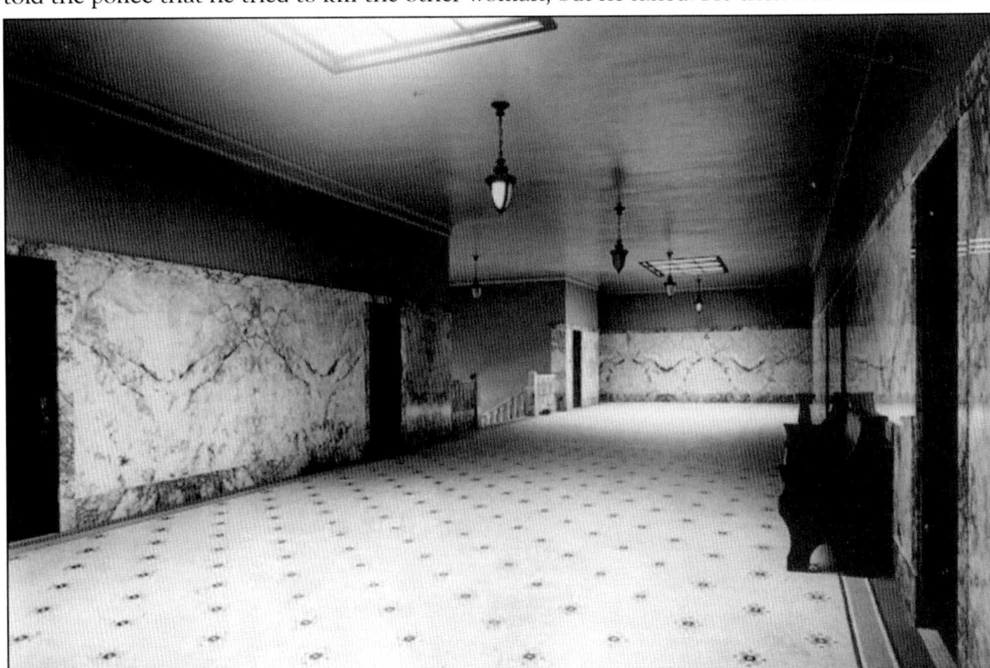

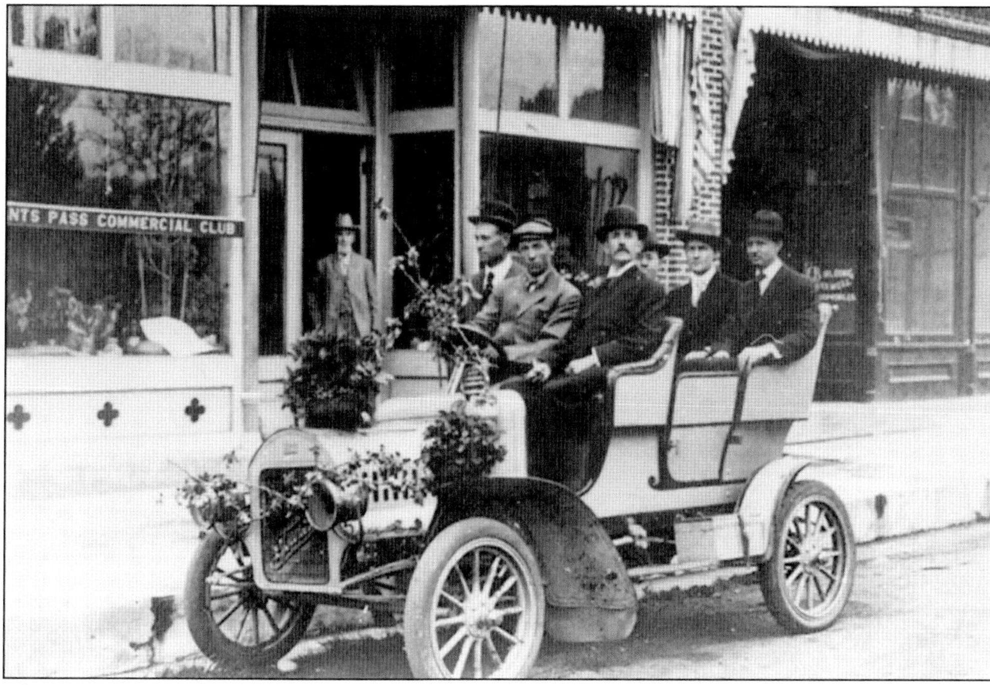

The Grants Pass Commercial Club was a predecessor of the Grants Pass Chamber of Commerce. In the above photograph, club members pose in front of their office. Below, they are taking part in a Grants Pass Rose Parade. The Commercial Club visited outlying areas in the county to ascertain the needs of the rural residents and to inform them of the work they were doing to promote the county. The *Rogue River Courier* reported that on a trip to Williams in 1909, "The hour of starting was eight o'clock in the morning and promptly at that time the automobiles left Sixth Street in front of the Commercial Club, keeping the proper distance between each vehicle so as to avoid each other's dust. They hurried along Sixth Street, crossing the bridge and passing through south Grants Pass and were soon on the road to Williams."

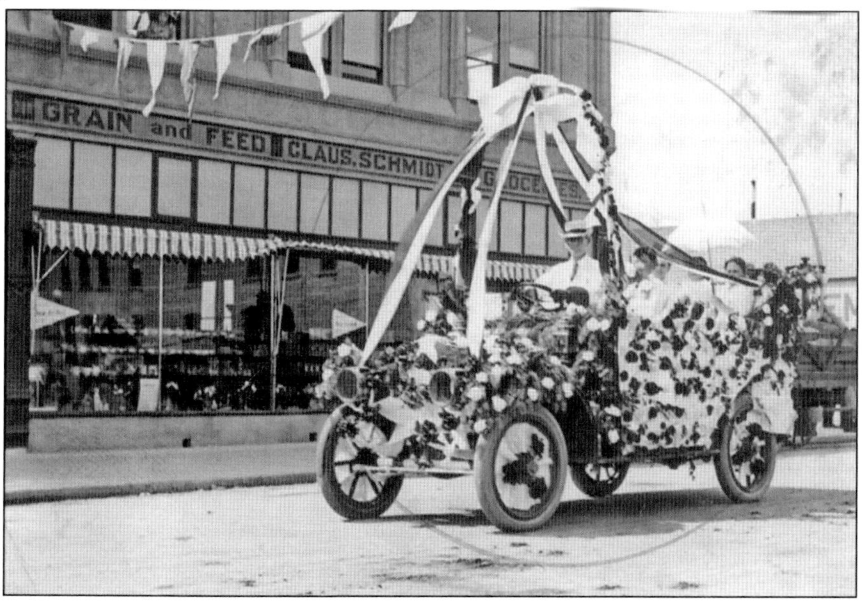

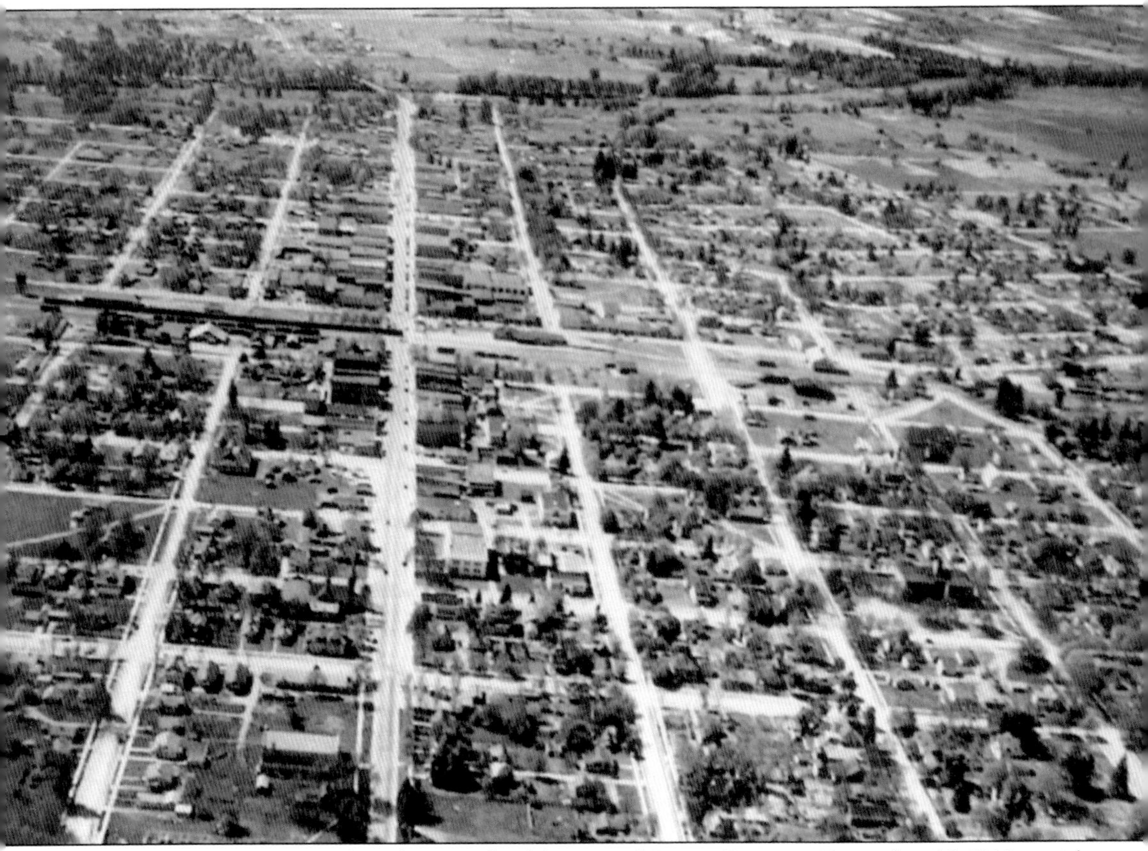

Harry Andrews summed up the growth of the city of Grants Pass in a December 16, 1910, article in the *Rogue River Courier*: "Here in Grants Pass we have much to look back upon with feelings of satisfaction and pride. As a community we have made rapid strides in the development of our city, not only in matters pertaining to public improvements but also along lines of education and social tolerance." He went on to write, "The issuing of $45,000 for a high school building. The elegant new passenger depot erected by the Southern Pacific Railroad and the commodious express building are two structures significant of the growth of Grants Pass. The erection of modern pressed brick and steel front business blocks is another indication of the progressiveness of our city."

Three

INDUSTRY

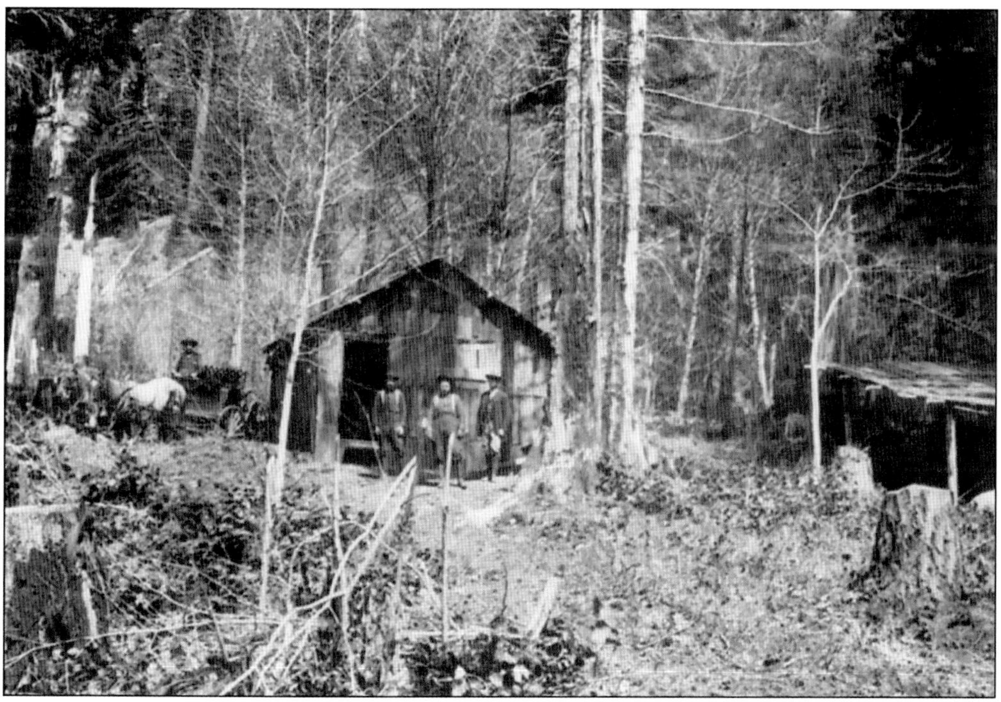

The earliest mining in Josephine County started in the early 1850s and was done along the French Flat; Galice, Althouse, Josephine, and Canyon Creeks; South Umpqua River; and Sailor's, Allen, Scotch, Shelly, Butcher, Taylor, Fyre, and Caro Gulches. Early in the mining boom, a pick, shovel, and gold pan were the only required tools. Miners also used rockers and sluice boxes, which trapped the gold at the bottom of a wooden box as water and material from the bottom of the riverbed ran through it.

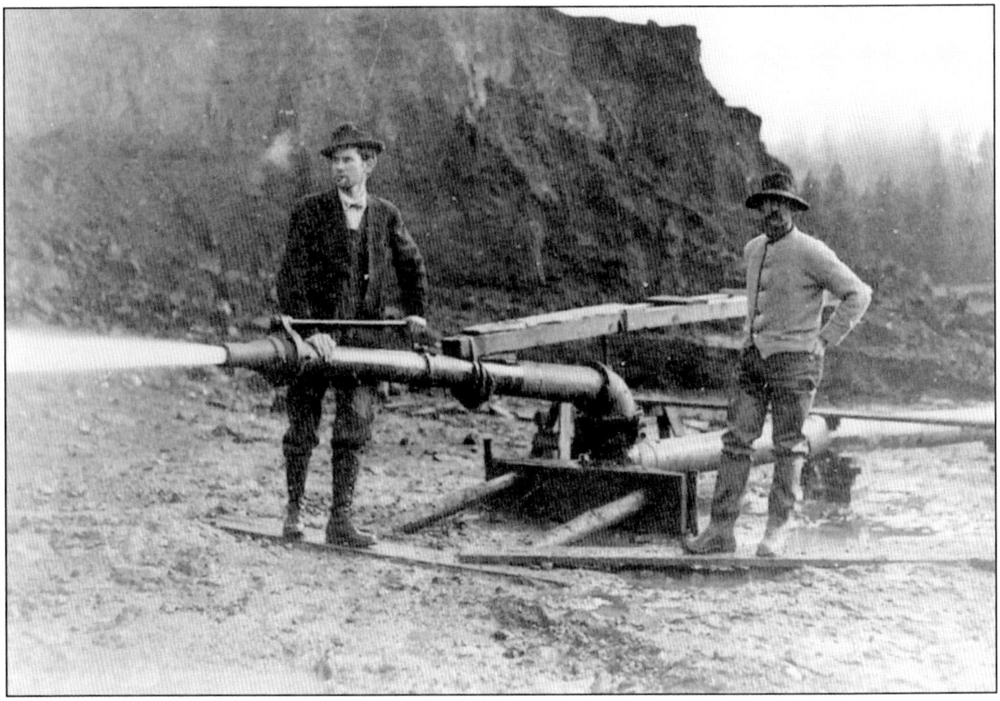

When the first miners arrived in the early 1850s, they were able to find gold by using gold pans and sluice boxes or rockers. Once that gold had been removed, they had to come up with a more elaborate method to extract gold from the natural resources. This involved hydraulic mining, wherein hydraulic giants sprayed huge streams of water onto an area.

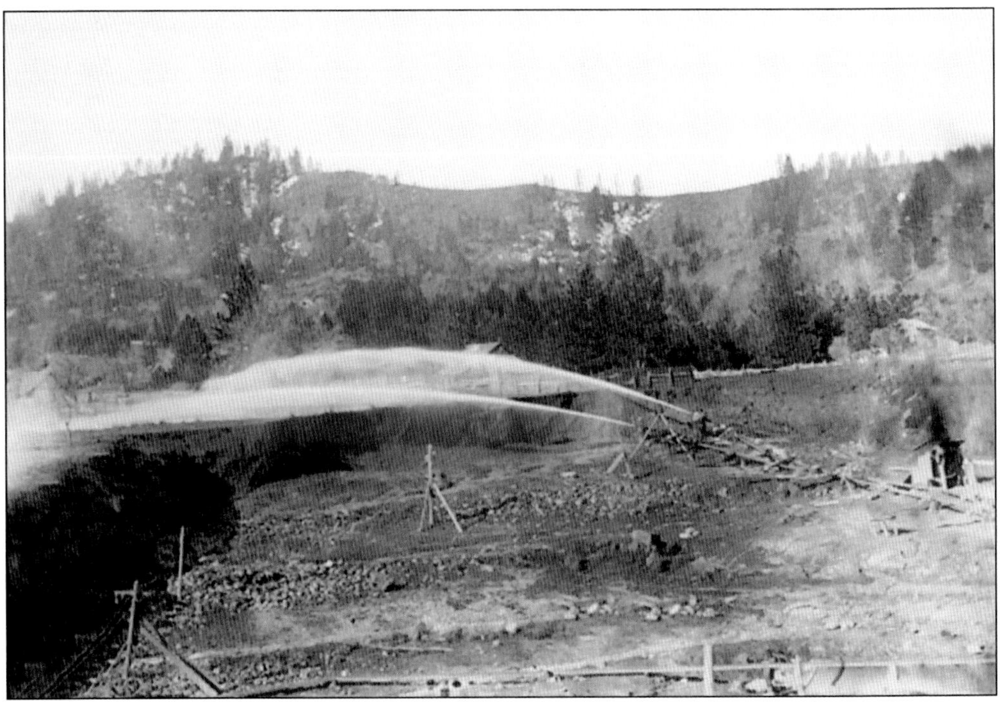

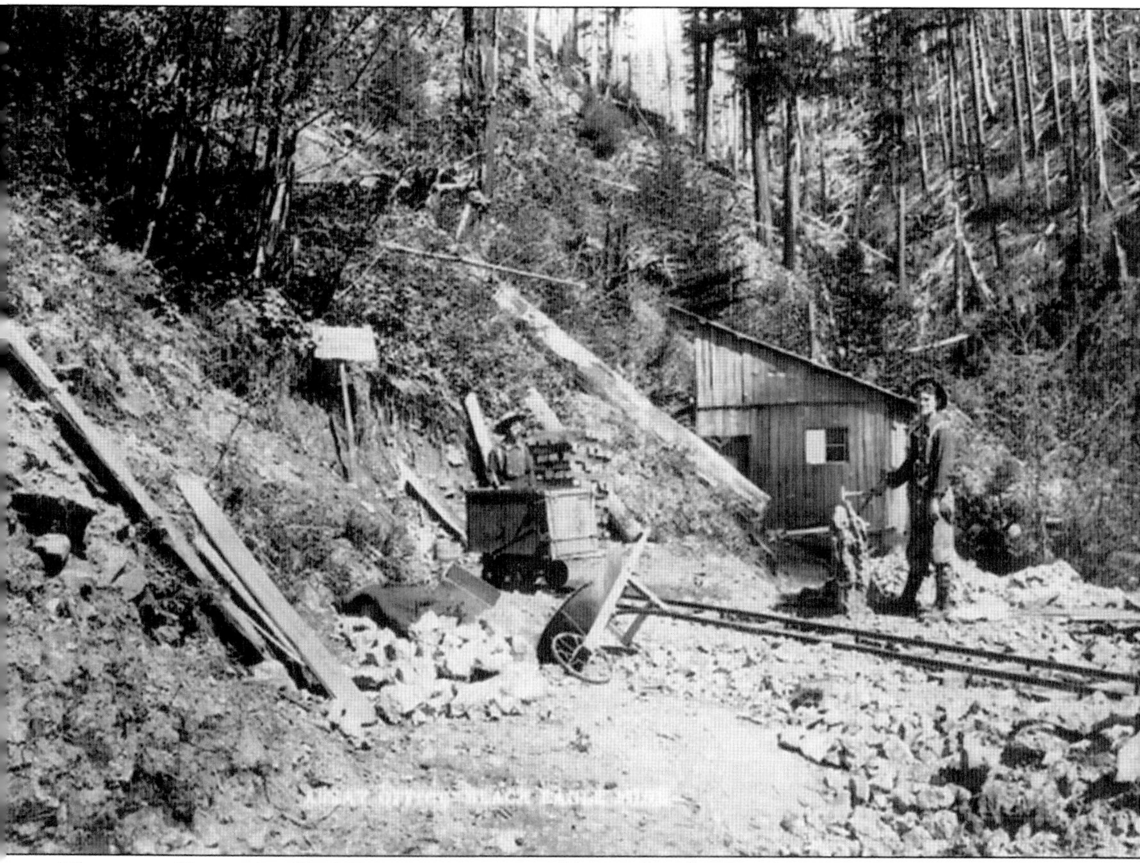

The assay office at the Black Bear Mine is pictured here. Shortly after the start of the 20th century, a company bought the mine and was able to once again extract ore from the property after it had sat dormant for a number of years.

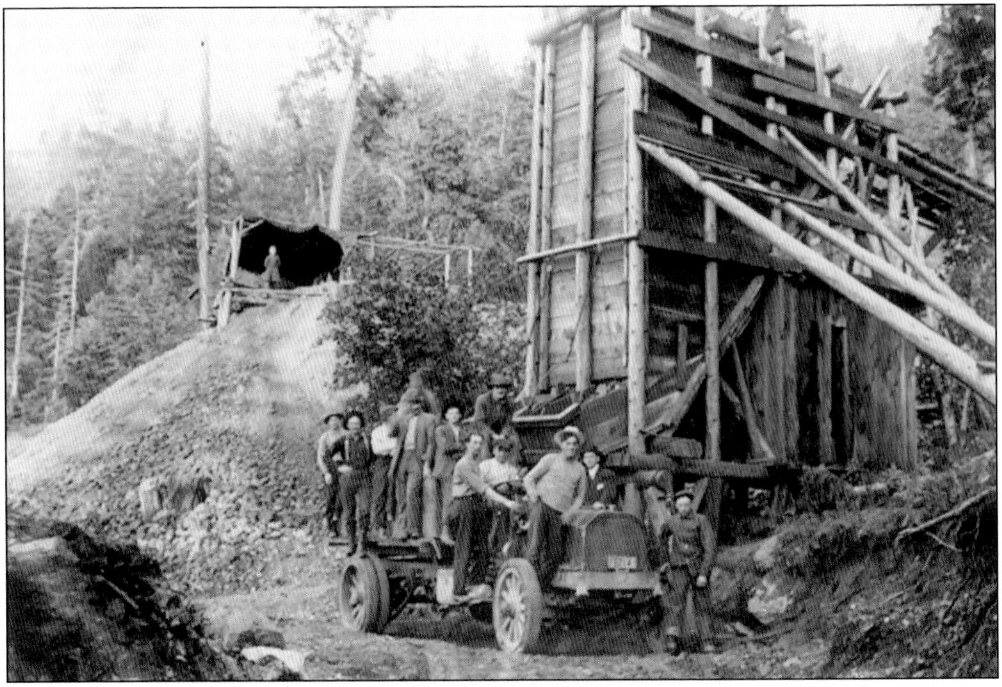

In 1911, an article from the Seattle Power, Mine, and Factory paper stated, "Josephine County has made a good showing during the past few weeks. Some truly remarkable strikes have been made. Mining men from all parts of the west are flocking to Grants Pass and are going out into the hills prospecting. The prediction is made that several thousand miners and prospectors will flock to this section within the next few weeks, and it is believed that many new finds will result from this additional prospecting. In fact, the excitement now evidenced seems to indicate one of the record gold rushes of western America."

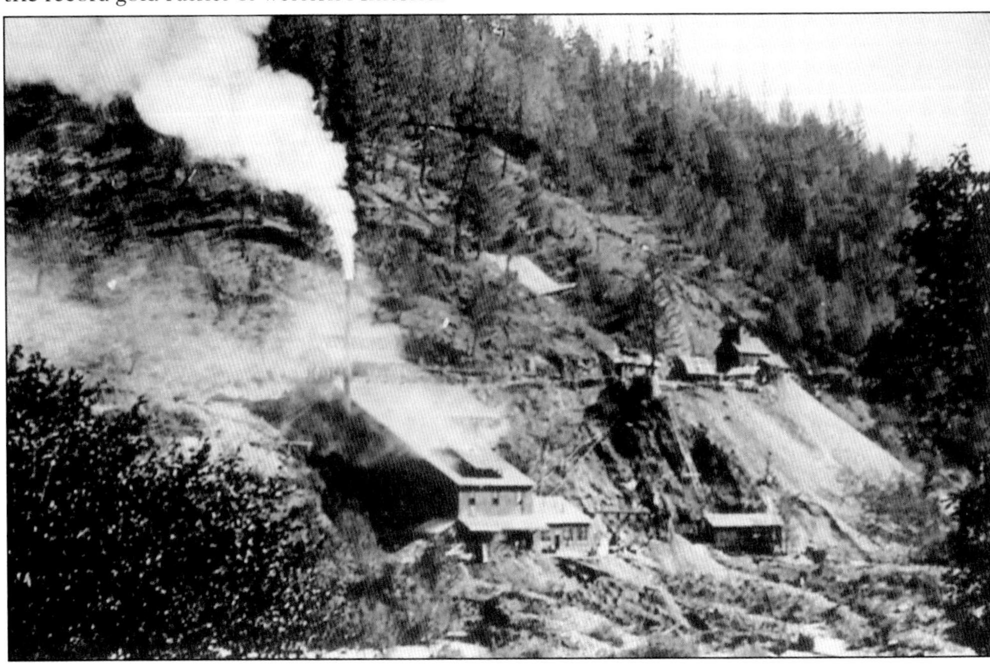

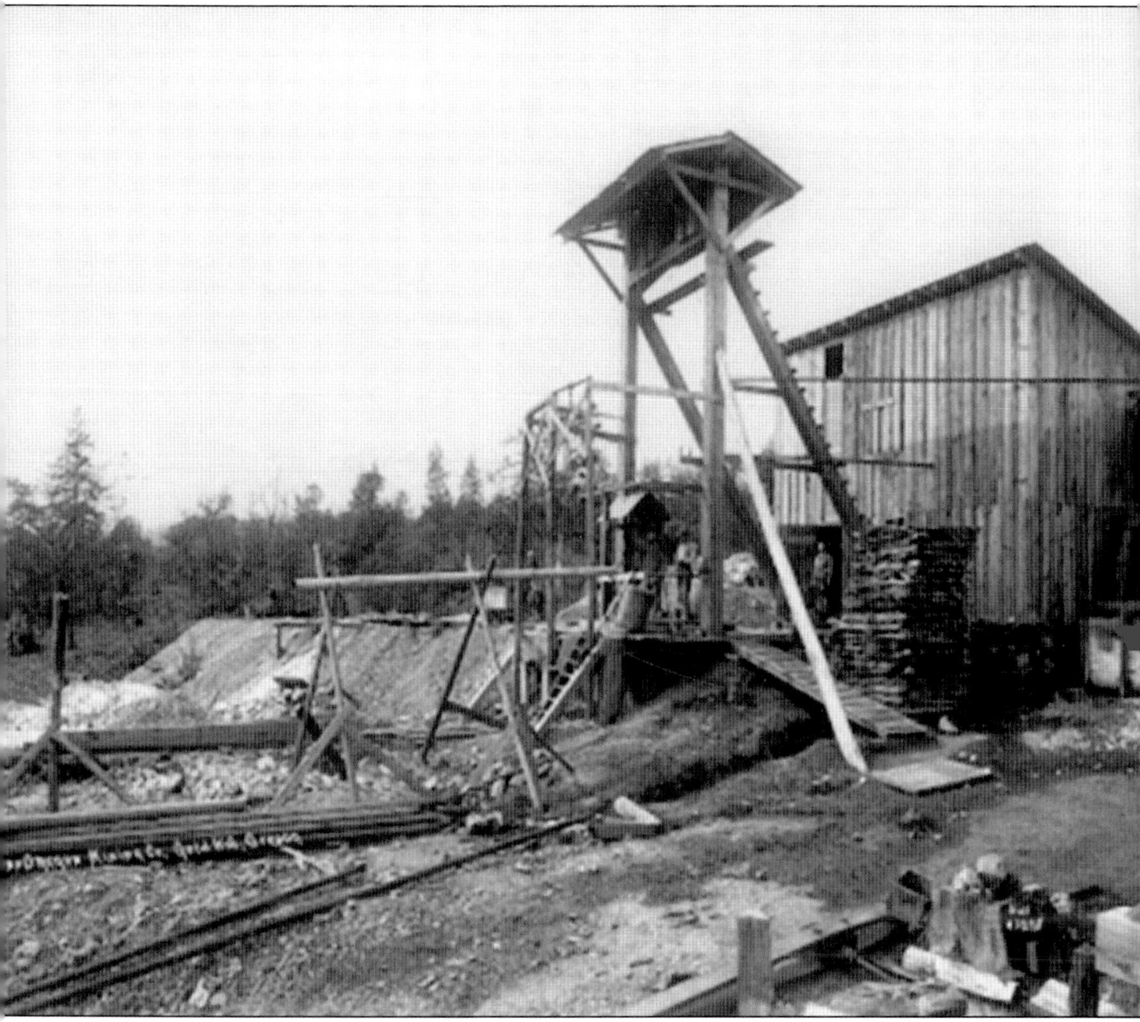

A study done by the University of Oregon near the beginning of the 20th century declared that there were 47 minerals in Josephine County—more than in any other county in Oregon. The minerals included the following: calcium, copper, gold, silver, iron, lead, graphite, barite, calcite, celestite, chlorite, chromite, chrysocolla, chrysotite, cinnabar, garnet, gypsum, hematite, ilmenite, aragonite, galena, arsenopyrite, molybdenite, monazite, olivine, iridosmine, magnetite, malachite, pyrite, siderite, talc, tenorite, rhodonite, pyrolusite, quartz, and sphalerite.

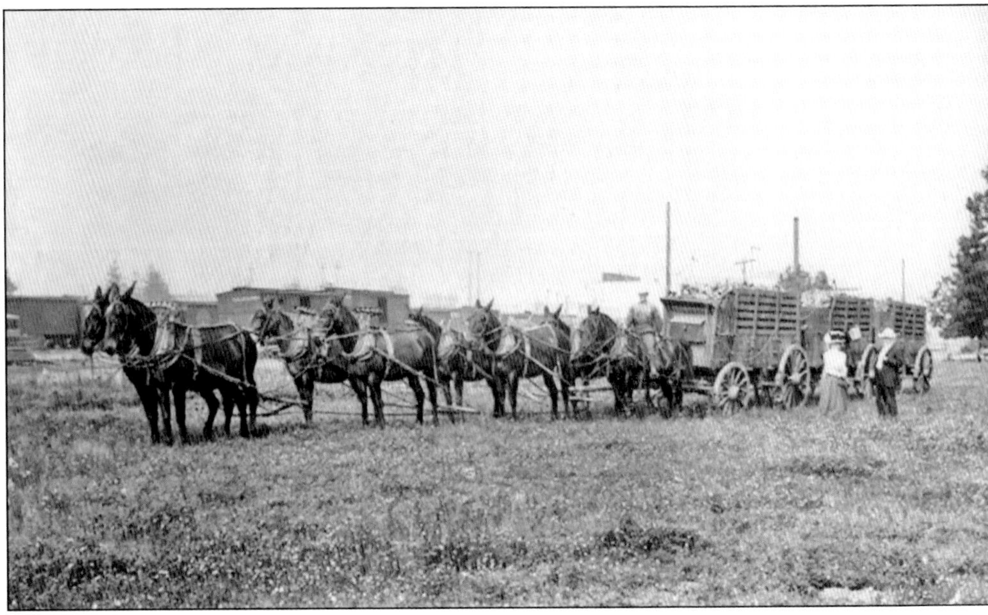

The above photograph shows three carloads of coke waiting to be hauled to a mine. Below is the Almeda Mine. In 1910, the *Rogue River Courier* reported, "Among the mines which are very active is the Almeda which is getting ready to blow in the 100-ton smelter. The company has three carloads of coke at the depot in Merlin and as soon as these can be hauled to Almeda increased work at the big mine will be started and added development undertaken."

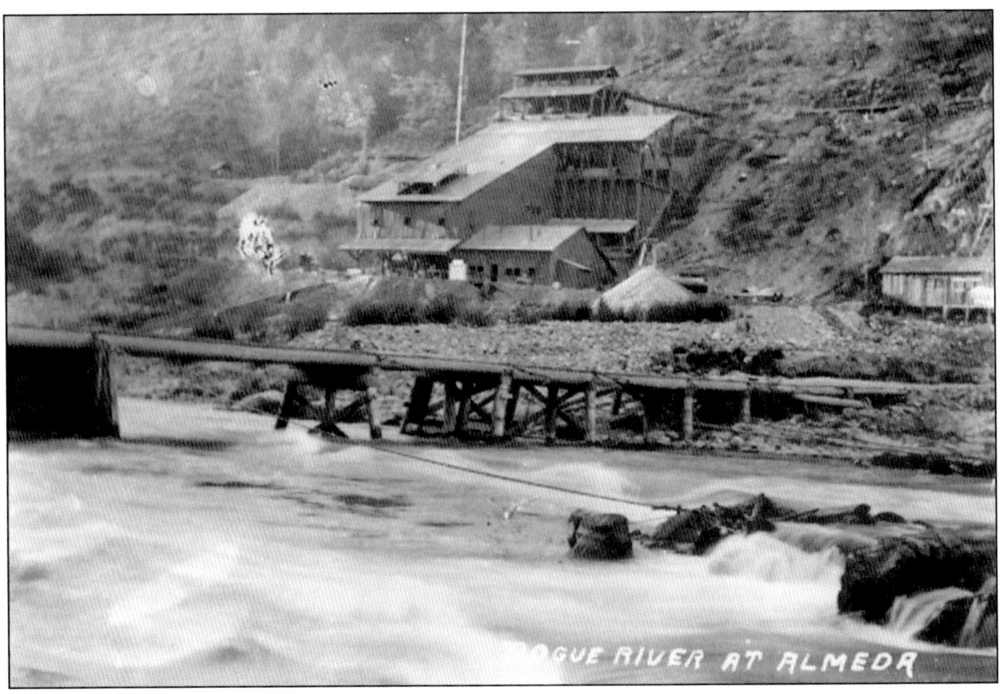

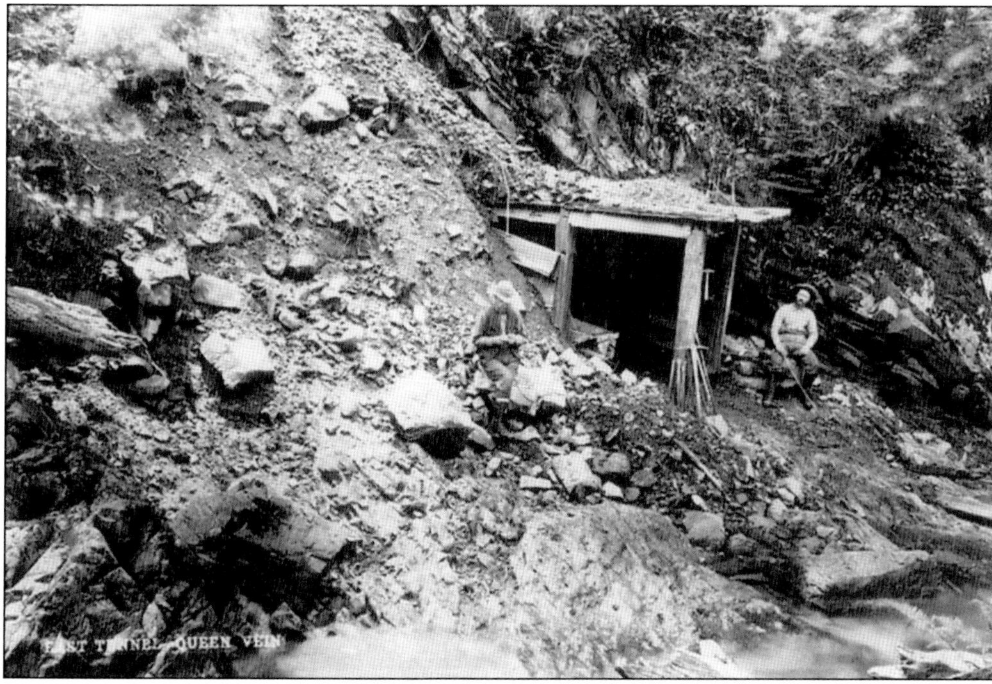

The east tunnel of the Queen Vein is shown above, and the west tunnel is below. The Commercial Club, speaking to the gold-mining industry in Josephine County, said, "This district in former years was regarded as being an exclusive placer mining region and while it is still the home of the model hydraulic mine of this state, yet its quartz mining industry in importance and value outweighs all other classes of mining."

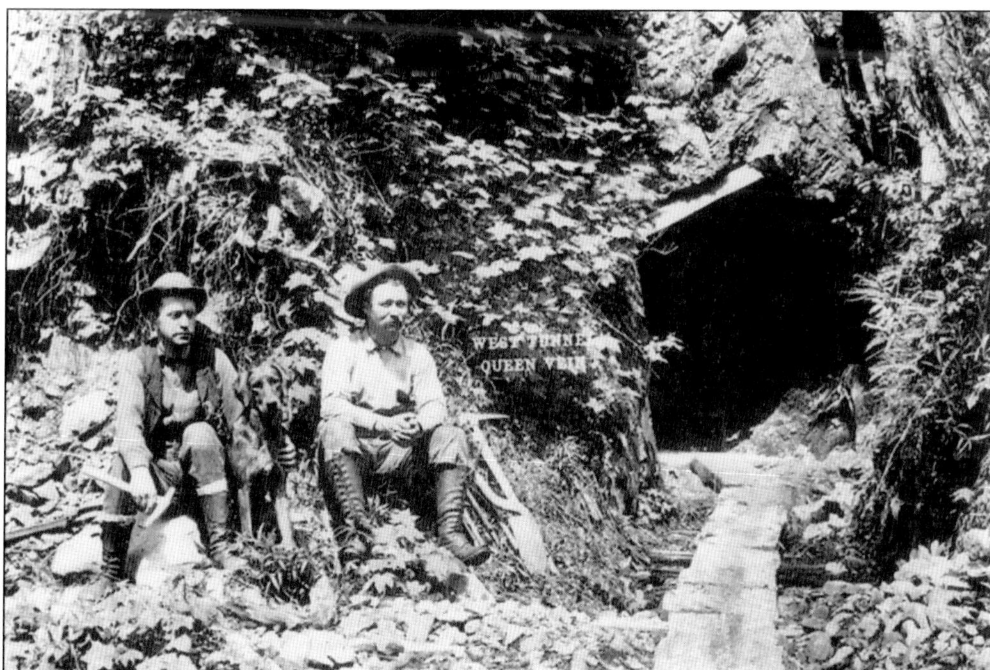

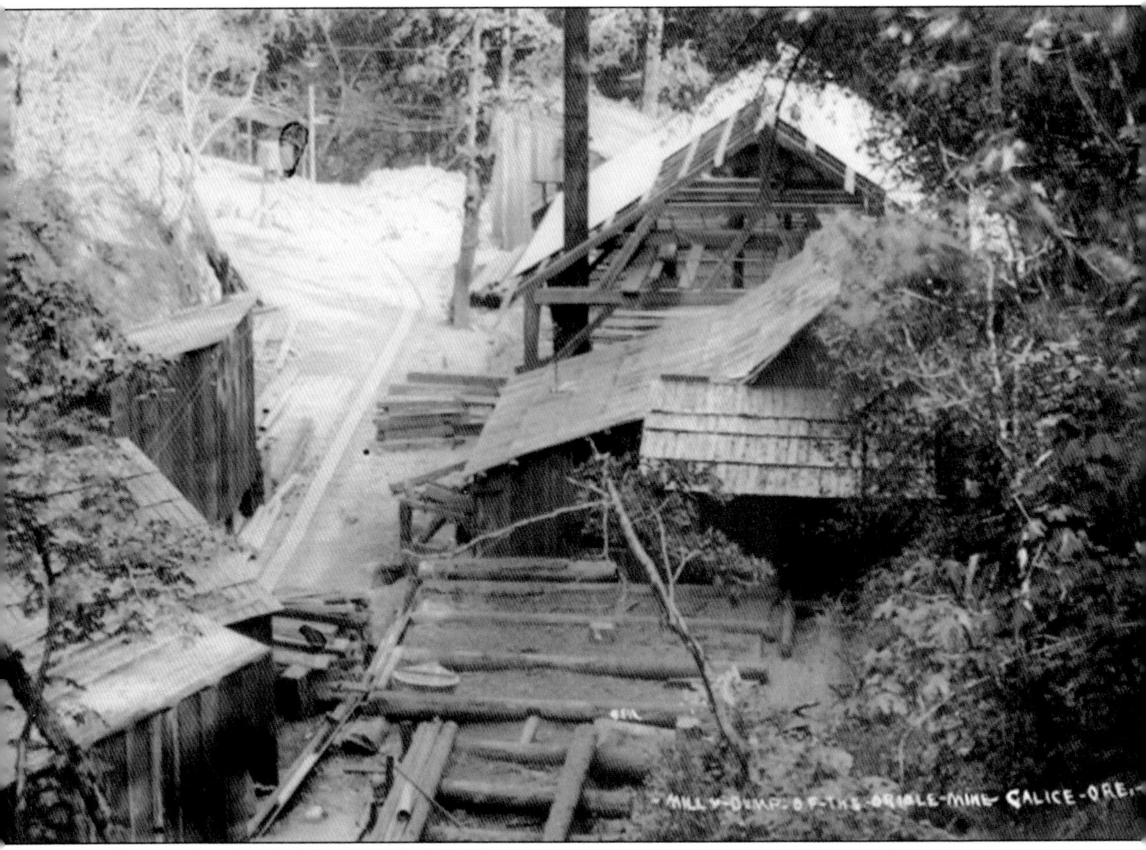

This is the Oriole Mine in Galice. In 1909, the mine's owners constructed a 10-stamp quartz mill, which ran on electricity generated from water power. The current from the water provided power for the compressor and lights. The following year, the *Rogue River Courier* reported, "The big Oriole Mine is proving to be a wonder—a veritable 'Lluvia de Oro.' The high grade ore in evidence on the surface outcroppings has recently been encountered by the 900 foot tunnel at a vertical depth of 600 feet, thus proving the fact that its wonderful values are not confined to surface deposits. The big vein, which is 100 to 200 feet in width, is composed of siliceous quartz strata of generous and variable size, ranging from one to 20 feet in width and interlaced with ribbons of metamorphic slate."

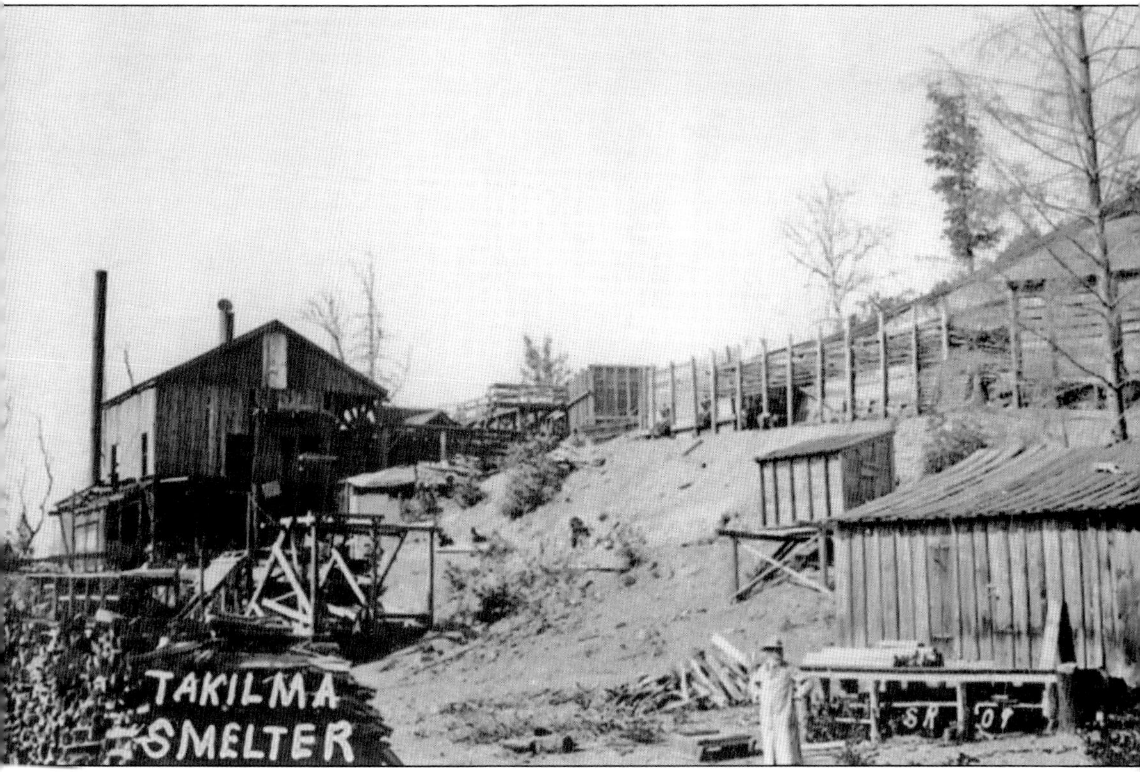

Copper ore in the vicinity of the Takilma Smelter was of such a good quality that, at times, up to 125 tons was smelted per day. The smelter could only run for three months of the year due to the ruination caused by rain and mud on the roads. If there was not as much rain in a given year, it could operate for six months. In the early 1900s, the 42-mile trip from Grants Pass to the Takilma Smelter took four to five days for a round trip. A load of coke was taken to the smelter, and a load of matte was brought back and then shipped by rail to a refinery in Tacoma, Washington.

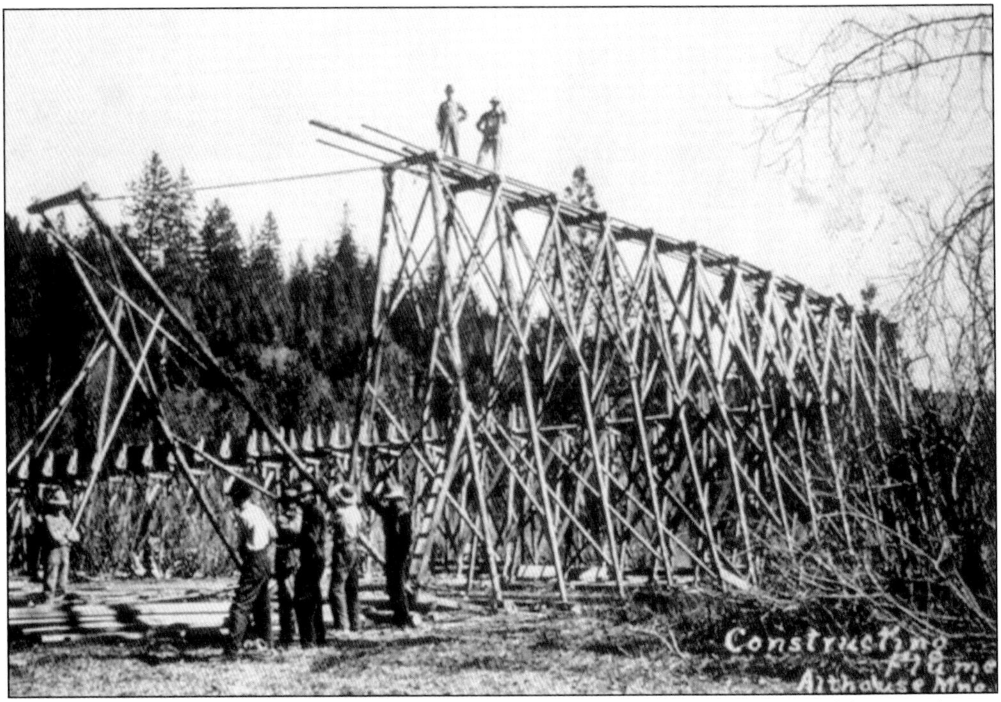

Althouse Mine got its start when three brothers—Samuel, John, and Philip Althouse—began mining on the creek that they later named after themselves. The brothers, who were from Peoria, Illinois, were pioneers of 1847. They named the Illinois River after their home state. In the above photograph, their company is constructing a flume. The below photograph shows their excavator; this equipment is a far cry from using picks and shovels.

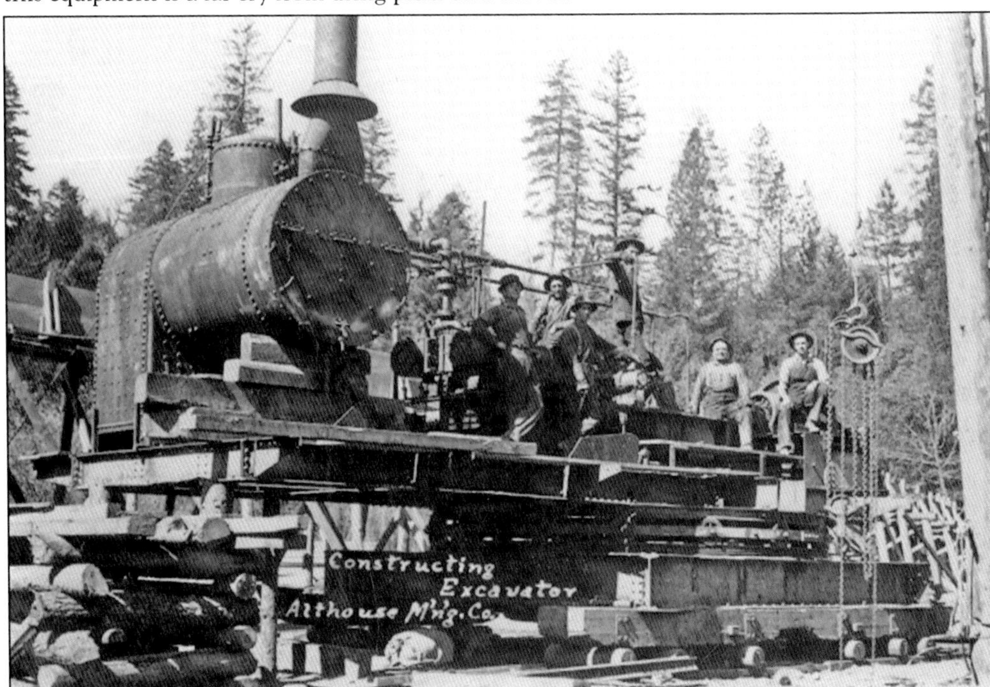

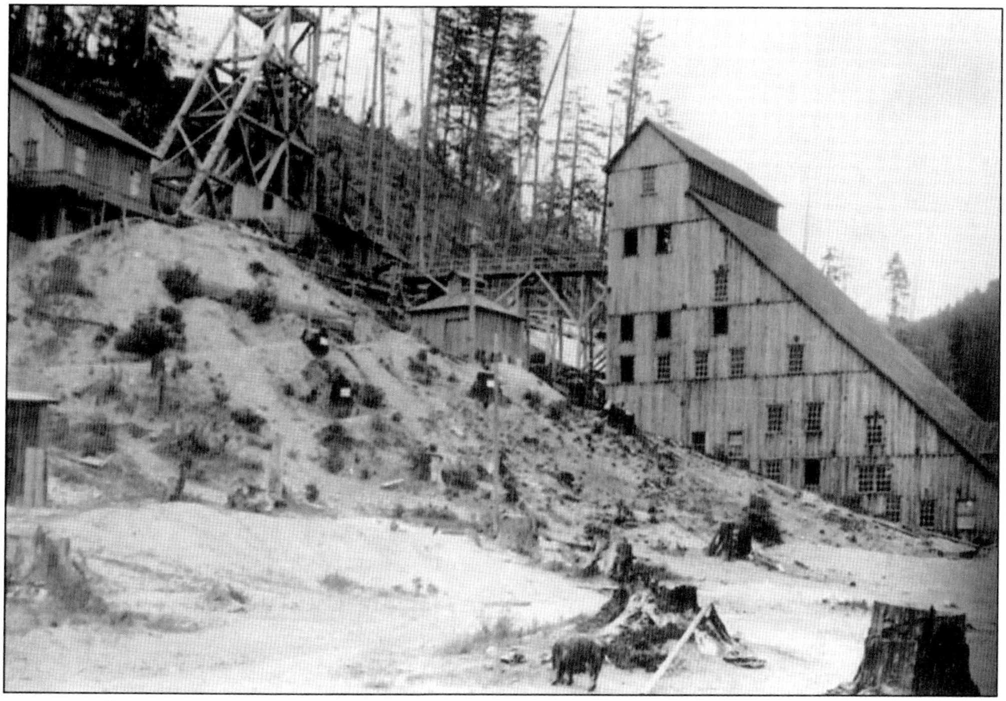

In 1905, the Grants Pass Mining Association provided a reference room filled with volumes of books on mining from all over the country as well as maps detailing all of the mining in Josephine County. The association advertised, "The use of the room is free to the general public and mining men. They can avail themselves to the use of and make the room their headquarters when they are in Grants Pass. Stationery and desks are at their service free of charge for any correspondence they may wish to do and the leading daily papers, mining, and other publications are on file for the use of those who wish to spend an hour or more in reading. The library and minerals exhibit room is open daily from eight o'clock in the morning to nine o'clock in the evening."

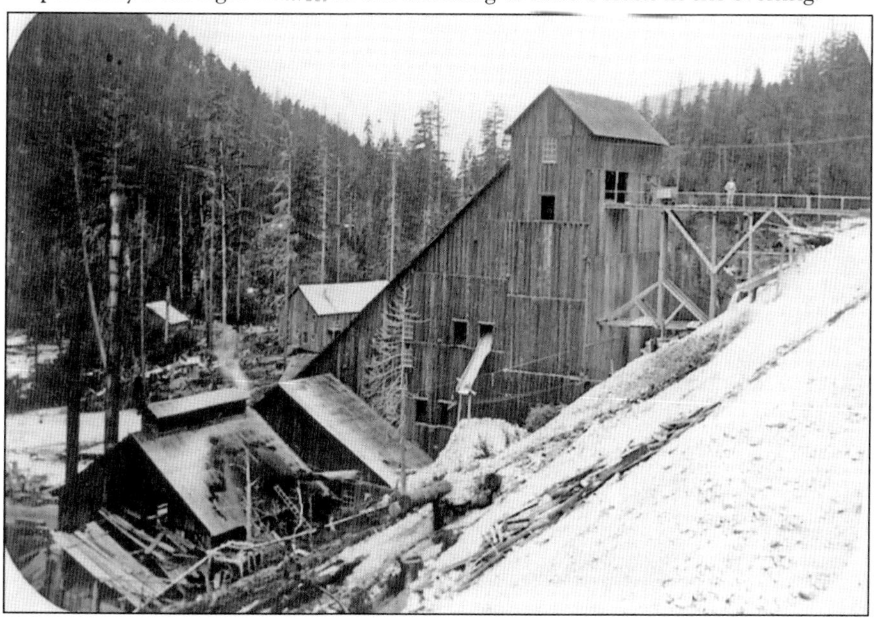

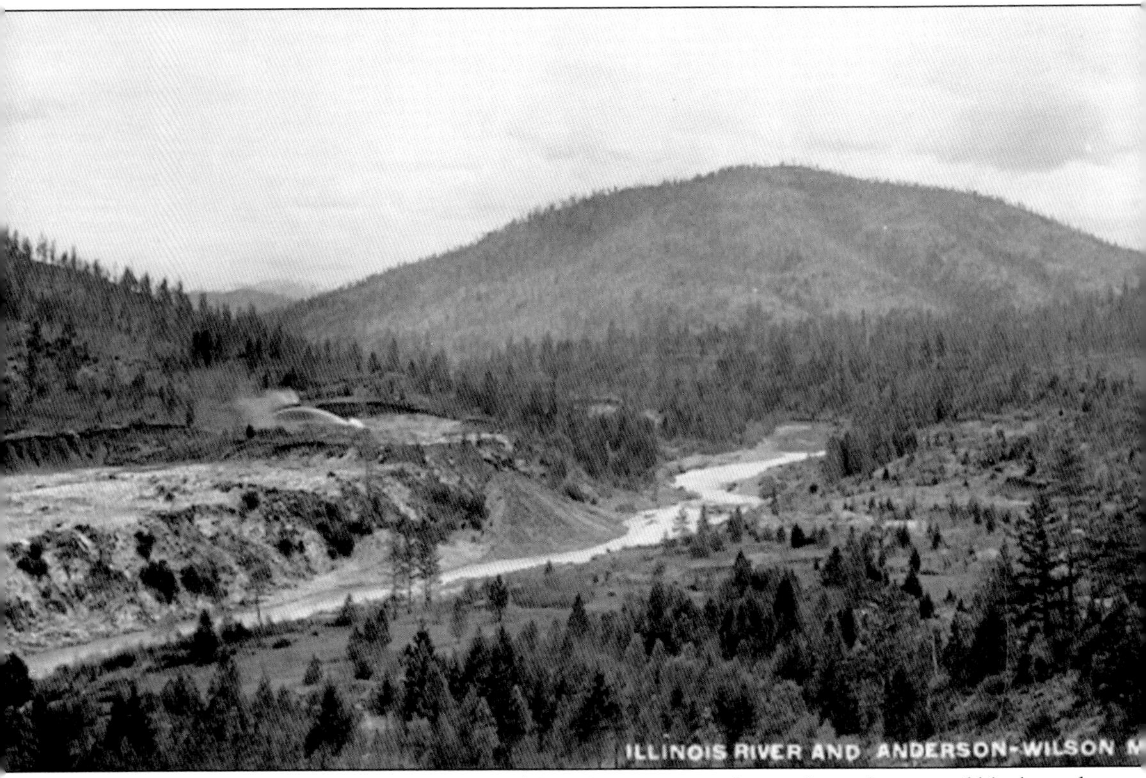

The Anderson & Wilson Mine is pictured. J.W. Sweet patented a machine that mined black sand, and he enjoyed success with it in the California mines. He and Mr. Lane brought that machine to the Anderson & Wilson Mine in 1913 to work for platinum.

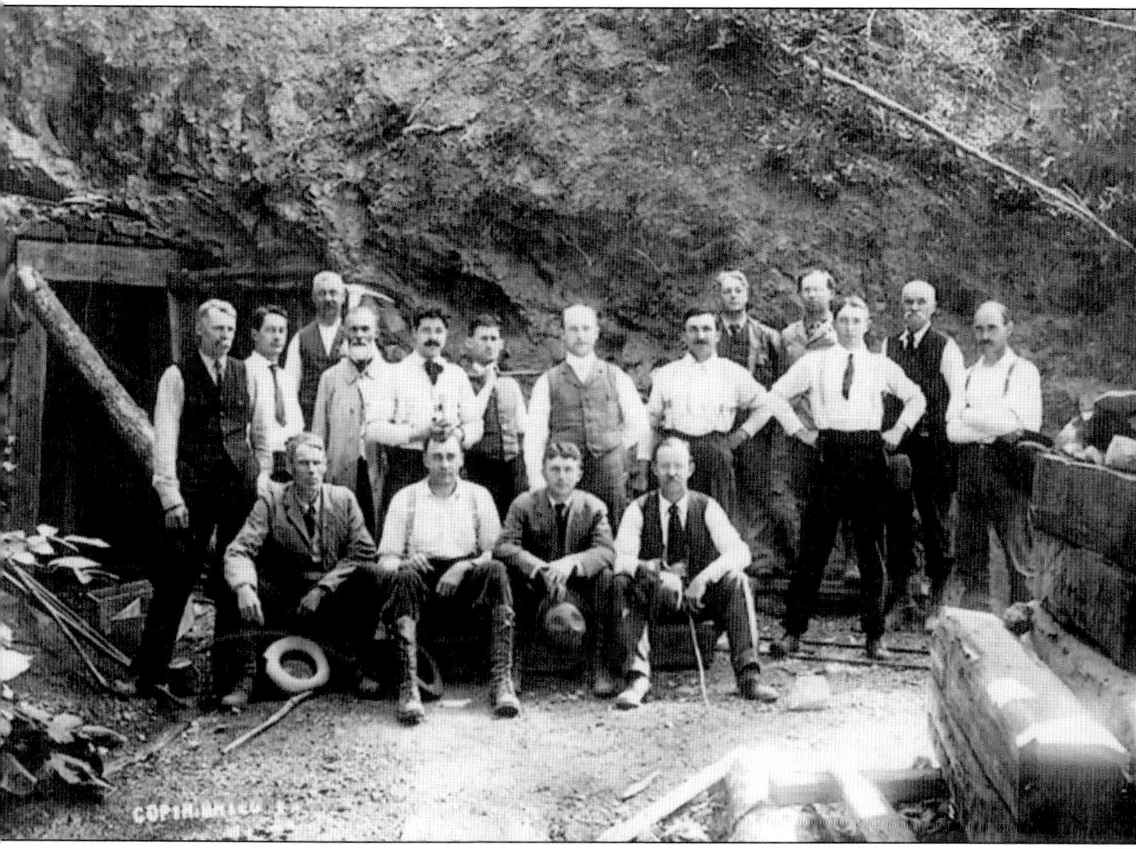

In 1900, the Mining and Commercial Club of Grants Pass made the following offer to mine owners: "If you own a quartz mine which has a tunnel in 100 feet or a shaft down 50 feet and are desirous of placing the mine on the market in order to further develop it, there are two ways of doing so. Sell an interest outright or else issue stock and sell the stock on the stock board. The mining committee will furnish a written recommendation with an expert report and this will tend to strengthen the confidence of mining investors in your mine. Or give an interest in the mine in exchange for cash and the committee will take a deed in escrow to secure the advance."

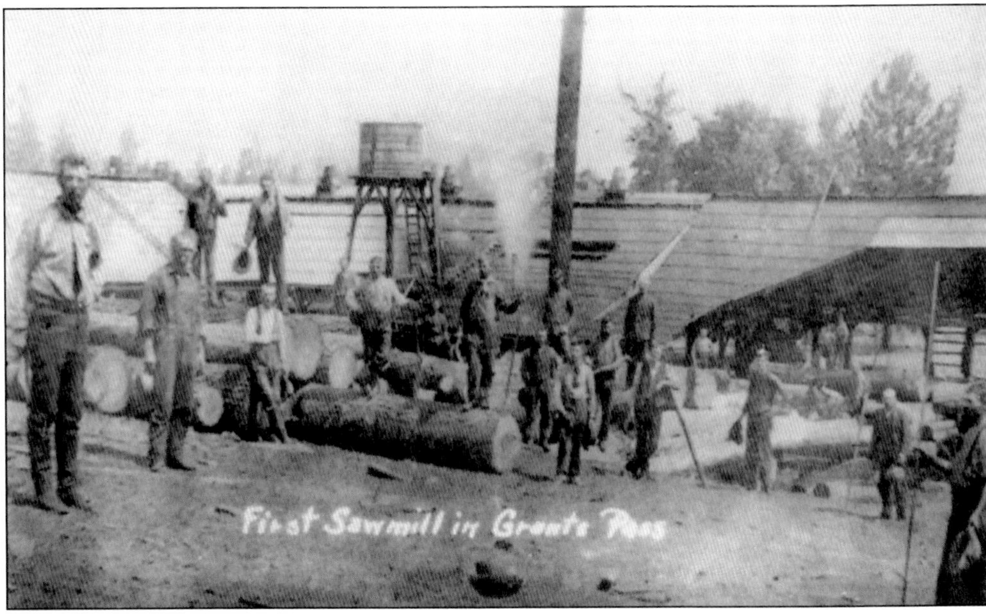

The first sawmill in Grants Pass is pictured above. In 1900, the *Rogue River Courier* reported, "Sugar pine has been used on the Pacific Coast for fifty years and it is used for exactly the same purposes as white pine on the east coast. Doors of sugar pine do not shrink or swell. It has no equal for pattern work, durability is unquestioned. It is used by boat builders in California. There is a ready market on the east coast for sugar pine. Grants Pass is at the center of sugar pine and yellow pine interests."

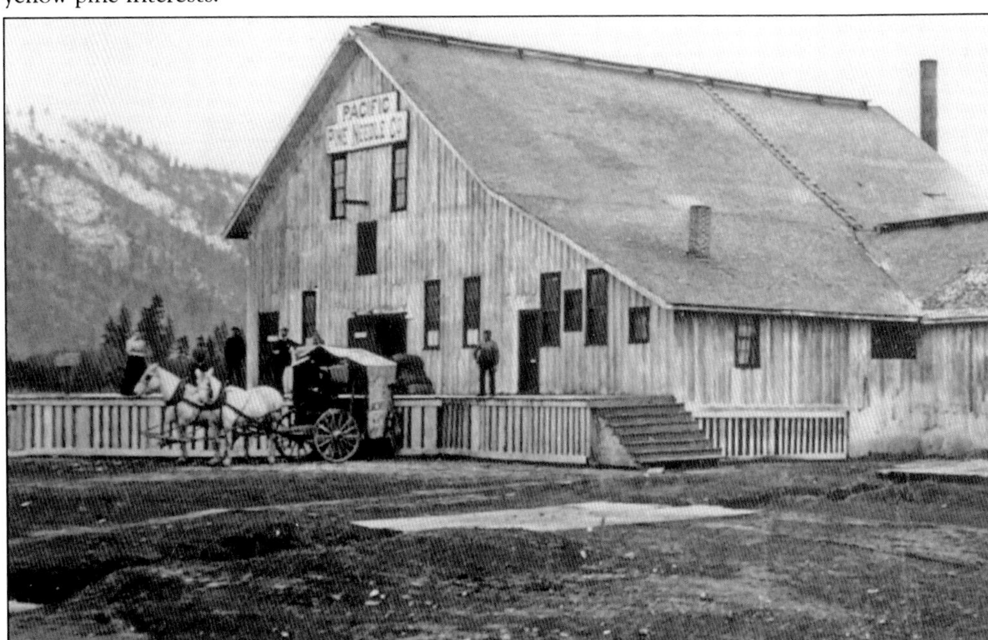

This is the Pacific Pine Needle Company factory. The factory advertised, "Pine needles wanted. The Pacific Pine Needle Company is ready to enter into contracts for the regular delivery of pine needles. Apply at the factory office."

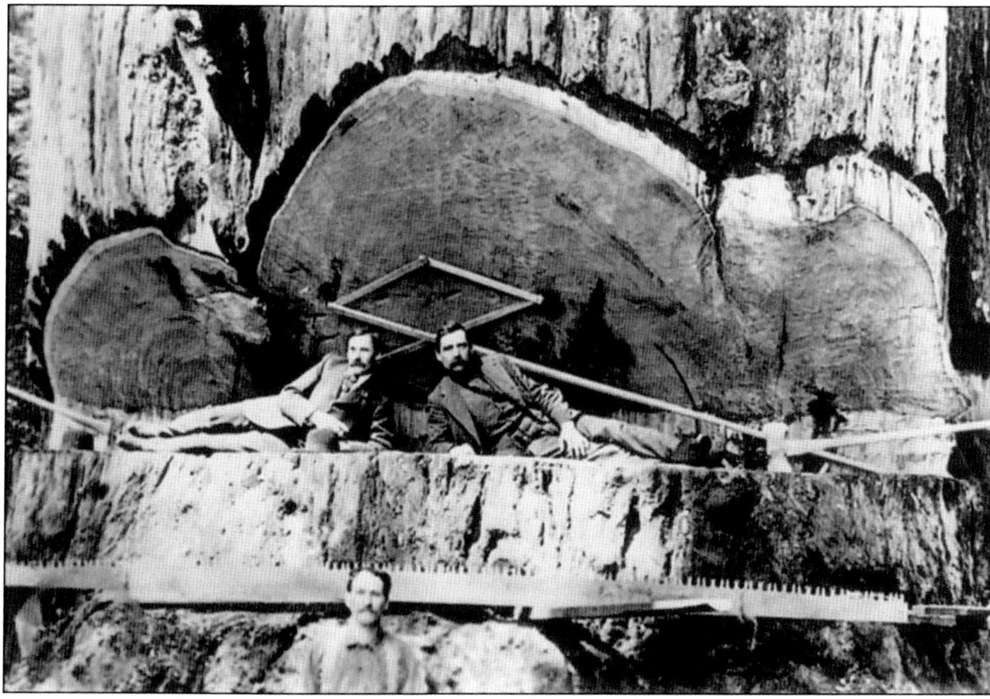

Every timber owner in Oregon was required to provide a "sufficient fire patrol" during the dry season. The patrol had to meet the approval of the State Board of Forestry. If a timber owner did not provide a fire patrol, the Oregon State Board of Forestry stepped in with their own fire patrol at a cost not to exceed 5¢ per acre at the turn of the last century.

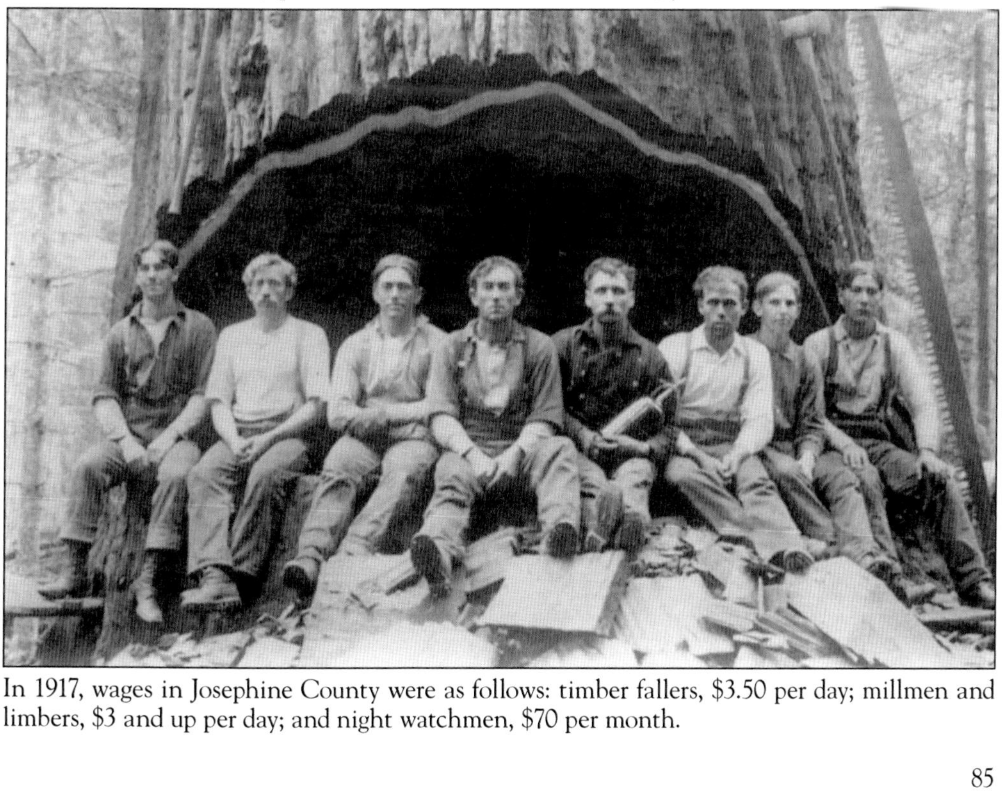

In 1917, wages in Josephine County were as follows: timber fallers, $3.50 per day; millmen and limbers, $3 and up per day; and night watchmen, $70 per month.

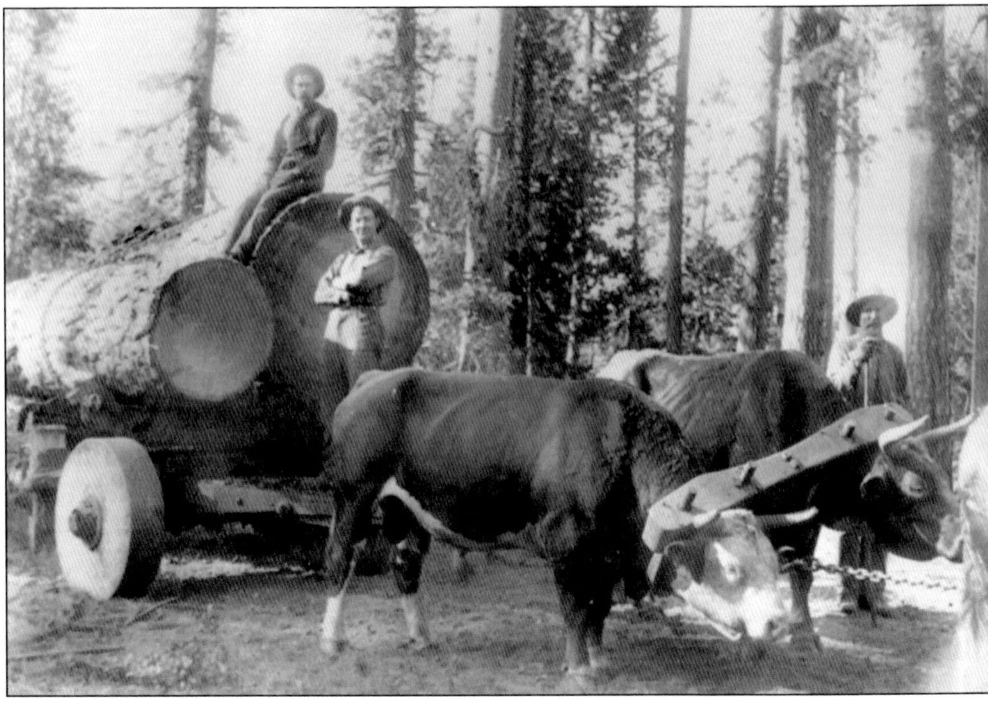

Oxen were a tremendous help in the 1800s. They pulled covered wagons across the plains, and once in Oregon, they were used to haul heavy timber, as shown in these photographs. Transporting lumber to the mills or the railroad was dependent on weather. Once the rains came, the roads became impassible due to the heavy mud.

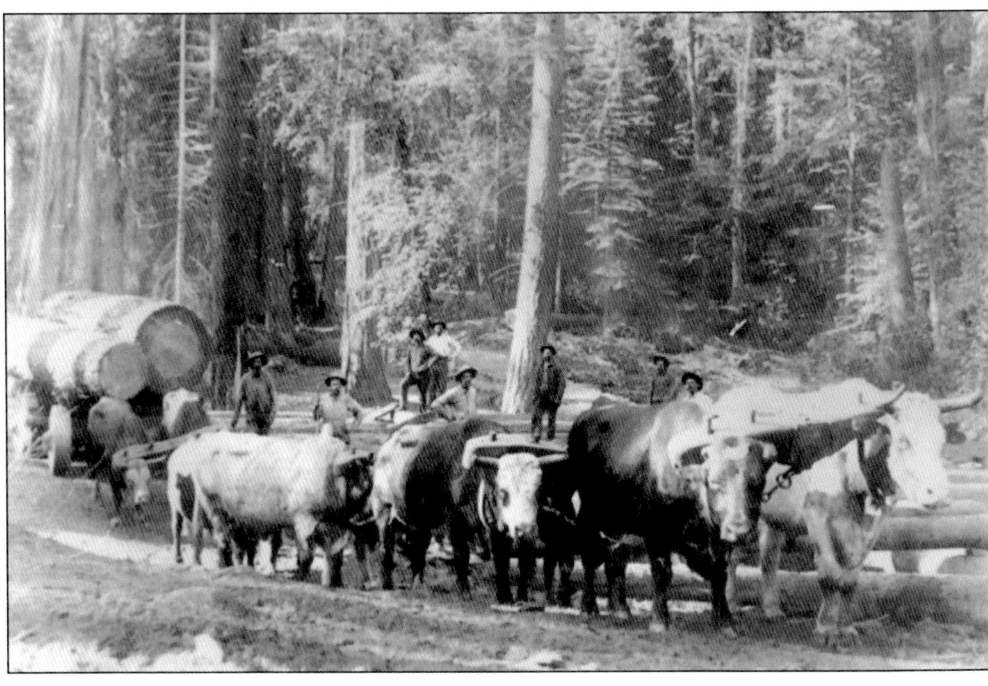

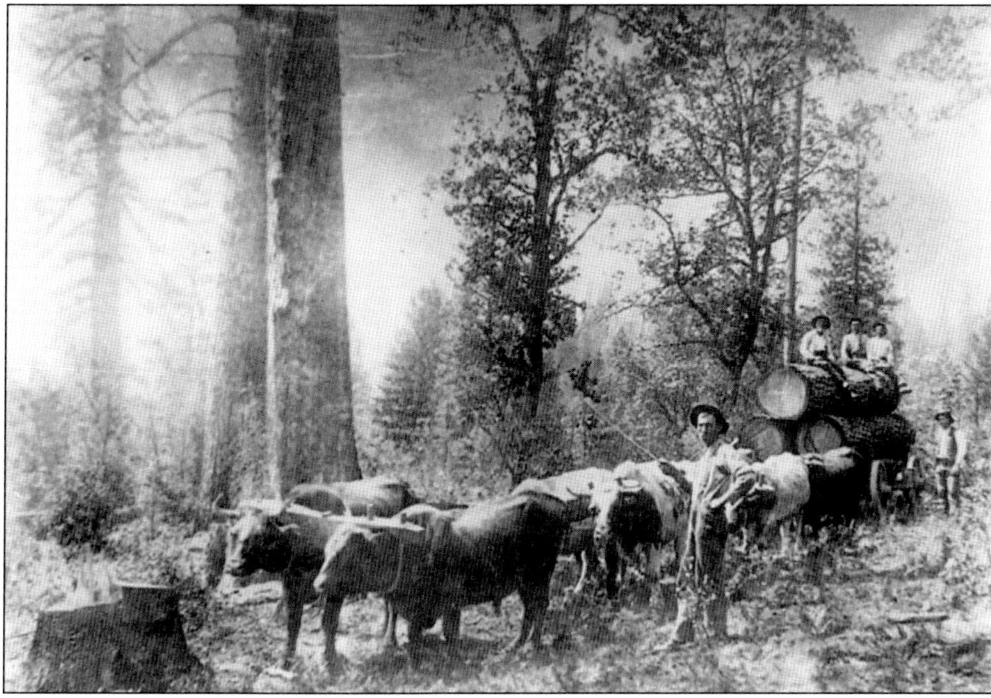

In 1905, the *Rogue River Courier* reported, "The lumber cut this season is sugar pine and is of a fine quality. The larger part of it will be shipped to Eastern factories."

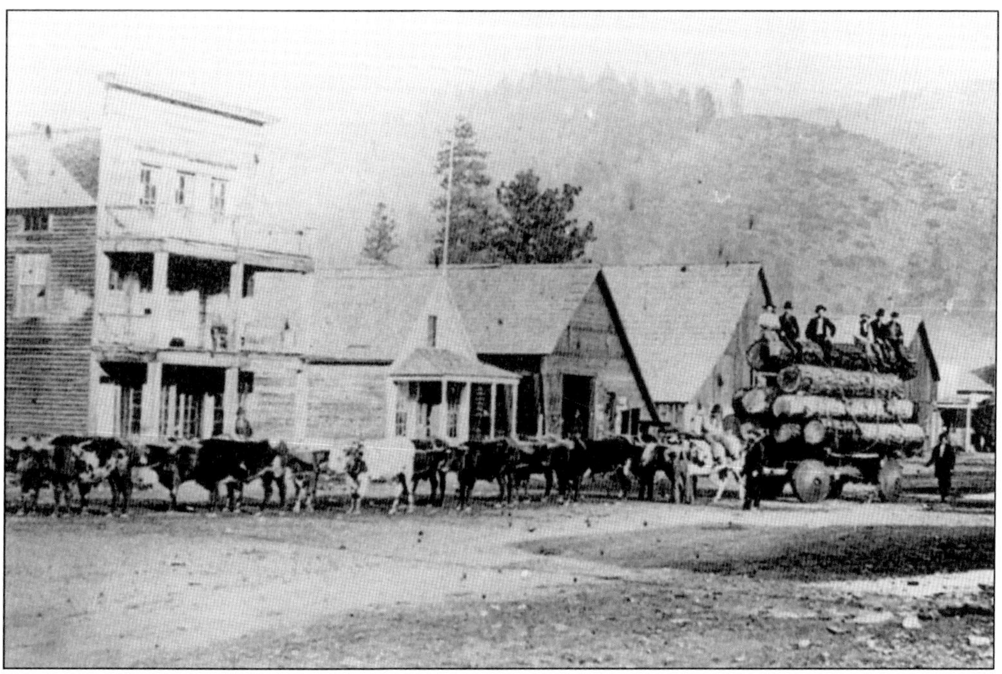

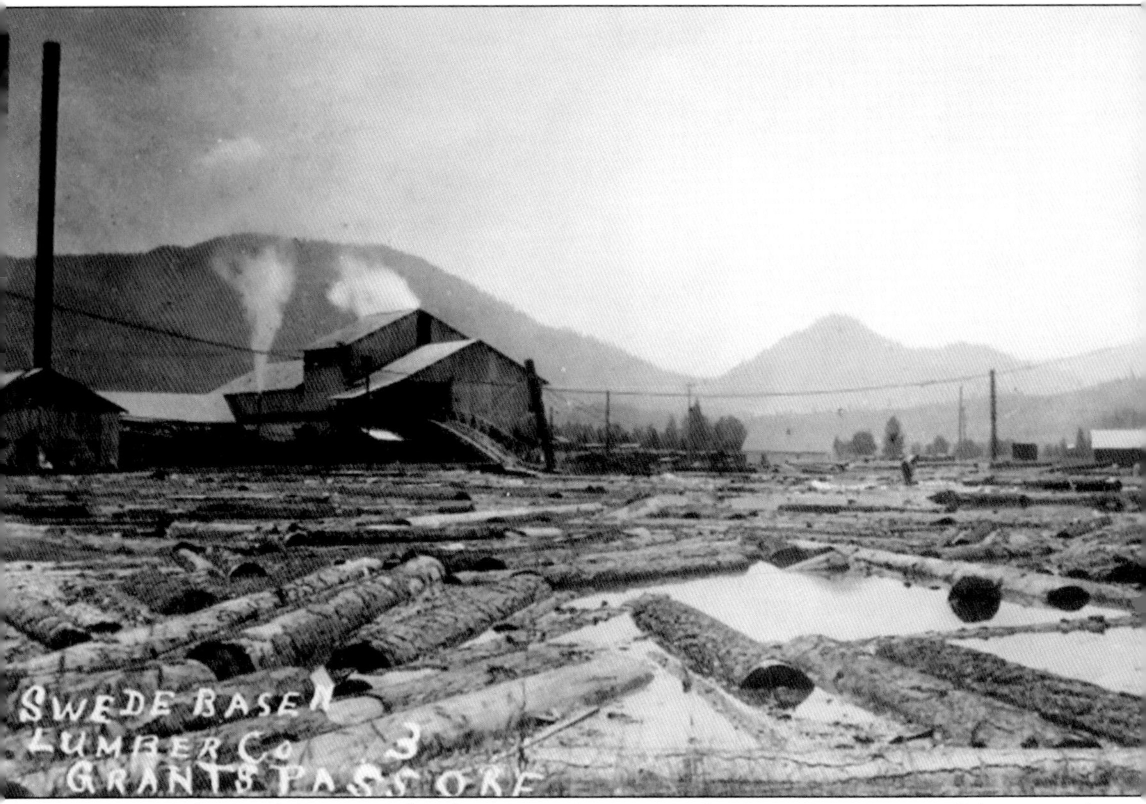

In 1918, the Swede Basin Lumber Company advertised in the *Rogue River Courier*: "Men wanted 50 cents and up per hour. Come out or write A.L. Allen, Wonder, Oregon." The newspaper explained, "Swede Basin Mill needs more men. A.L. Allen, in charge of logging operations at the Swede Basin Mill, was in the city today in an effort to secure men to work in the mill. He is advertising for 50 men and offering 50 cents and up per hour. There are now 50 men employed at the company. Lumber will be hauled by auto truck to the railroad terminus at Waters Creek and it is expected that hauling will be commenced within a few days, there being a large amount of last season's cut yet in the yards. The season's cut is expected to be about 750,000 feet."

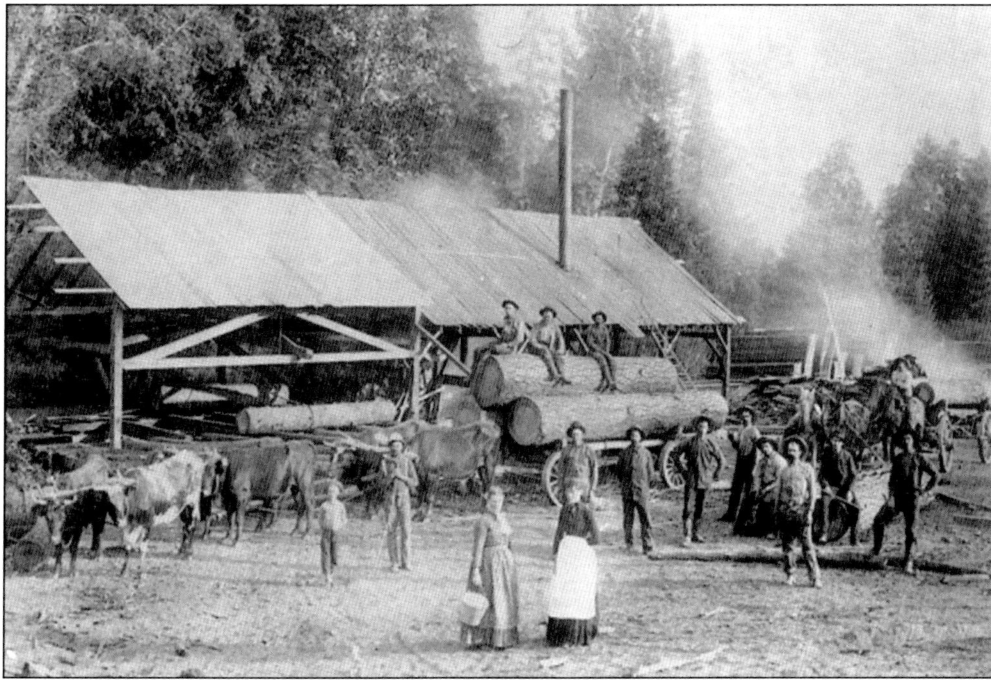

These photographs were taken in 1898 by the Southern Pacific Railroad as part of their advertisement for the Shasta Route. Pictured is the George J. Hiller Mill on Riverbanks Road near Wilderville. In the above image, George J. Hiller is sitting on the log holding a yardstick at the right; Hiller's mother, Christina Hiller Brandt, is standing in the forefront holding a pail; the small boy in the foreground is Holman Peters, and his father is standing next to him.

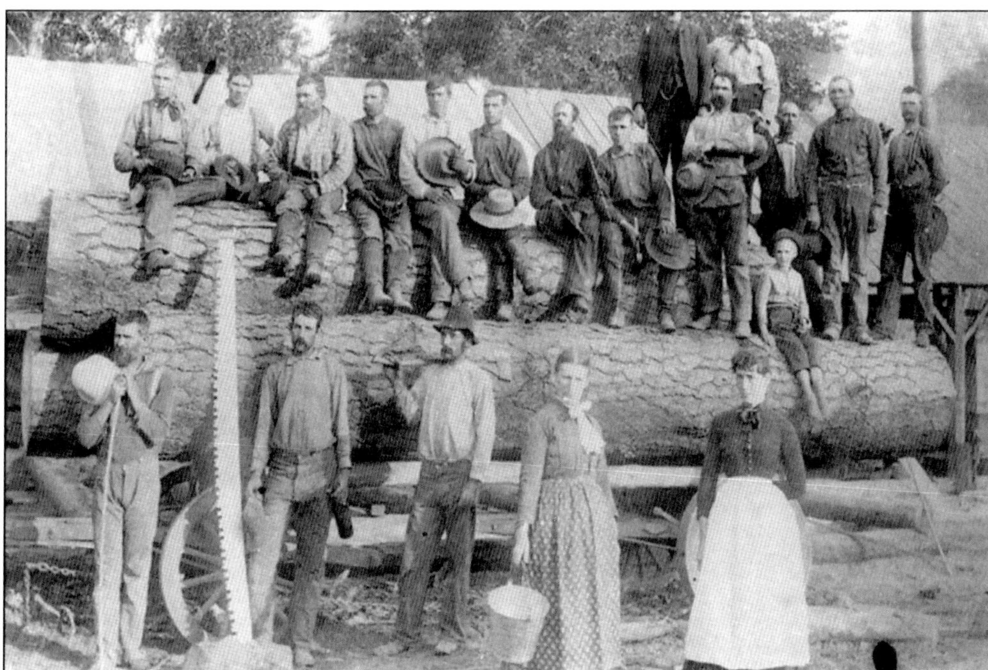

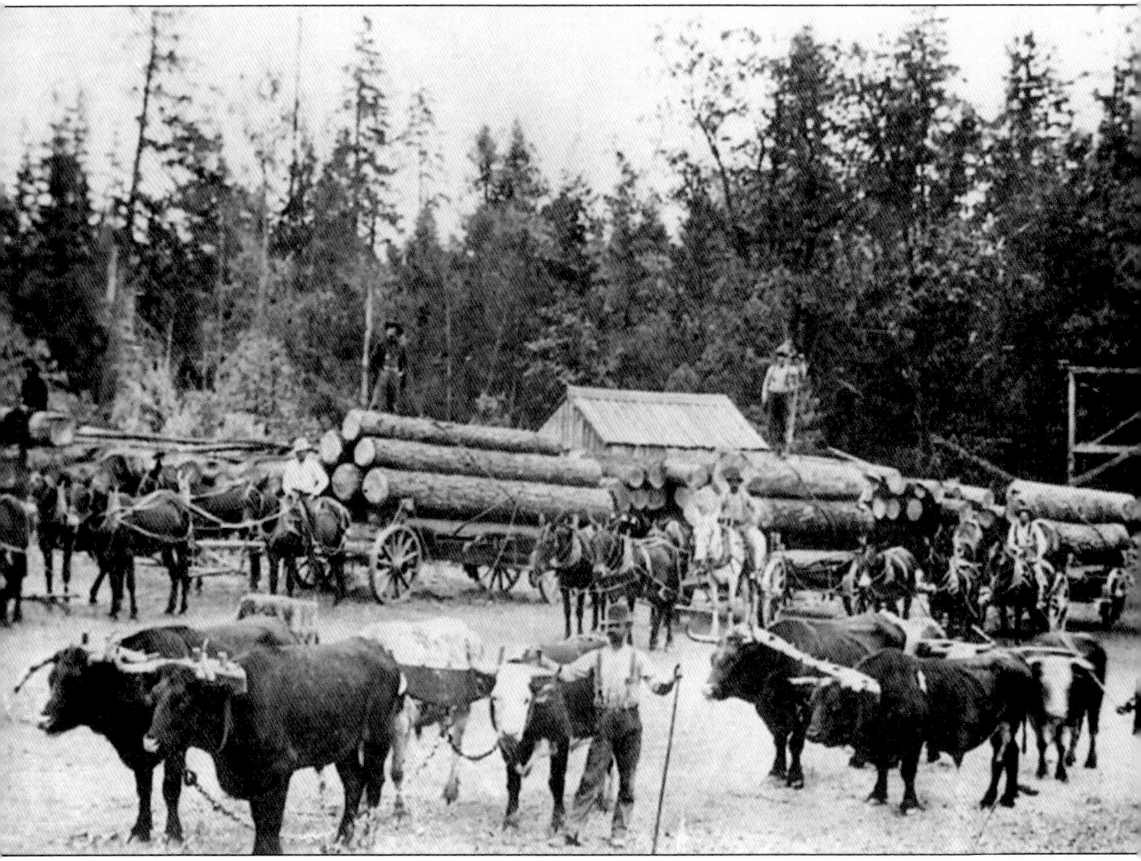

This photograph was taken in the Shan Creek area. In 1908, the total amount of timber sold in the United States was 386 million feet for a value of $850,000.

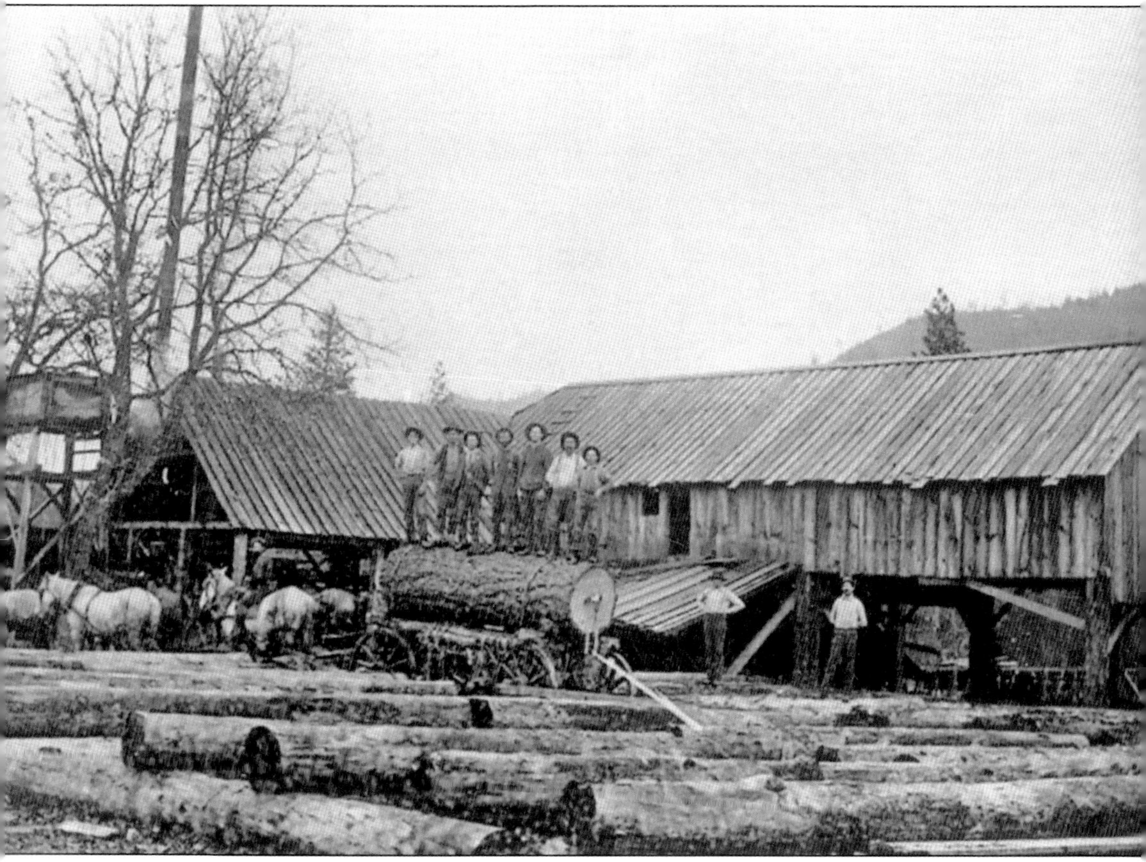

The horses pictured here are getting ready to haul a load of logs. There were instances wherein a company had to move its entire sawmill once the nearby timber had been cut. In January 1903, the Golden Drift Mining Company moved its sawmill, because it was unable to haul lumber any distance due to what the *Rogue River Courier* reported as "fearful conditions of the road which are little else than a mass of seemingly bottomless mud, so badly that they are cut up by the teams and wagons hauling the massive timbers. Some of the timbers are 30 to 40 feet in length."

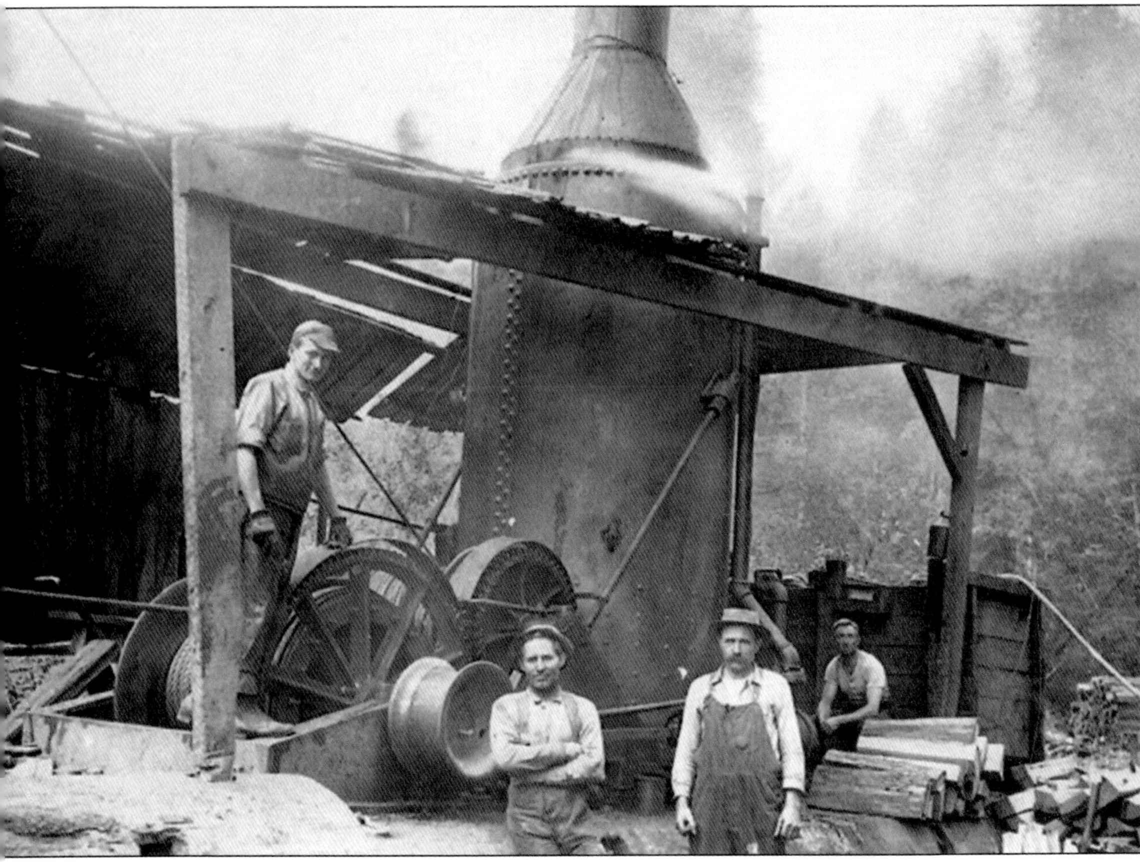

Donkey engines were in great demand for use in hauling timber to the mill and clearing stumps. They were also used to tow machinery to the mines.

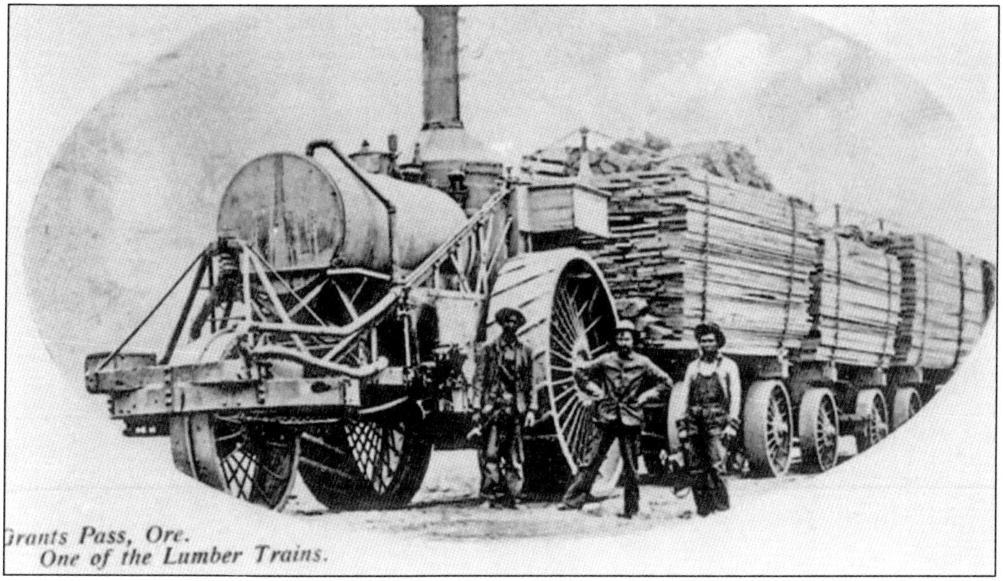

On July 8, 1910, the *Rogue River Courier* reported, "The monster traction engine hauling its modern lumber special of 40,000 feet was passing over the new steel bridge at the foot of 6th Street when one of the long sway braces which support the huge structure gave way. The county court issued an order preventing traction engines and heavily loaded wagons from crossing the bridge. The importance of this bridge to Grants Pass and that part of the county south of the river cannot be fully realized until it is put out of commission. The county court has stationed a watchman on the bridge who has instructions not only to prevent heavy loads from crossing but to compel all teams to pass on the west side of the bridge, so as to be far from the weakened part."

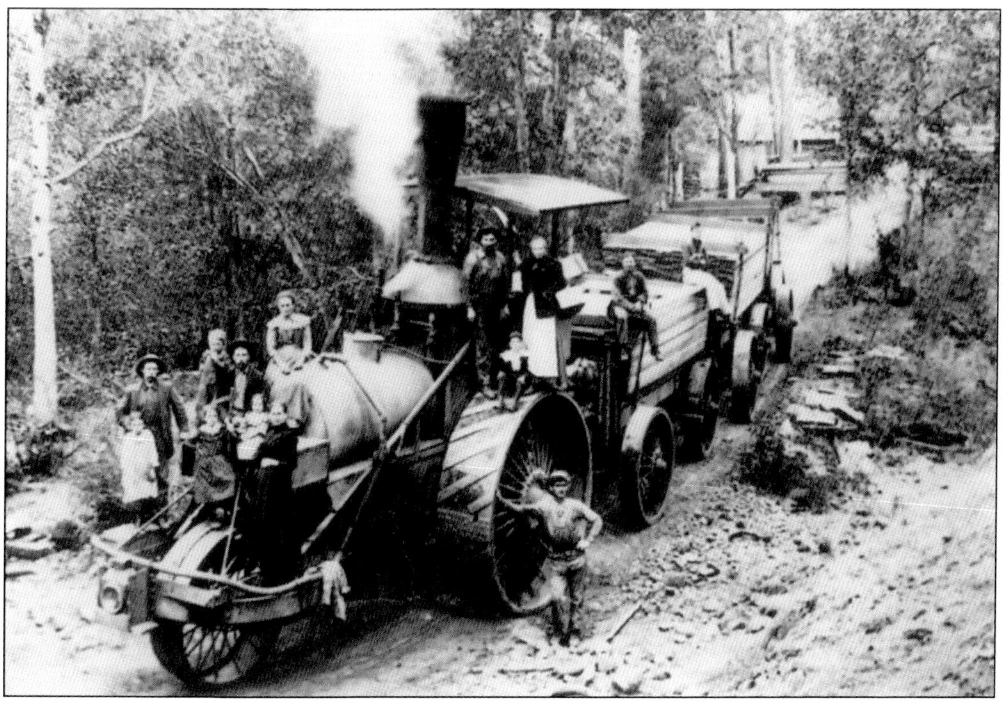

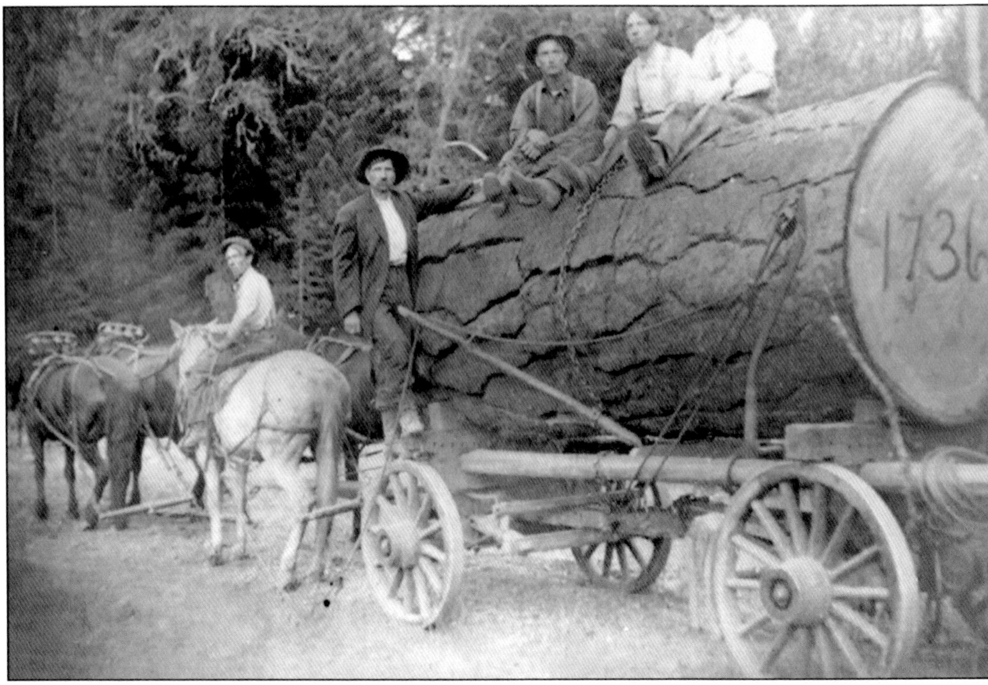

In 1906, the *Rogue River Courier* reported, "The state of Oregon has approximately 300,000,000,000 feet board measure of standing timber. It is a much greater amount than is possessed by any other state in the Union. Commercially the value of the standing timber when manufactured into lumber and sold at the rate of $12 per thousand board feet would be $3,600,000,000. This is a sum in excess of the total amount of currency in the U.S. at the present day." One of the largest timber sales in Josephine County took place in 1906. The sale was for 3,880 acres of pine and yellow fir for $100,000. In May 1916, John A. Dale advertised 275 acres with an estimated scale of three million feet of merchantable saw timber for $3,500.

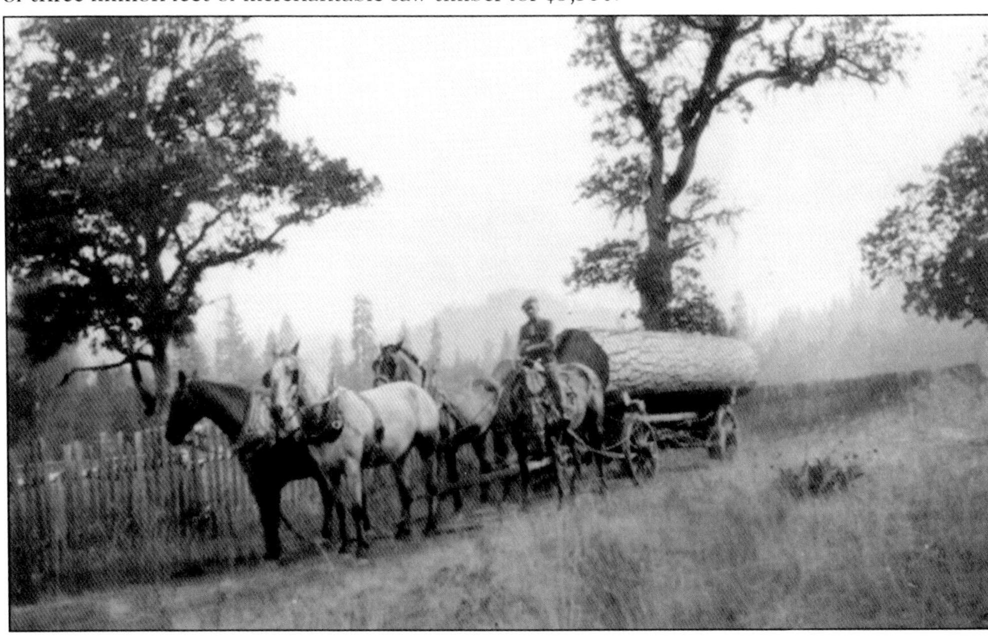

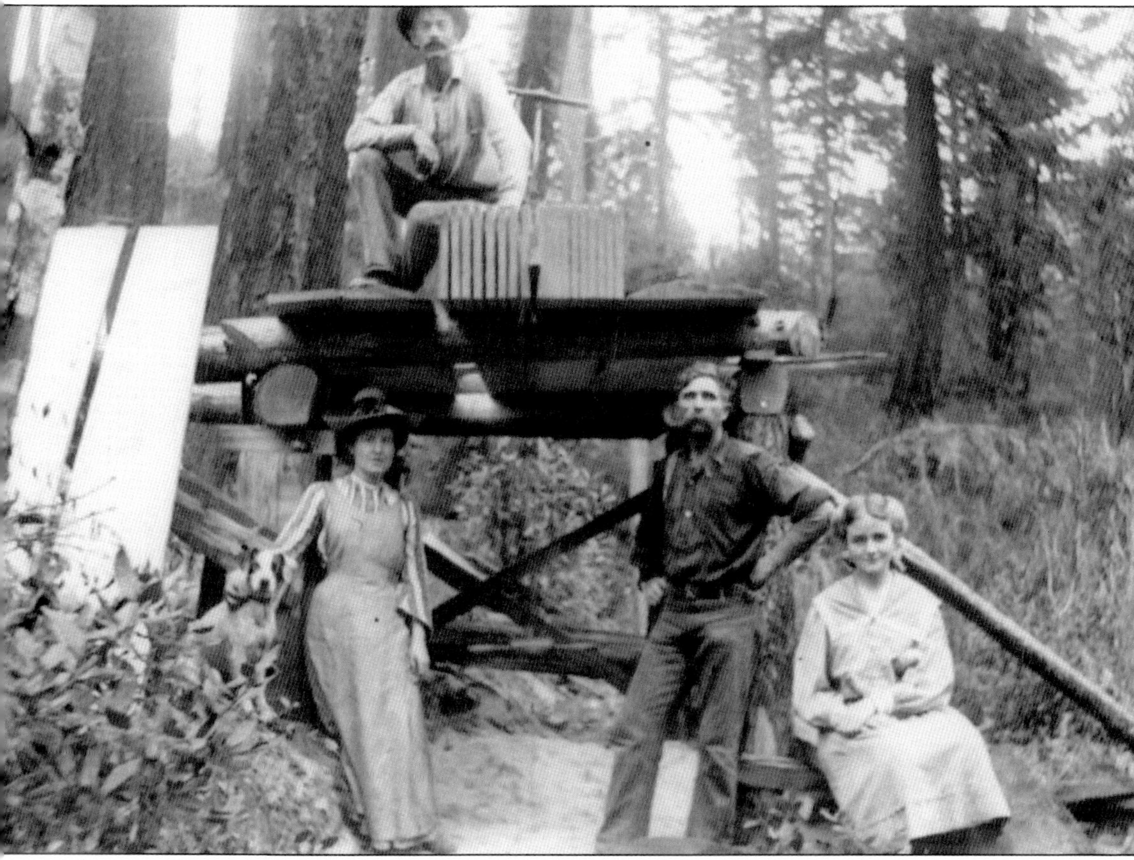

Whipsaws, like the one pictured, were used throughout Josephine County to cut timber before it was hauled to the mill.

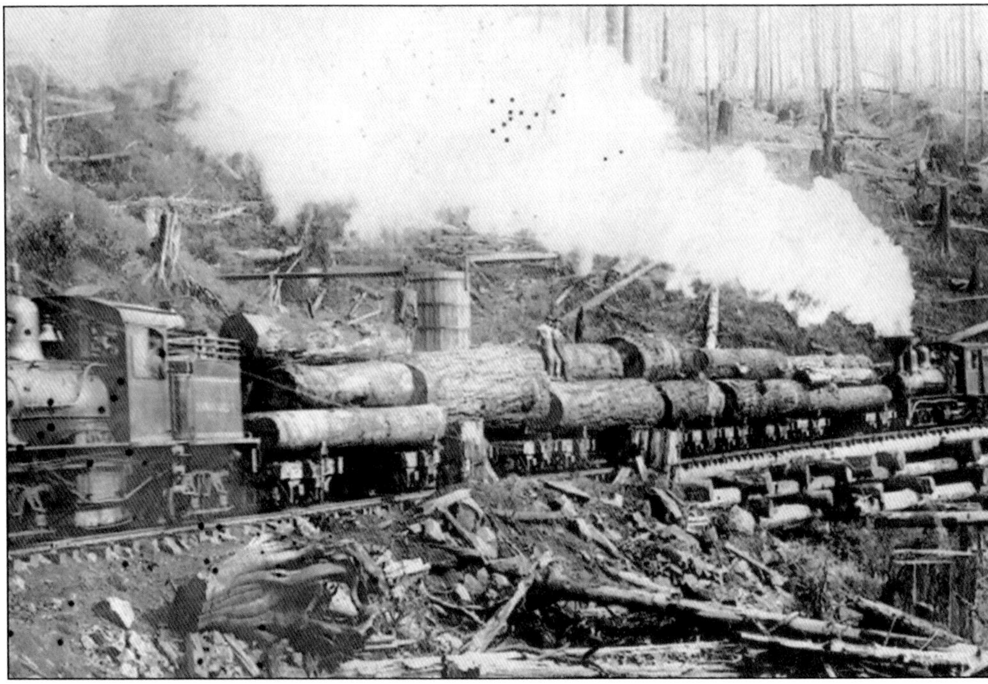

Hauling timber by railroad (above) could cost as much as 1.5¢ per pound in 1917. Later, when trucks (below) were available, timber was hauled directly to where it needed to go without being constrained by the railroads. This also lowered the cost of getting the timber to the buyer.

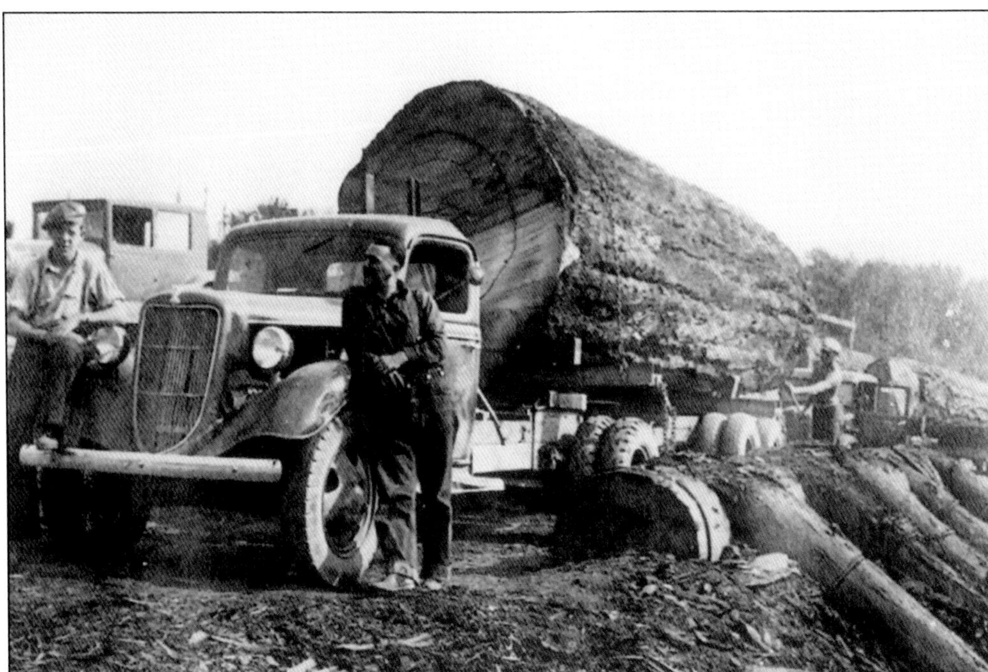

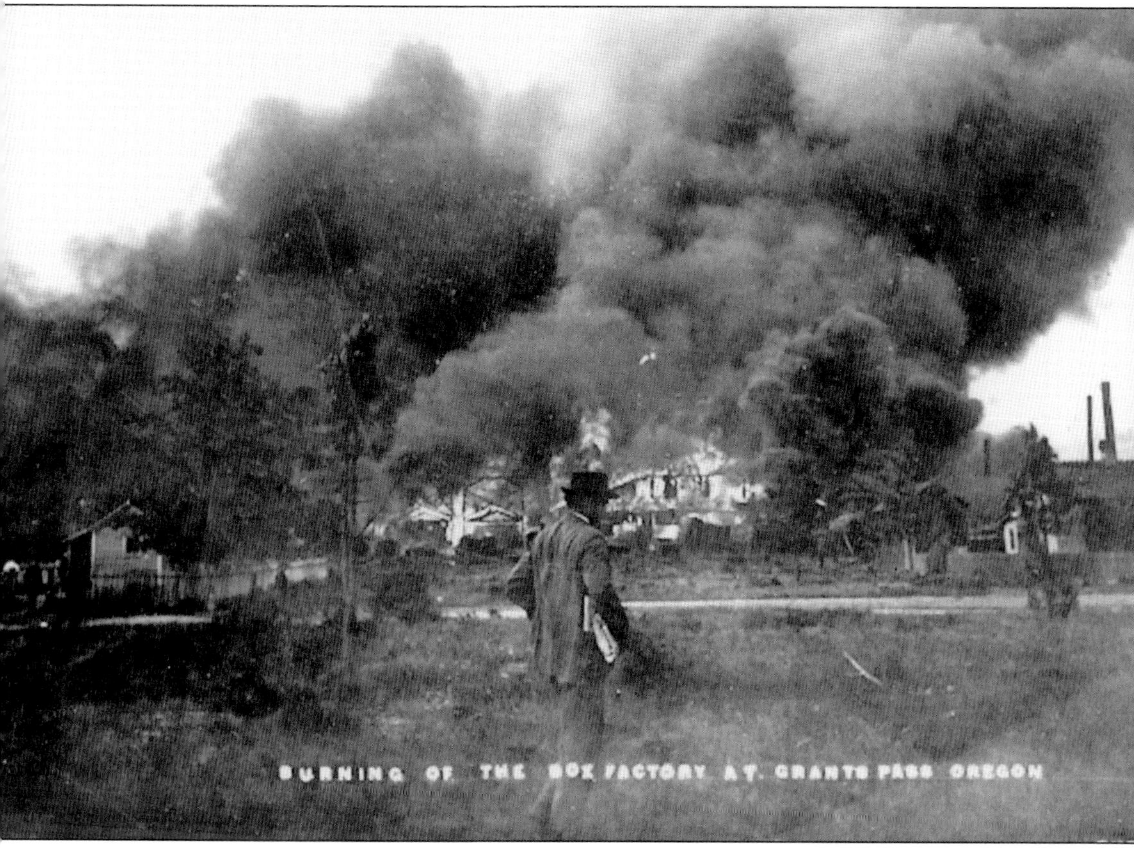

Hammond C. Kinney was born in Quebec, Canada, in 1850. He moved to Orleans County, Vermont, with his family when he was a child. As a young man, he headed to Idaho and worked at a sawmill. He arrived in Grants Pass in 1885 and immediately helped organize the Sugar Pine Door and Lumber Company. The following year, he built a box factory and opened a general merchandise store. He lost the box factory to fire in 1889 and again in 1902 (pictured). He rebuilt the factory both times.

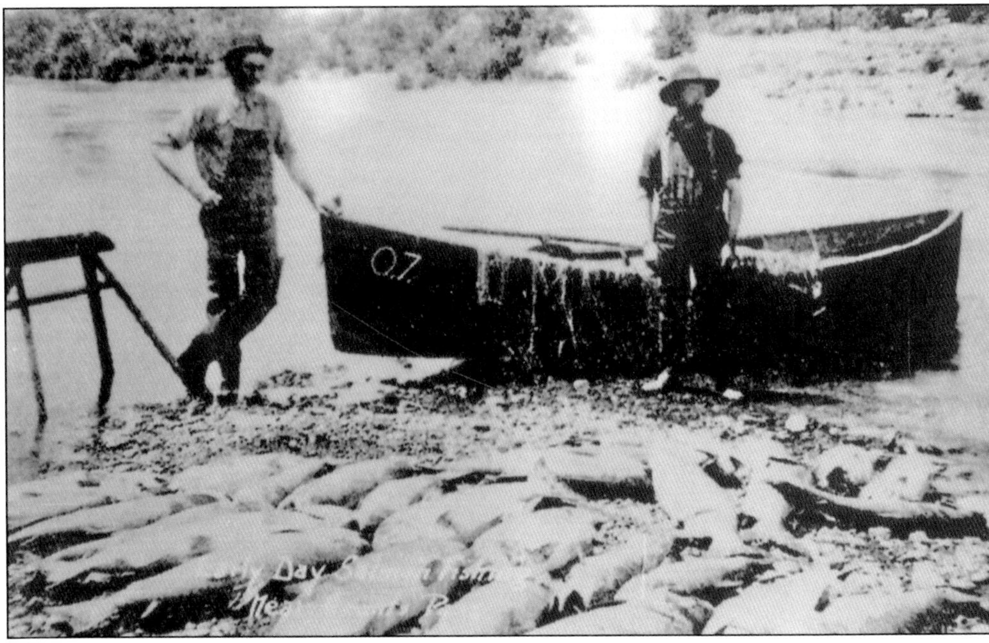

In 1919, Josephine County was featured in the monthly brochure of the Standard Oil Company, which described the Rogue River as the "best fishing stream in America." The brochure also read, "Camping grounds every hundred yards, plenty of wood everywhere, splendid shade under beautiful pine trees. Rogue River is on the Pacific Highway leading from San Francisco to Portland, about half way between the two cities. Scenic in the extreme. It is not unusual for steelhead trout to be caught in this river weighing from four to 18 pounds. It is not uncommon for a lad to catch 150 pounds of fish in one day. Plenty of small and big game within 50 miles of populated centers. Climate ideal and especially healthful for ladies. Try it."

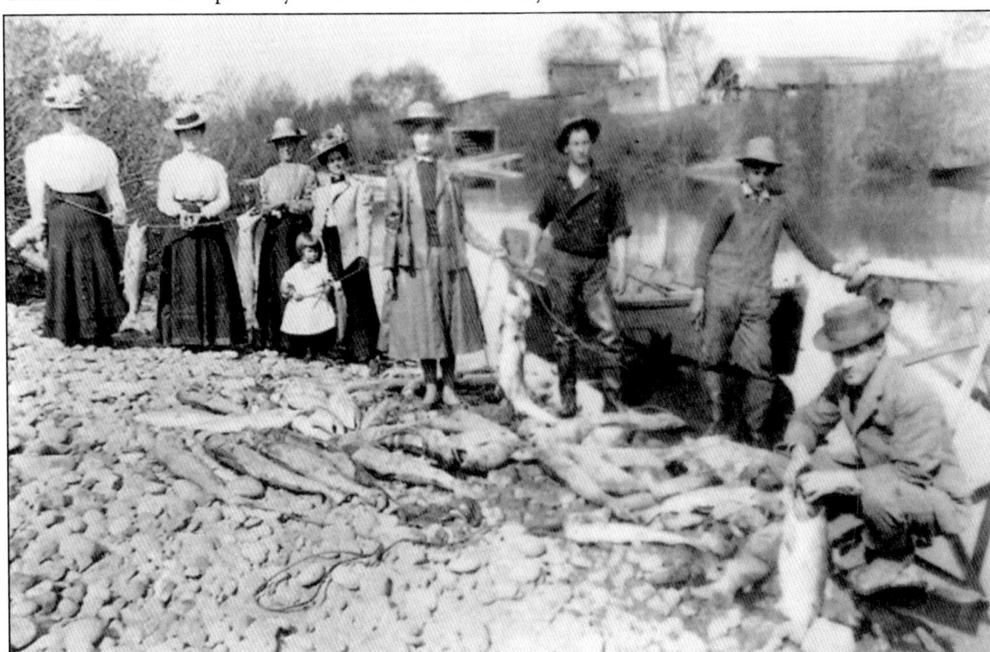

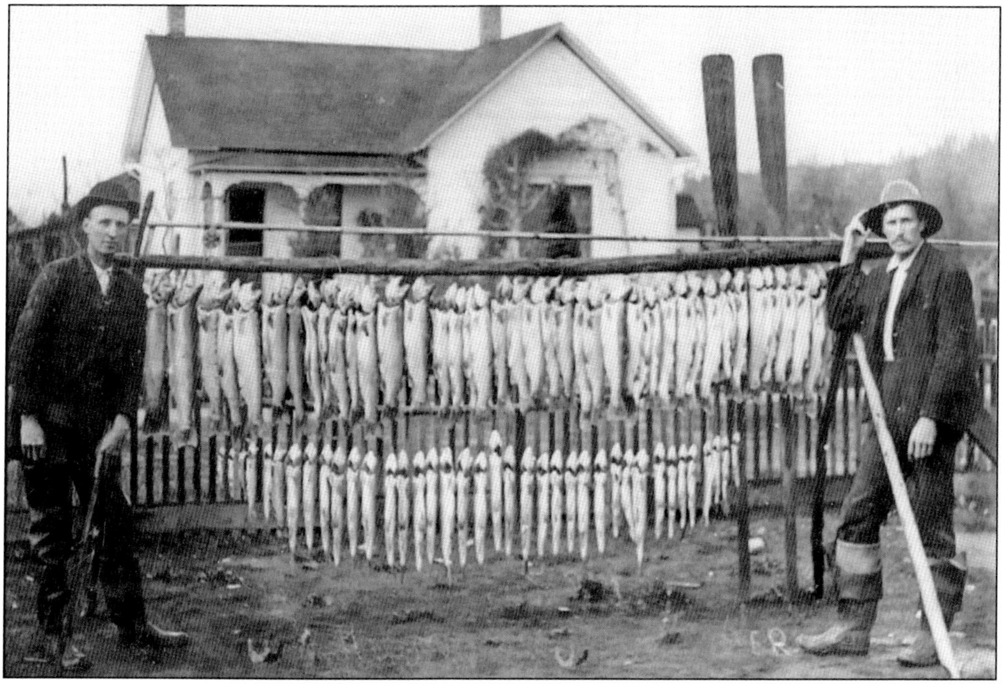

In 1909, the *Rogue River Courier* reported, "In that 'Queen of all streams' our beautiful Rogue River, which is a grown up mountain brook, the finest fly fishing on the American continent can be found. Nova Scotia, New Brunswick, Maine, Canada and the famous Restigouche are completely outclassed. The fish in this stream rise freely to the fly and one never knows whether the next fish will weigh one or 20 pounds or any weight between the two. The large fish are as plentiful as the small and it is not uncommon to catch more than one can carry. Hundreds of tons of the Royal Chinook salmon from the Rogue River are shipped annually during the fall and winter months. All this with an environment as wild and picturesque as any to be found."

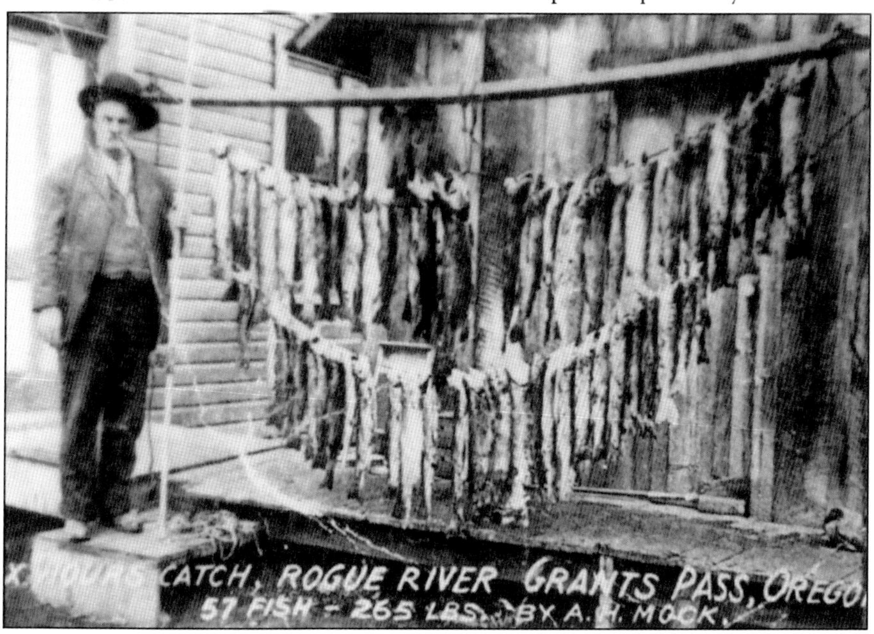

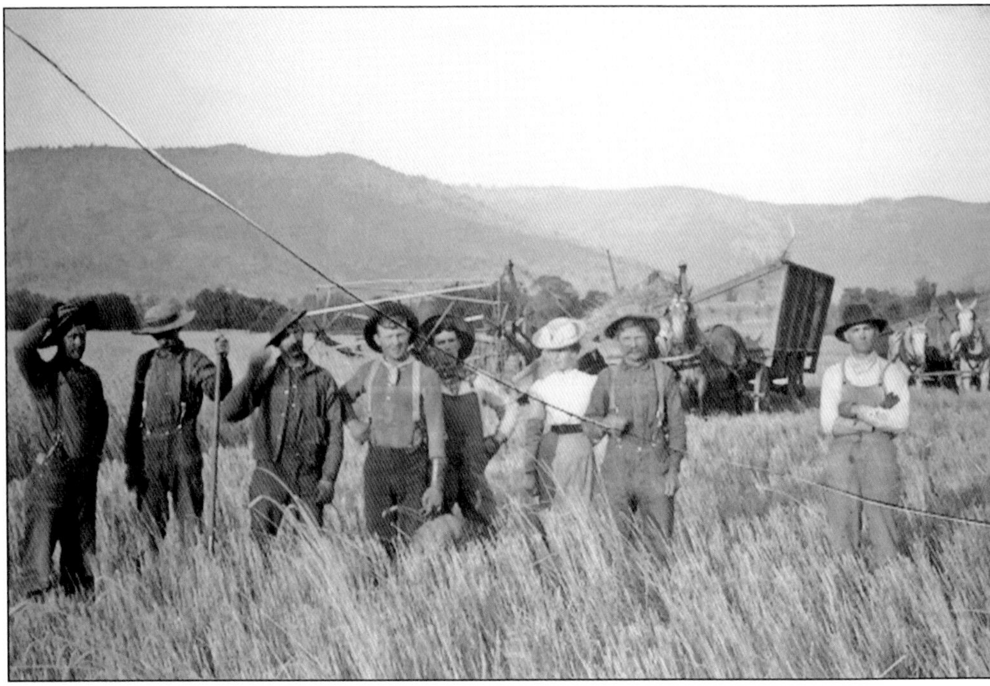

In 1917, the Grants Pass Commercial Club boasted, "Anything put in the ground that gives returns elsewhere will do equally well at Grants Pass. There are growers here who will say they get better returns than are harvested elsewhere. . . . The demand for hay in the local market is always greater than the production."

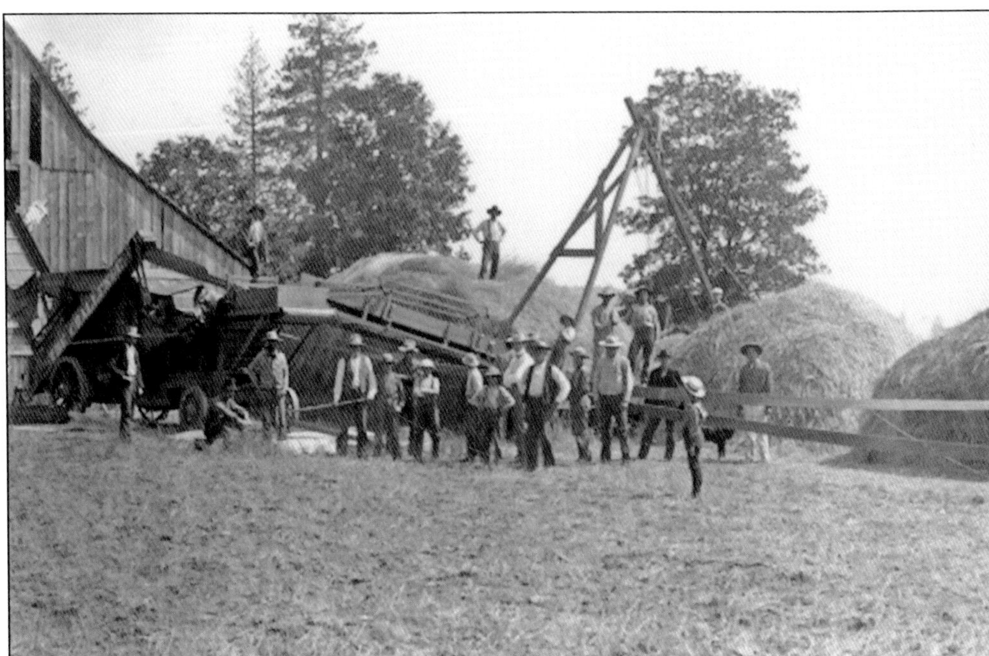

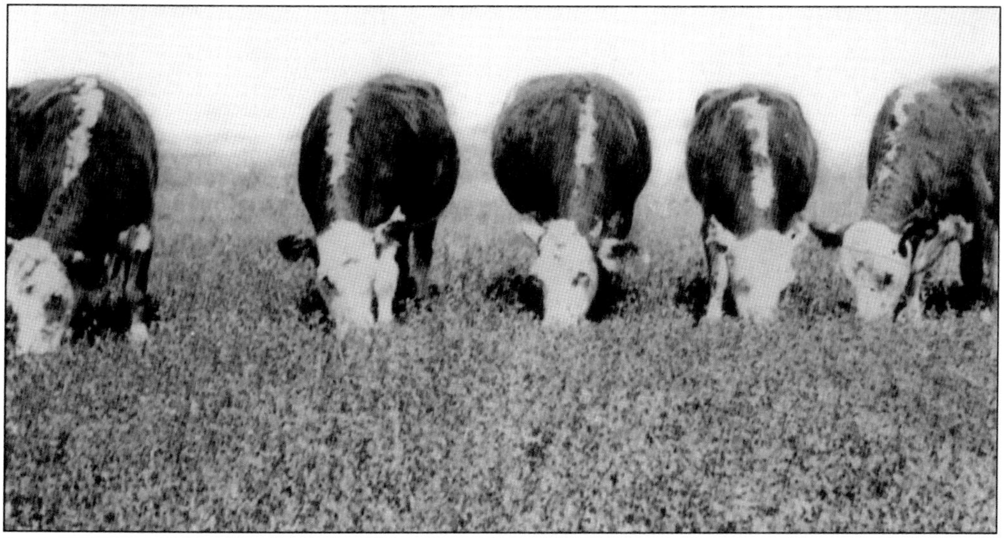

In the 1920s, ladino clover was introduced into Josephine County. It was similar to white clover but nearly twice the size. It was brought over from Italy and planted in small batches in Oregon. The Grants Pass Chamber of Commerce used this photograph to promote the crop.

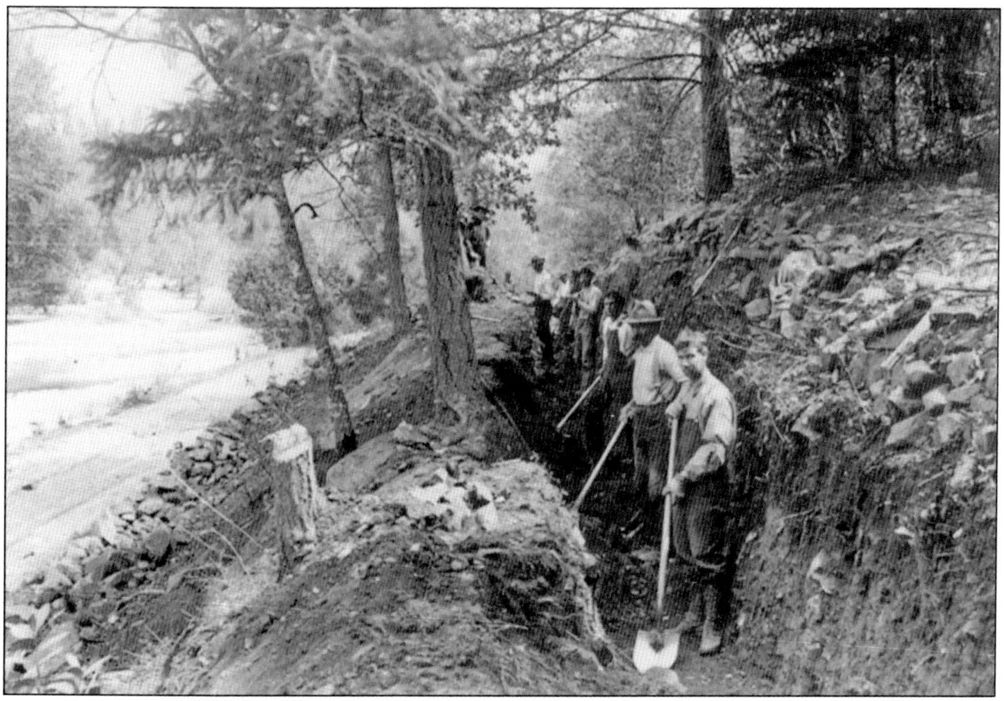

In 1909, the *Rogue River Courier* reported, "Opportunities offered the man who wants to make a profitable investment. There are vast sources of newly created wealth. This has been done by the building of the 50 miles of irrigation ditches. These ditches more than double the producing capacity of every acre of land under them, consequently doubling the value of the land after adding the cost of ditch construction."

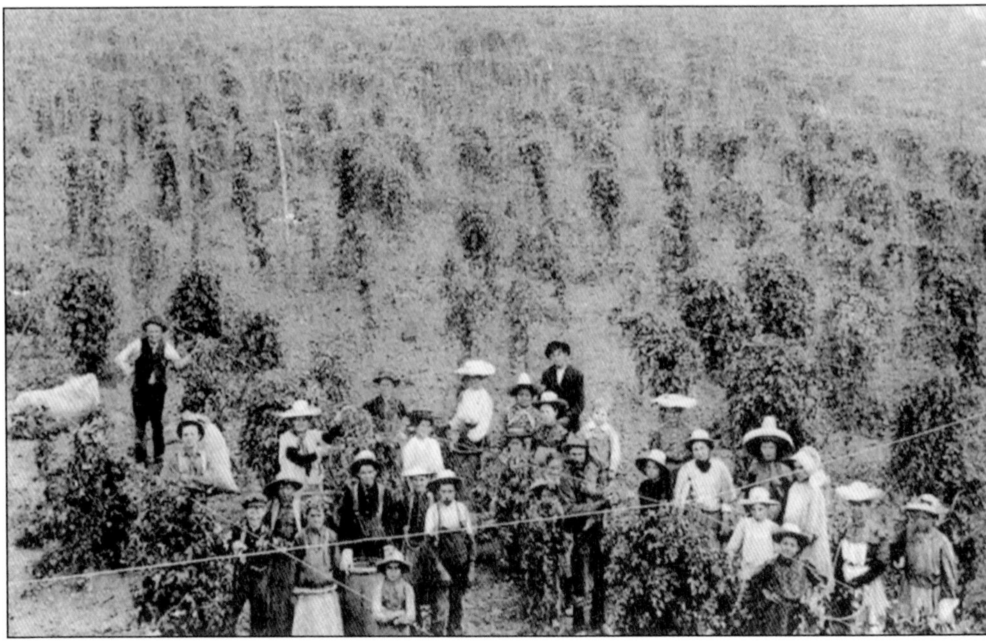

In 1906, the price for hops ranged from 7¢ to 11¢ per pound. The concern for local growers was that large brewing companies were experimenting with cold storage. This meant that the companies could purchase the crops and hold them over until the next season, thereby purchasing less hops the following year. In 1906, local hop grower C.G. Ament stated that he received 10¢ per pound for his crop of 75 bales of hops, but that it did not cover all of his expenses.

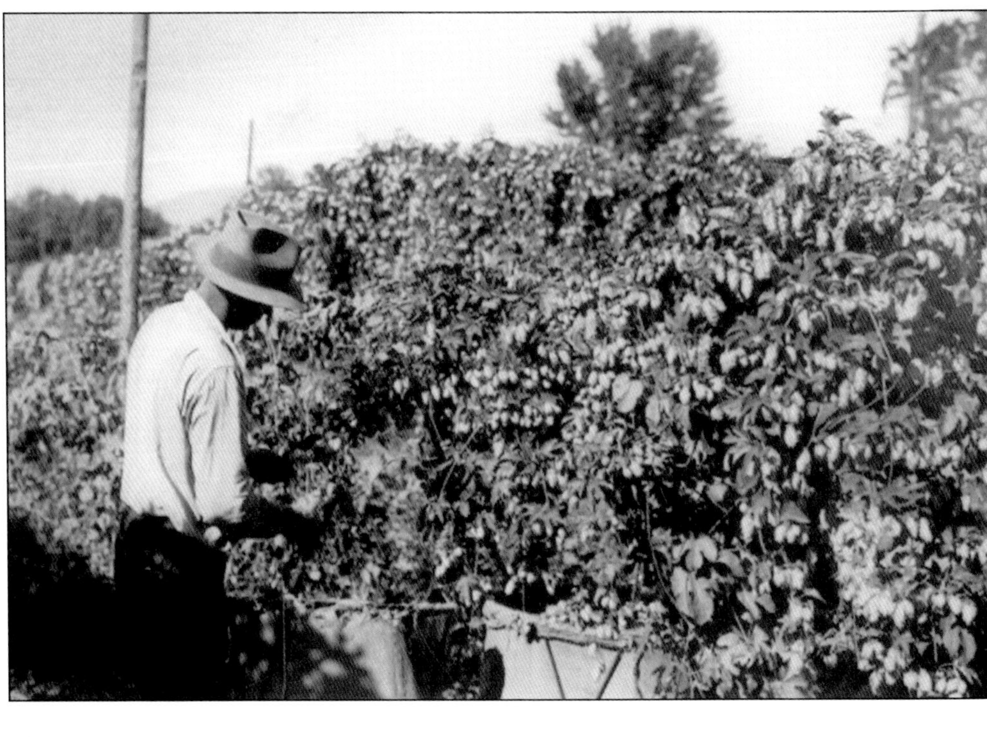

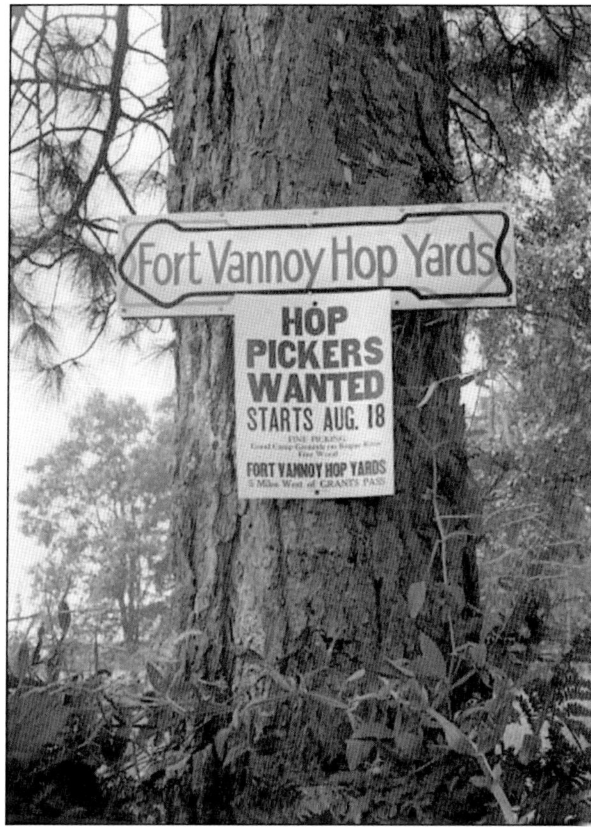

Pioneer James Vannoy operated a ferry at this spot in 1852. The fort was constructed during the Rogue River Indian Wars, and pioneers sought protection here. Pioneer A.G. Rockfellow wrote about his experience at Fort Vannoy, recalling being stationed as a guard with another soldier by the name of Doc Miller. Rockfellow wrote, "I had just had my turn standing at that place and watching by putting my head out from behind the tree when Miller came to my relief and took my place. I think it could not have been more than five minutes when a gunshot report rang out from the direction of the cabins and simultaneous with the report of the gun, Miller fell over by my side dead with a bullet through his head." The Fort Vannoy Hop Yards are pictured here.

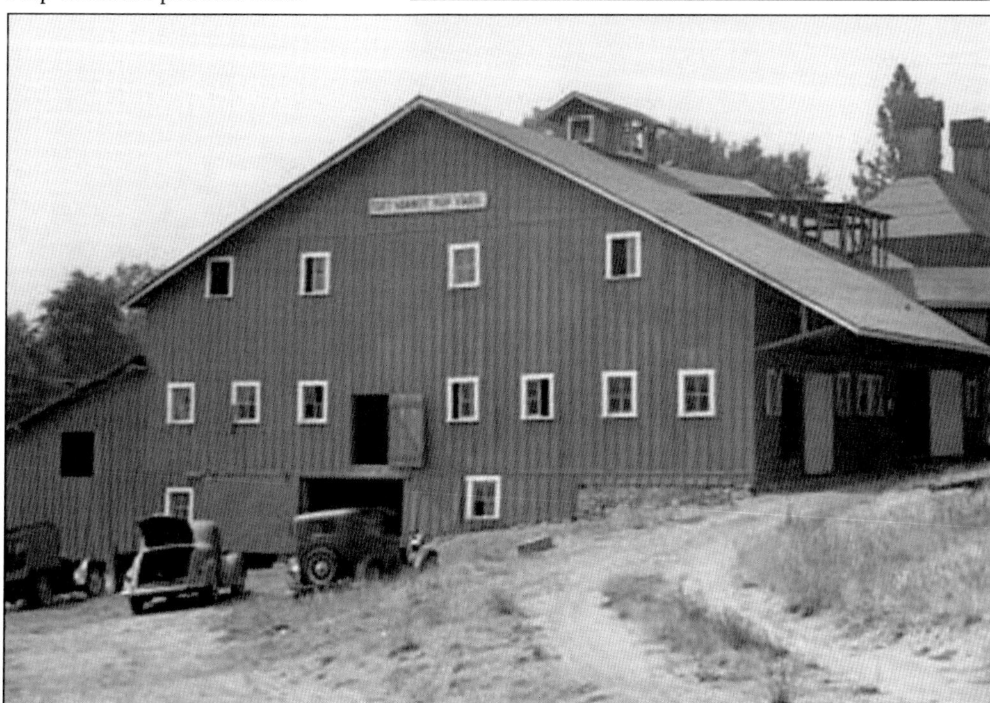

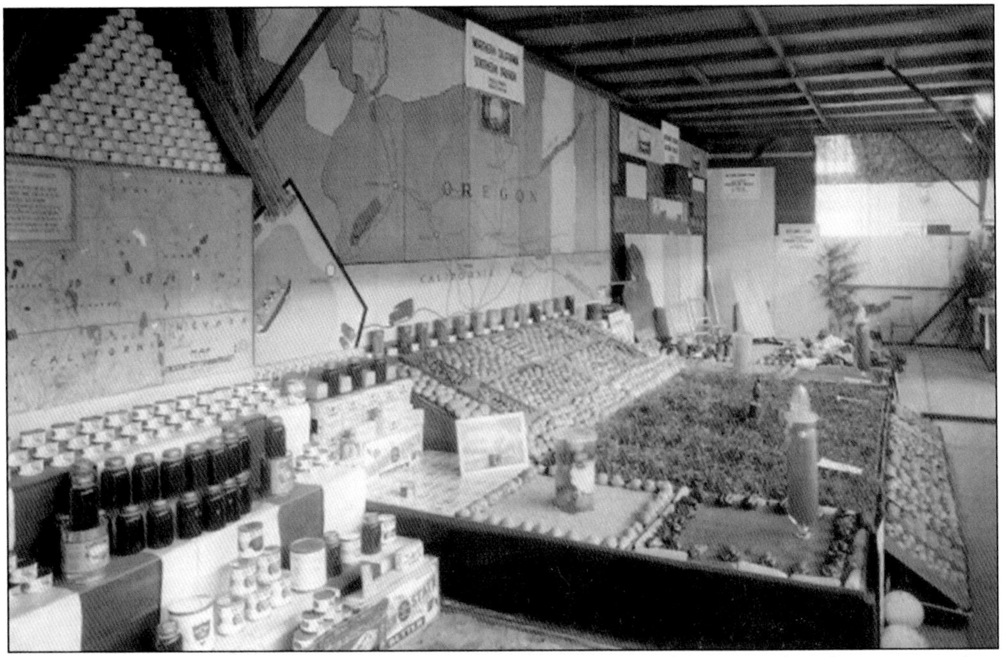

The products displayed here are under a map of Oregon and California. After Oregon won first premium at the Pan-American Exposition in 1901, the *Rogue River Courier* reported, "Now that Oregon has won first premium at the Pan-American Exposition, the labeling of Oregon fruit as California fruit should be strictly prohibited. We do not care to have Oregon products run down in this matter."

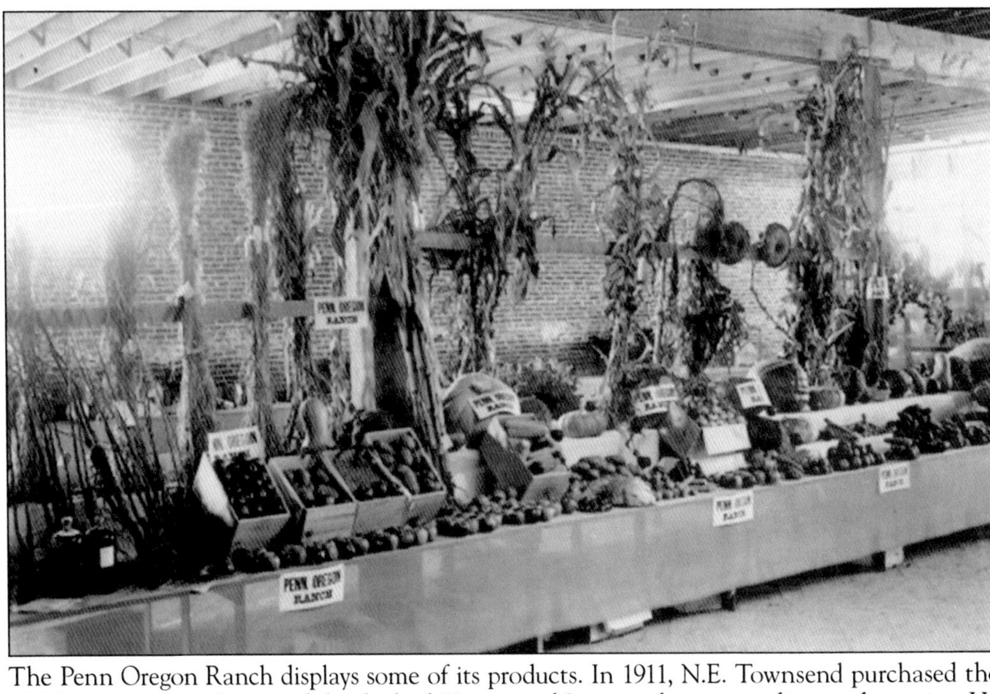

The Penn Oregon Ranch displays some of its products. In 1911, N.E. Townsend purchased the 1,300-acre ranch and reported that he had 12 men and 9 teams plowing, seeding, and spraying. He had 100 acres of alfalfa, 200 acres of grain seed, and 100 acres of potatoes, cabbage, and squash.

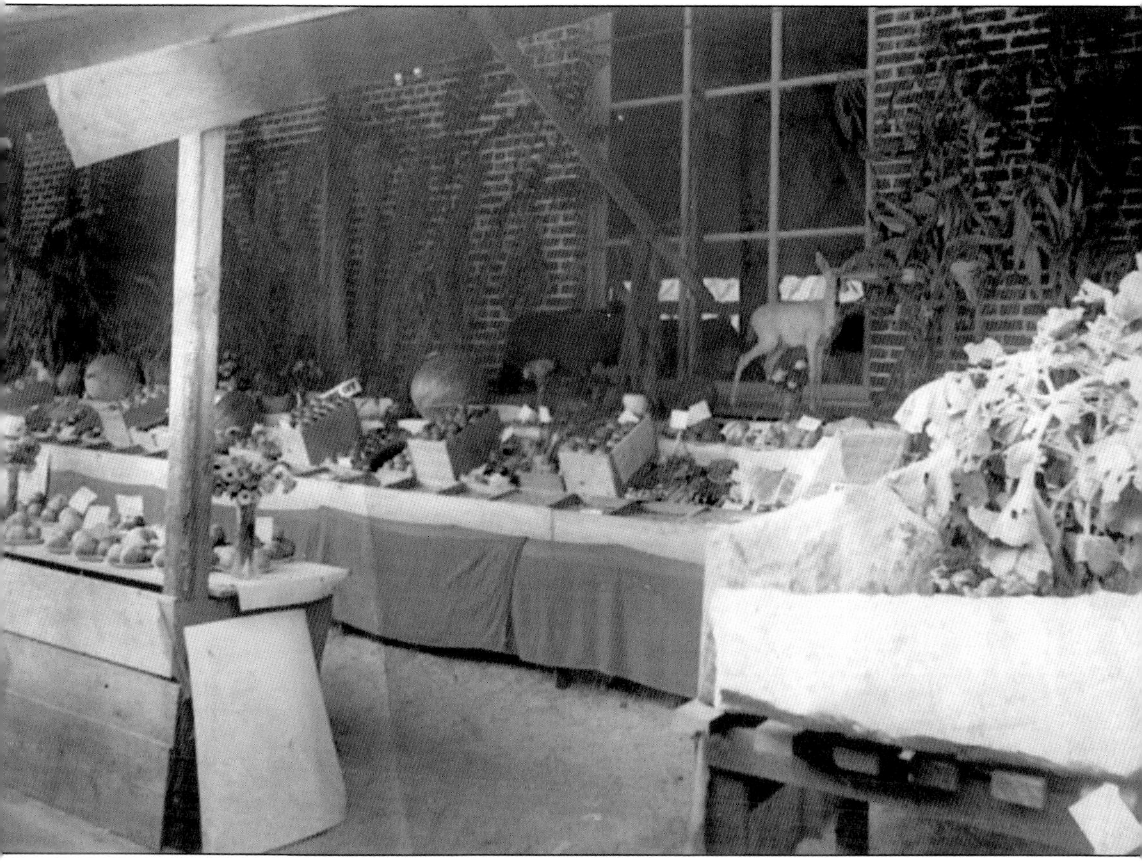

In preparation for their fourth annual exposition, the Grants Pass Commercial Club stated, "Every farmer, gardener, fruit grower, stock raiser, and miner should begin now to make preparations for exhibiting the best that skill can produce. We certainly can show fruit, vegetables, grains, grasses, lumber products, cattle, hogs, horses, and colts which would be hard to beat in any county. Everybody get busy. So come along Williams Creek, Illinois River, Sucker Creek, up the river, down the river, and every section of the county. Excursion trains will run from Spokane, Seattle, Portland and all immediate points so that our exhibit will be seen by thousands of people. The Southern Pacific Railroad will make a special effort to bring in everybody to see the wonderful exposition of the products of the far-famed Rogue River Valley. Let every citizen of this valley lend a helping hand in making the display worthy of the occasion."

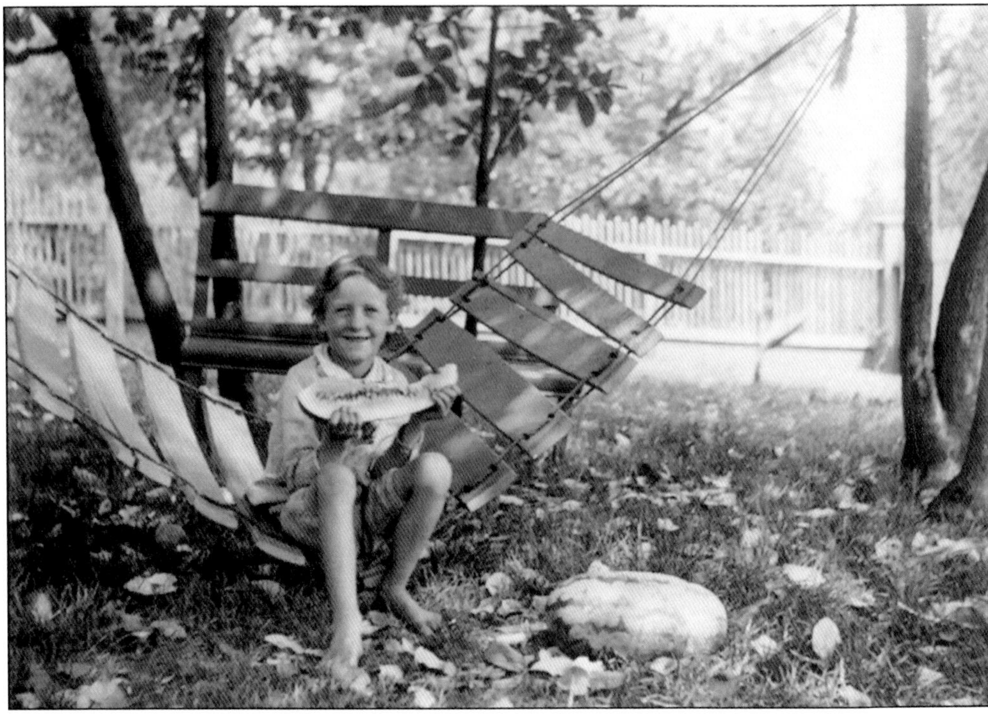

In 1903, the *Rogue River Courier* reported, "The sandy soil of the Rogue River bottom seems to be especially adapted to the growth of melons and the Rogue River melons are not eclipsed in flavor or general desirability by those of any other section on the face of the earth. Grants Pass has attained a wide spread reputation as a melon depot and 30 to 40 car loads are shipped out every summer."

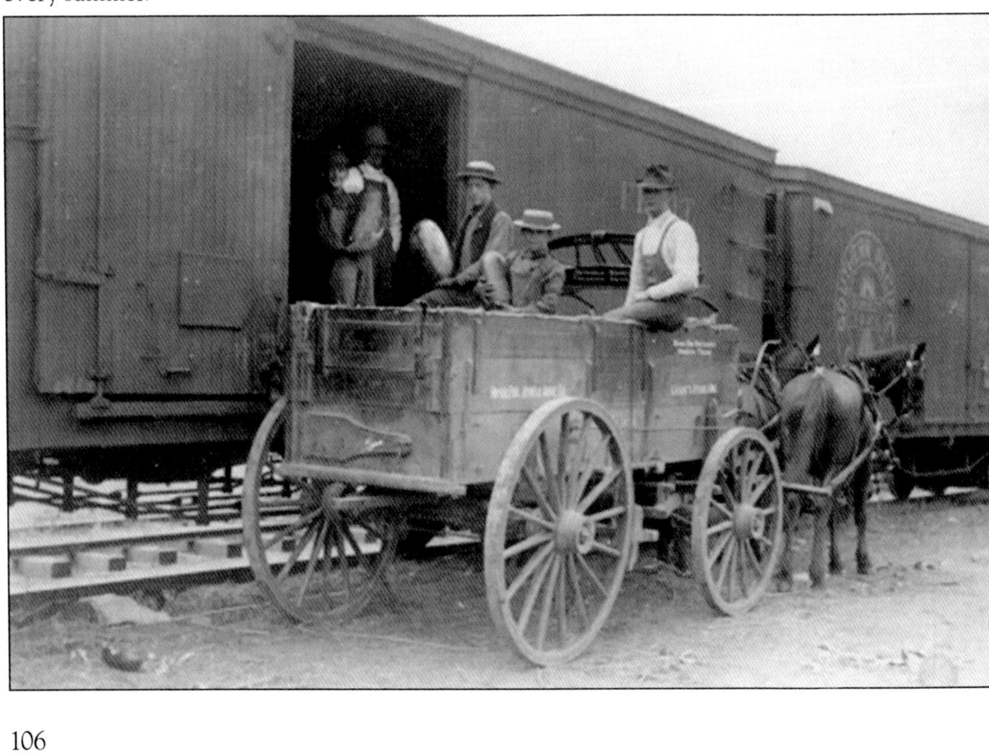

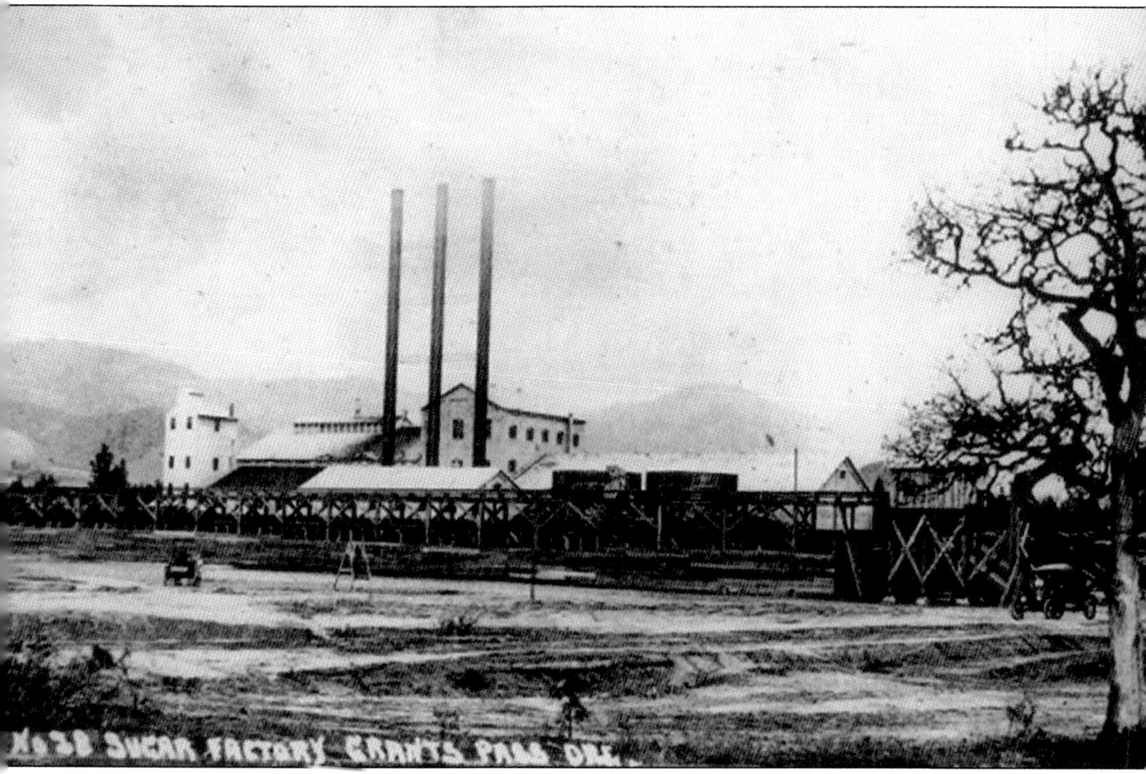

The Oregon-Utah Sugar Company planned to bring a "million-dollar business" into Josephine County, claiming, "Prosperity is surely coming to Grants Pass and to all of Southern Oregon." The company asked landowners in Josephine County to commit to raising a total of 5,000 acres of beets for five years, beginning with five to 10 acres. The growers were warned they would need working capital, as the cost per acre would be $35 to $45, with $6 to $12 for hired help due to the required thinning, hoeing, digging, and topping of the beets. When the factory was built in 1915, company officials said they had invested $1 million to bring the industry to Josephine County. However, it soon became apparent that there was not enough irrigation to support the amount of water the beets needed to thrive. After just two years, the Oregon-Utah Sugar Company pulled up stakes and moved the factory to Washington State.

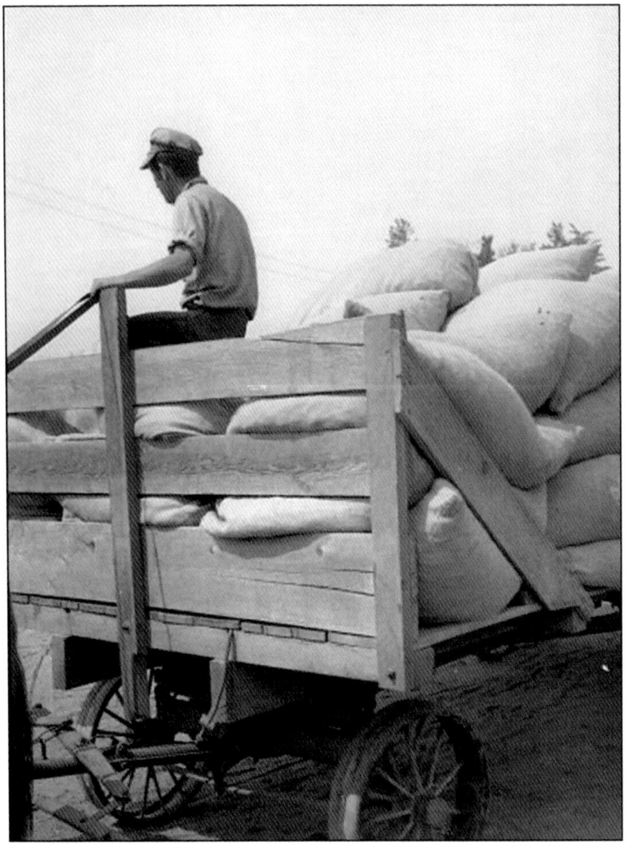

Crops grown in Josephine County 100 years ago included the following: pears, apples, peaches, tomatoes, grapes, cherries, strawberries, raspberries, blackberries, loganberries, gooseberries, English walnuts, hops, melons, corn, wheat, oats, alfalfa, and barley. While serving in France during World War I, Sgt. Oliver Morton wrote a letter home to Grants Pass, stating, in part: "Speaking of strawberries makes me think of the shortcakes you are probably having and wish I was able to eat a few with you. Strawberries are 40 cents per pound on the market here. I bought six apricots at the fruit store the other day and paid one franc and a half, almost 30 cents for them and they had no flavor." The white building at left in the below image was a tomato-packing plant located in Grants Pass that employed many men and women.

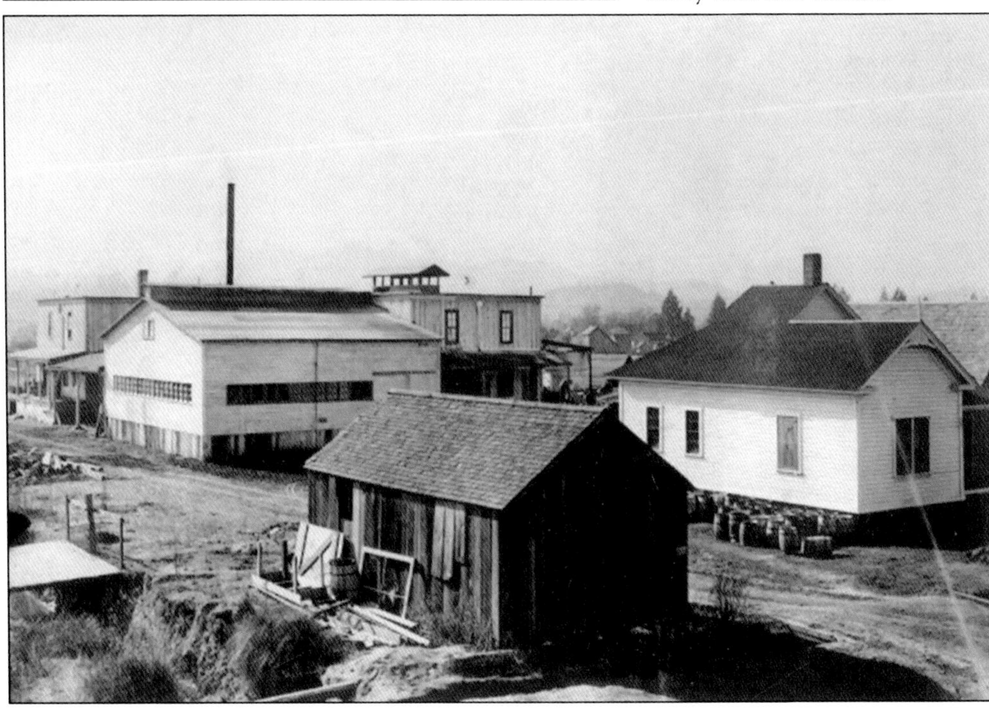

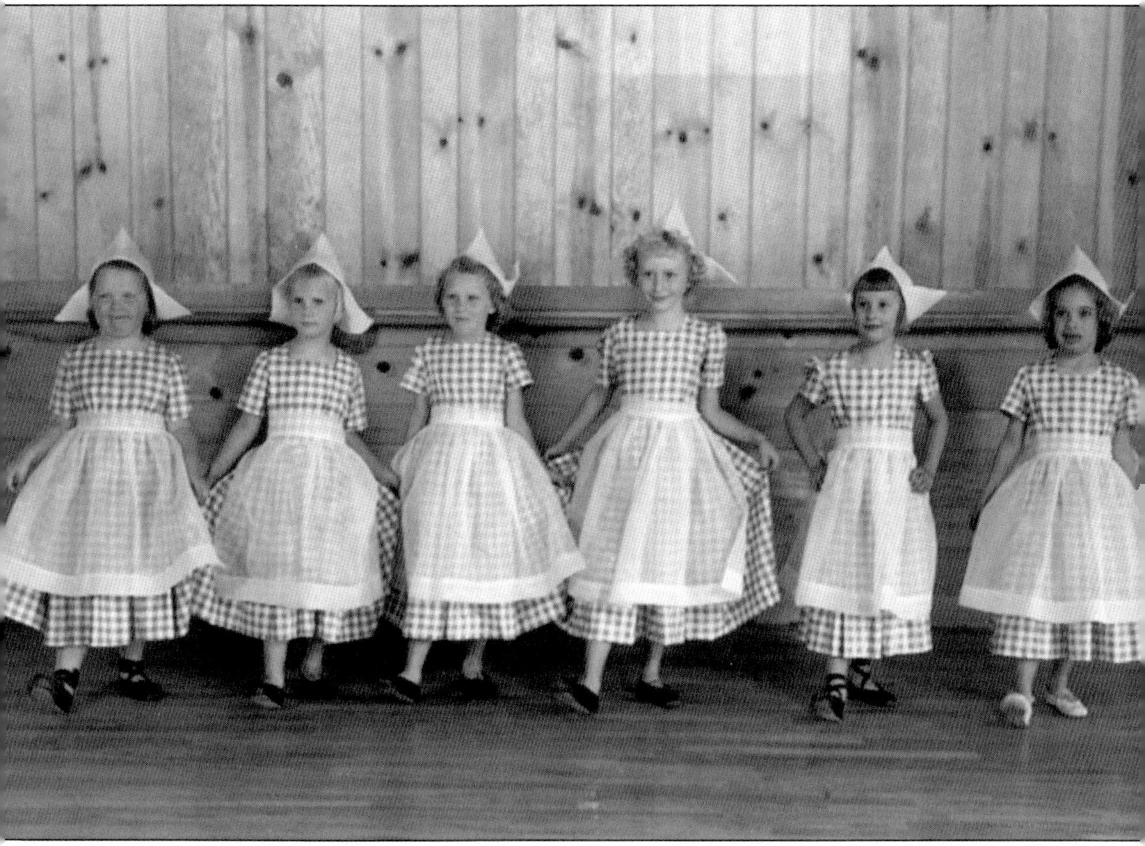

For many years, Josephine County was known for its gladiolus flowers. The first flower show was a small event held inside C.A. Winetrout's commercial garage located at the corner of Fifth and H Streets. Large crowds of people attended, and a decision was made to open the show to the public the following year. Soon, the show grew to include a parade and a festival. The young girls pictured are putting on a show for an audience at the flower show.

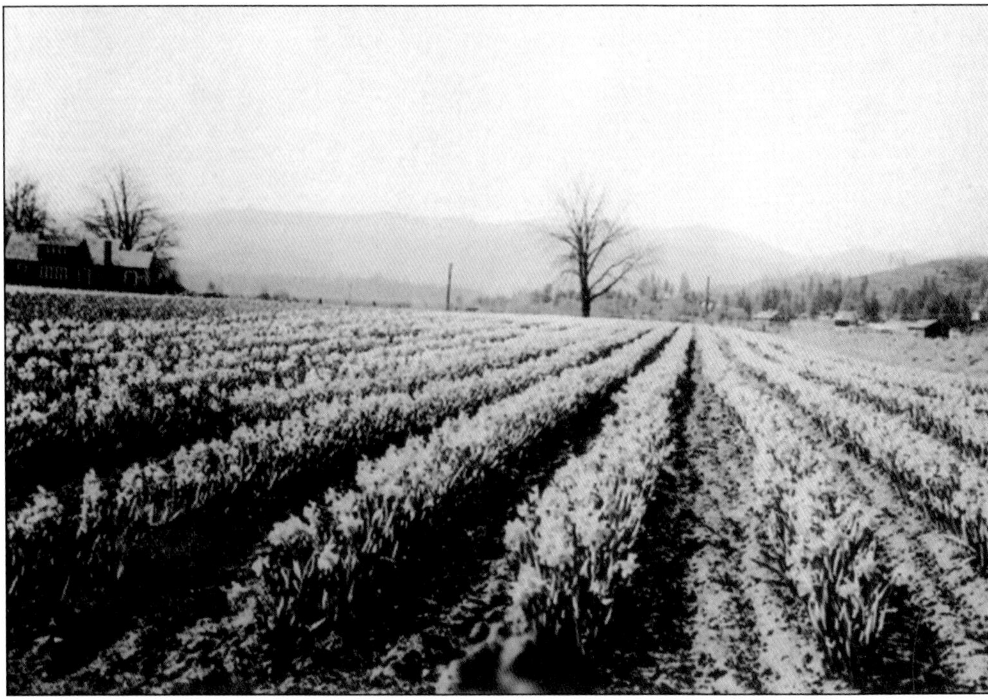

The gladiolus industry grew rather quickly in Josephine County. In 1927, there were approximately 28 farmers growing gladiolus bulbs on a total of 43 acres. The largest of the growers had six acres of the bulbs planted. Growers received between $300 and $600 per acre. Just one year later, there were approximately 350 acres of gladiolus bulbs planted in the county. That number continued to increase until it reached a peak of approximately 1,500 acres.

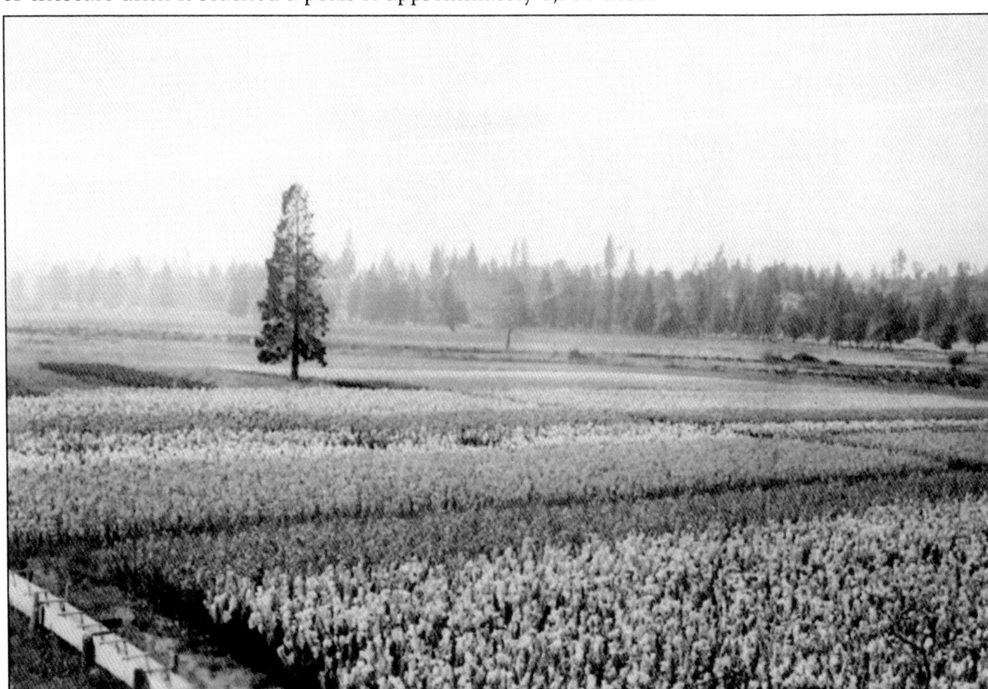

Four

TRANSPORTATION

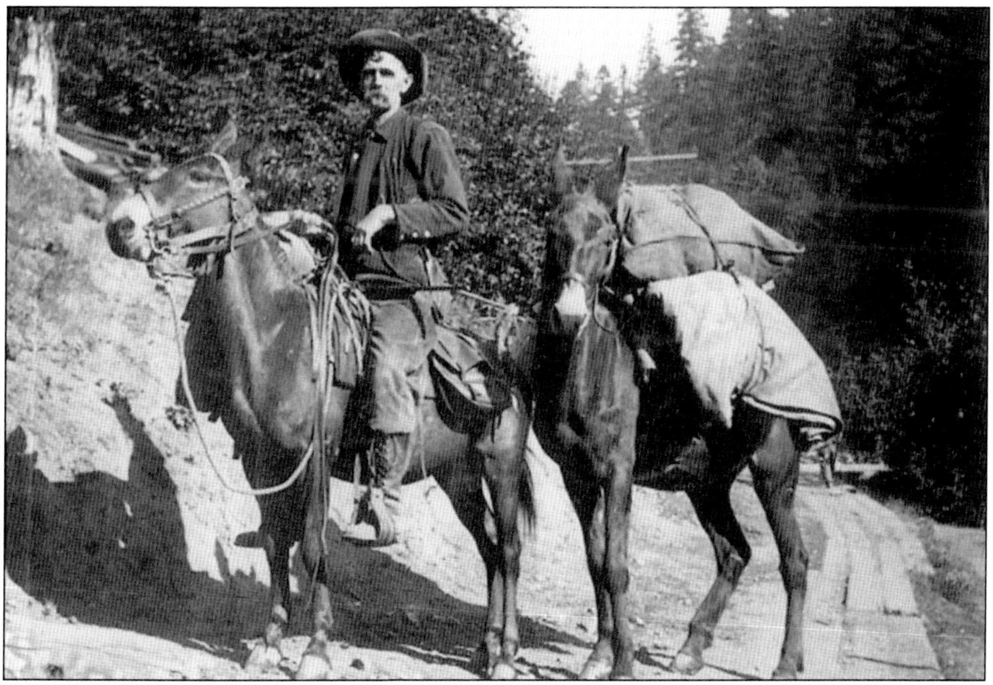

Pack mules were invaluable to miners. The July 14, 1911, edition of the *Rogue River Courier* included a report that, "Dan Hearn stated Sunday that a six mule pack train would leave Selma Monday morning loaded with supplies for the new gold discovery he and Jack Casey and others own one-half mile south of Higgins Golden Dream property in the Chetco District. Included in the supplies is a blacksmith outfit for sharpening steel, also good supply of steel and provisions."

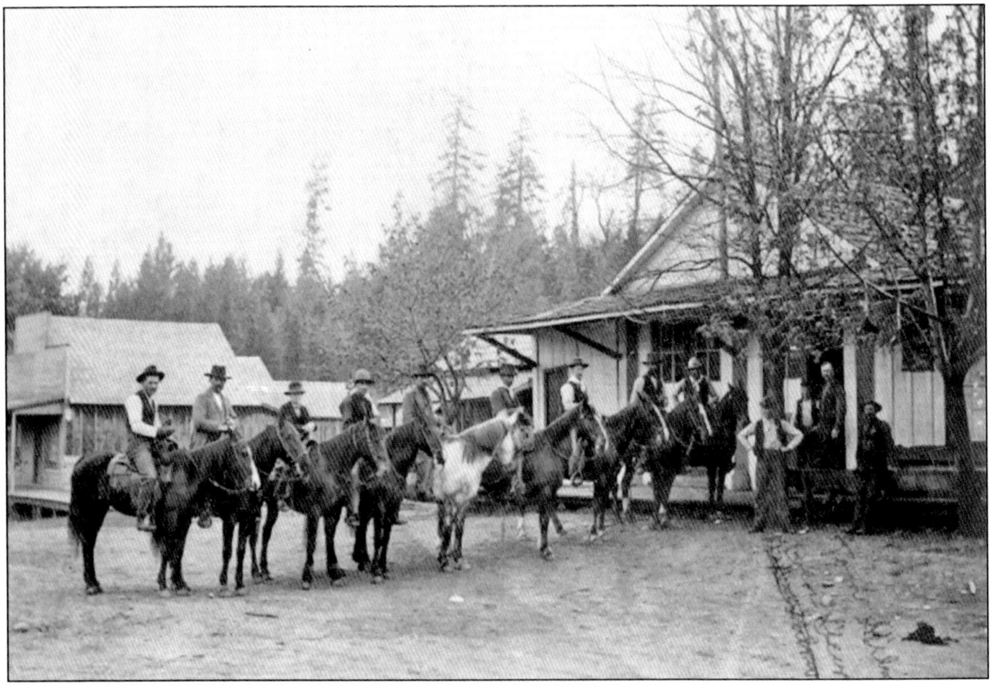

Horses proved to be necessary in the days before the automobile. Early settlers depended on horses and wagons to bring the supplies they needed, but there were times when the roads were impassable due to the weather. In March 1904, the *Rogue River Courier* reported, "For over two months it has been impossible for a wagon to get in and at the present time there is no telling when the road will open. Provisions and supplies of all kinds are running low and some of the miners are returning to first principals and are packing in supplies on their backs."

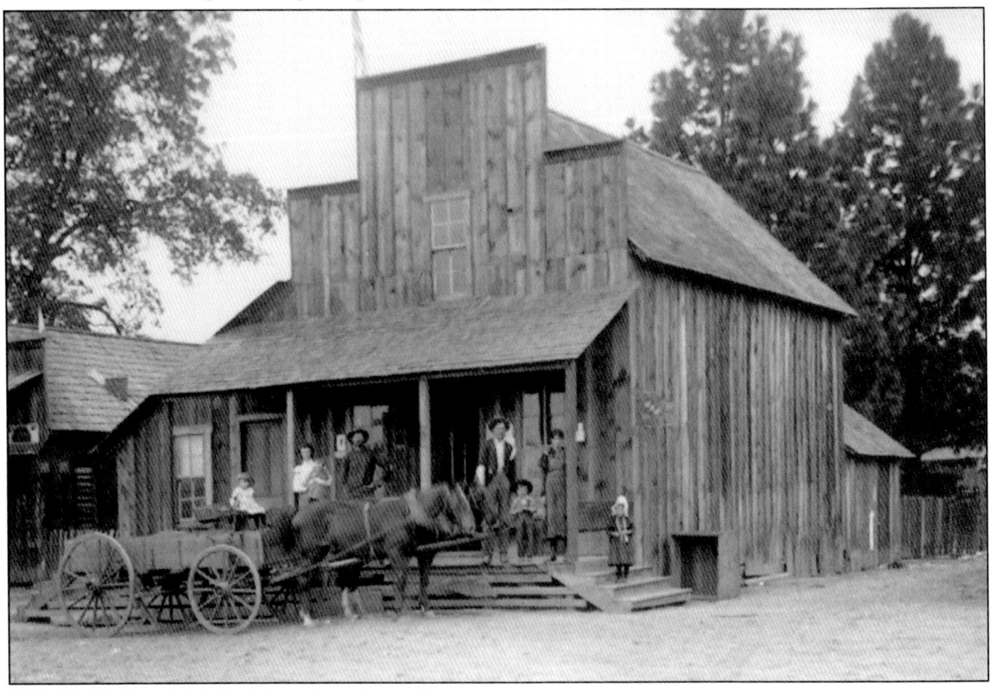

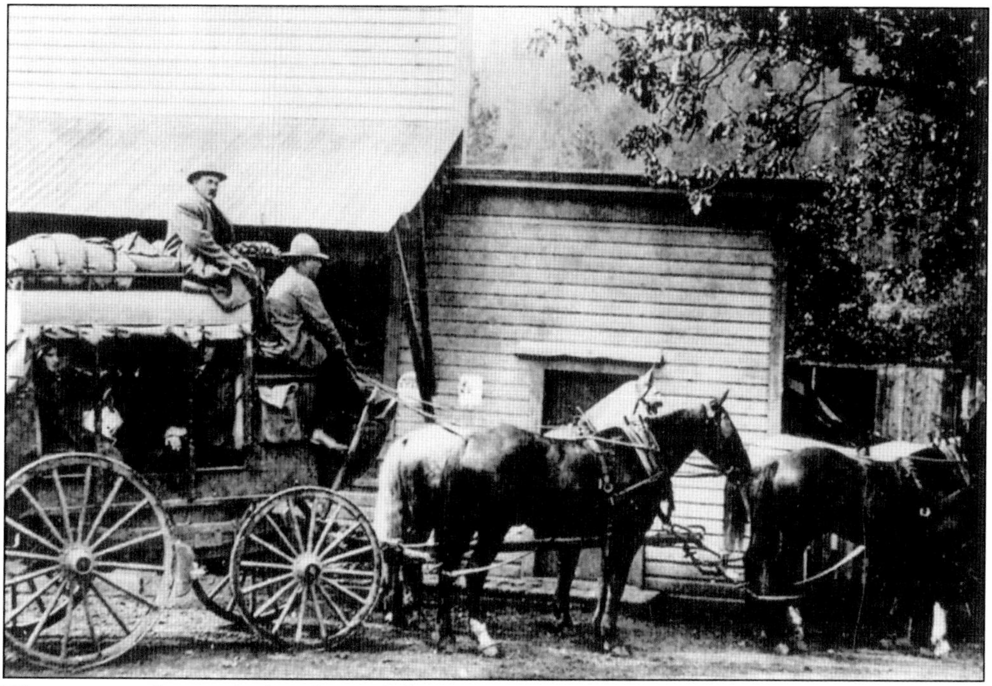

This stagecoach is parked in front of the Stringer Store and Wilderville Post Office. A "Most Wanted" poster hangs on the exterior wall of the building.

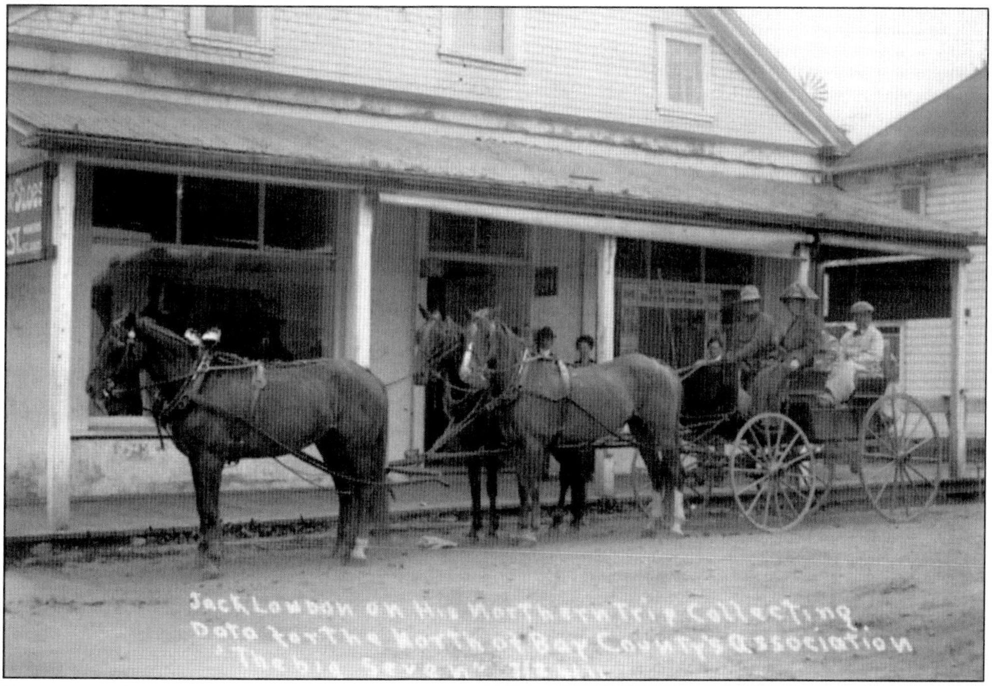

Famous author Jack London spent quite a bit of time in Josephine County. He stayed at the Wolf Creek Inn while writing and visited Crater Lake National Park while enjoying his visit to southern Oregon.

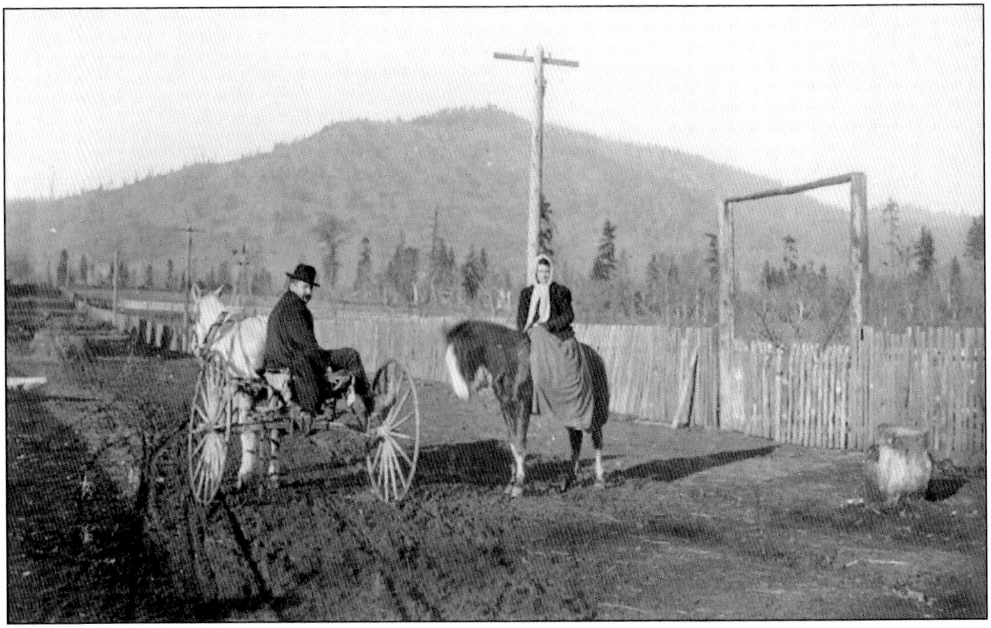

Jacob and Sarah Yokum are pictured above in the early 1890s. When automobiles first took to the streets, wagon teams had to share the roads with them. In 1912, the *Rogue River Courier* reported, "The team attached to the delivery wagon of the Grants Pass Feed Company took a spin down the road Thursday morning on its own responsibility. Seeing the Herreshoff automobile of manager Gorbett of the Rogue River Lime Company standing at the Oxford Hotel, the team made a dash for it, and one horse made a good running jump at the front seat. The horse will soon recover but the auto will be in the hands of the physicians and surgeons at the Fashion Garage for some days."

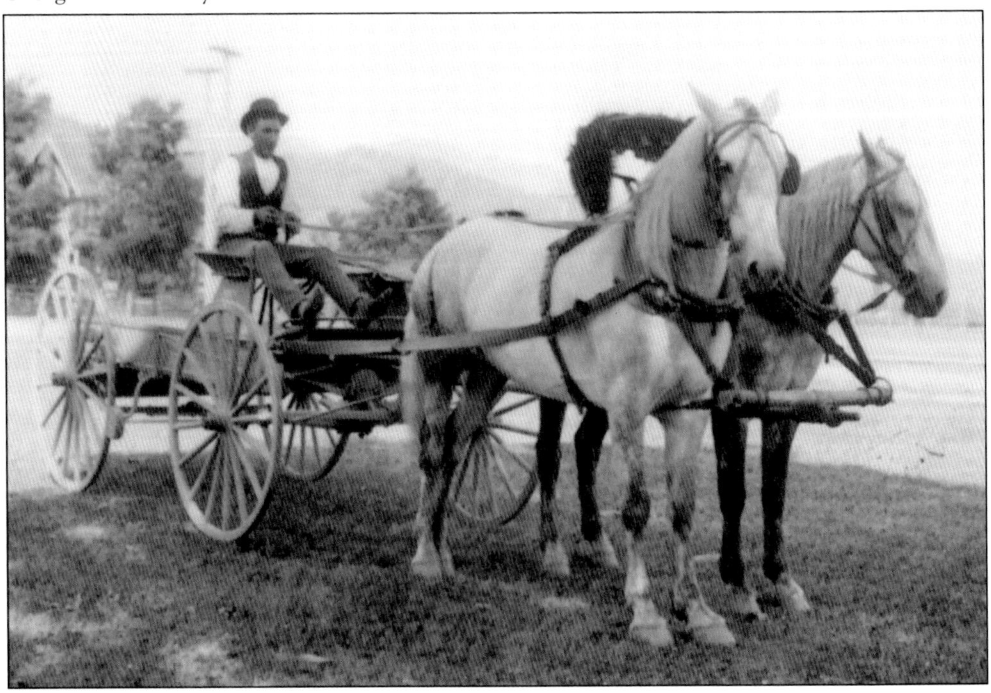

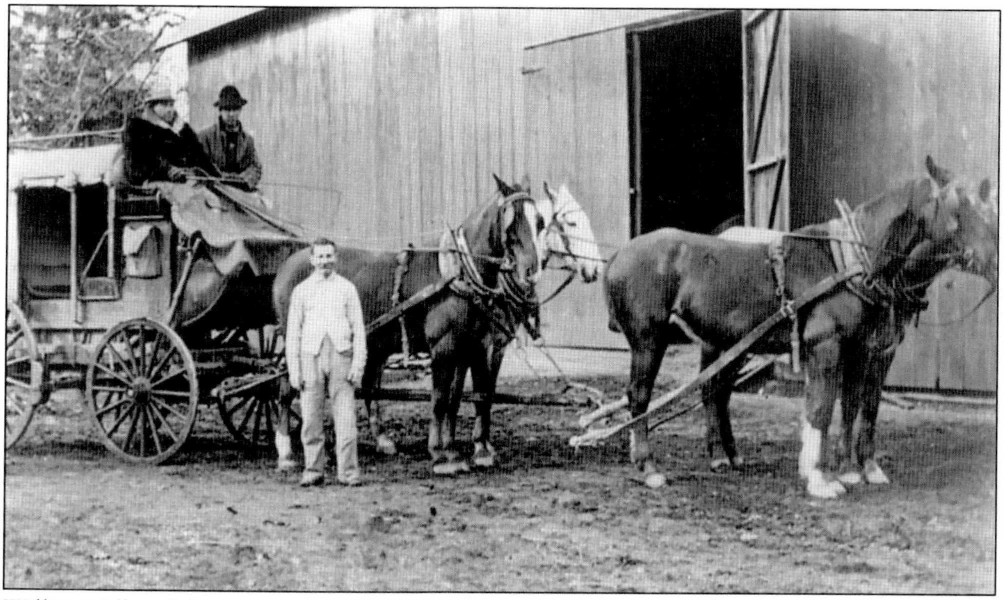

William Albert Massie is pictured in front of his stagecoach. He was born in 1850 in Powhaten, Ohio. As a young man, he moved to Illinois, where he taught school for a number of years. In 1885, he and his wife, Edith, arrived in Grants Pass. Two years later, they moved to Merlin. Massie was a school superintendent for Josephine County from 1890 to 1894 and drove the stagecoach for 23 years. He died in Merlin in 1917.

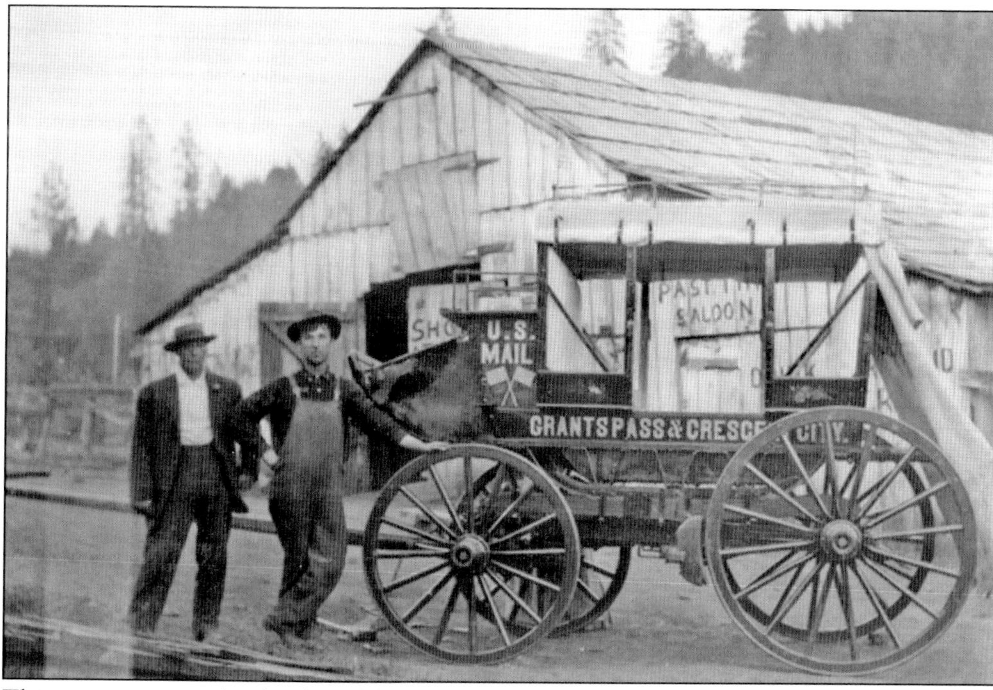

This wagon was used to haul mail from Grants Pass to Crescent City, California. In 1901, the residents of Crescent City petitioned their senator to ask the US Post Office Department to secure a 24-hour mail schedule between the two cities. They were tired of having to wait two days for the mail to be delivered and felt the overnight stop in Waldo was unnecessary.

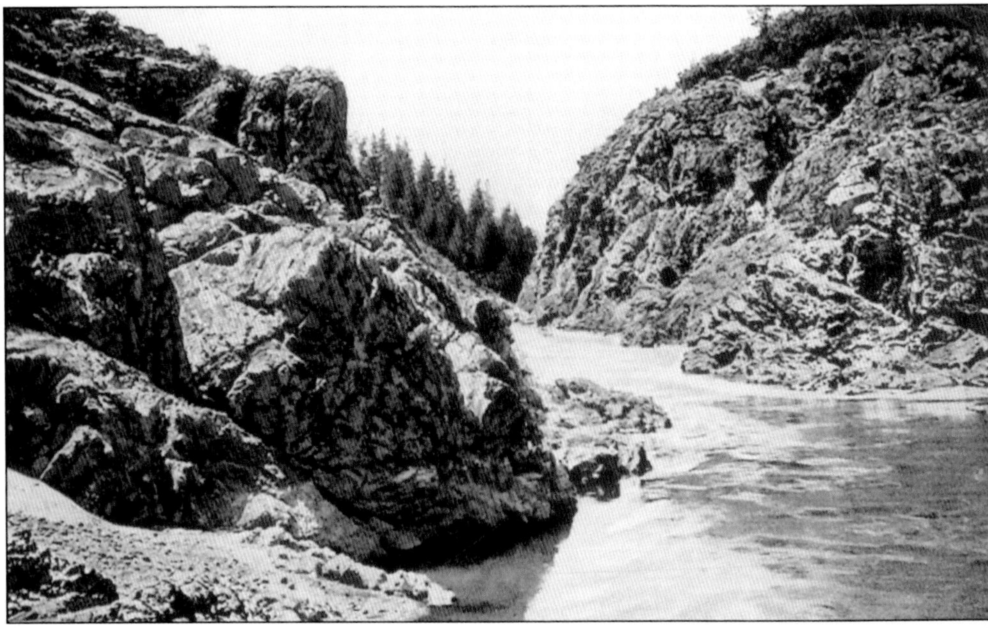

Navigating the Rogue River has always been challenging. For a period of time, there was much discussion about the potential cost savings of transporting freight via the Rogue River instead of by wagon roads. In 1907, the *Rogue River Courier* reported, "The first shipment of freight consisting of 3,900 pounds of hydraulic pipe, 3,500 nails, a boiler weighing 3,200 pounds, an engine of 3,800 pounds, and a lot of other materials and supplies, the total weight being 20,000 pounds. This was loaded on two boats that were built especially for this trip under the direction of Mr. Thurner of Grants Pass." Twenty days later, the boats arrived unharmed at their destination in Curry County. The first bridge across the Rogue River was built in 1886 at a cost of $7,000.

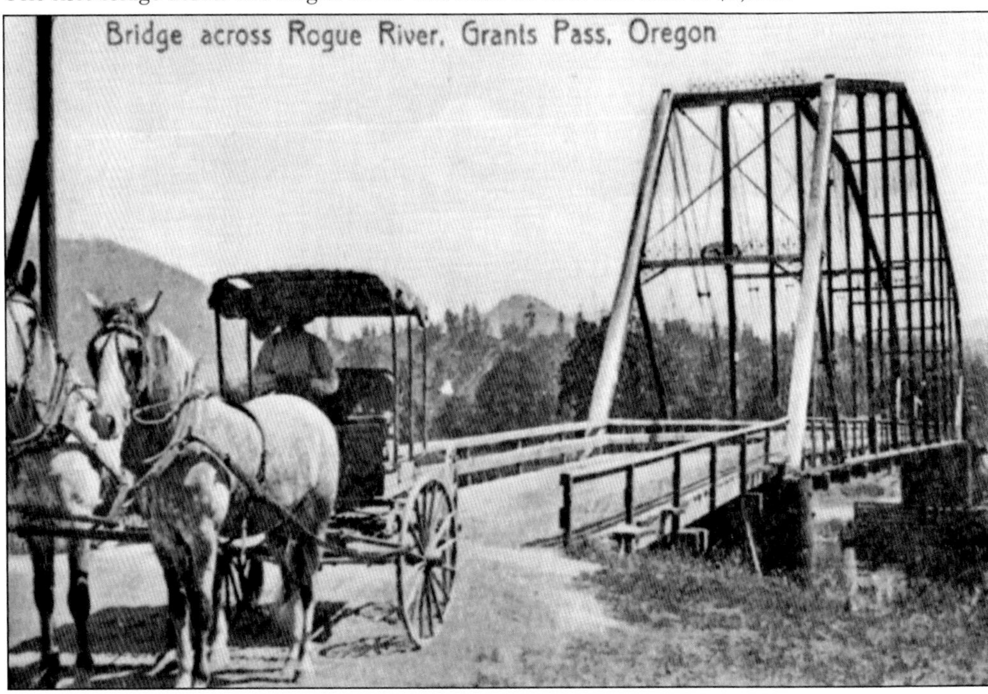

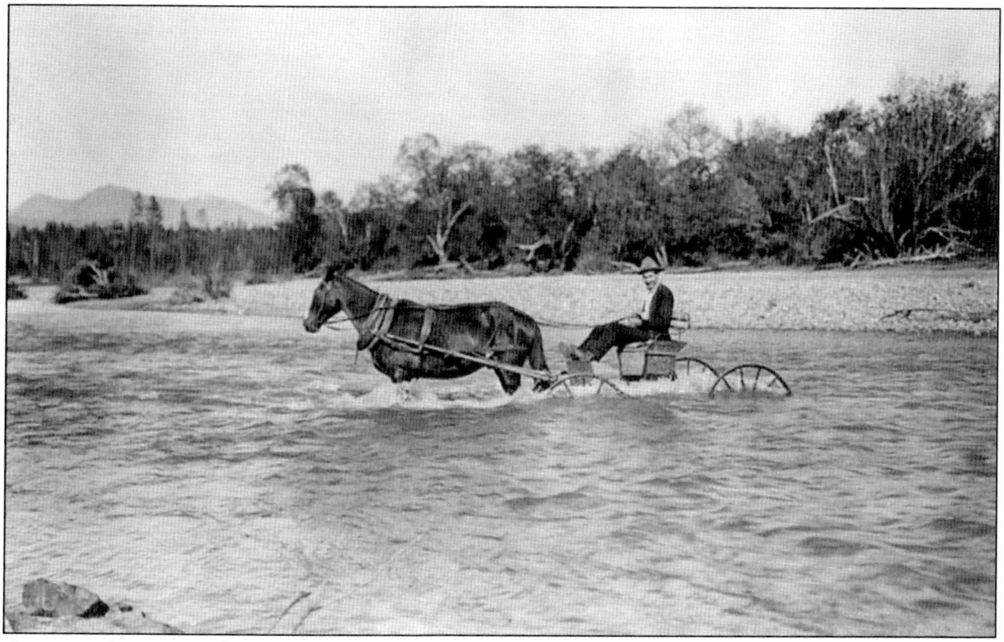

Crossing the waters of Josephine County proved quite difficult for early settlers. In 1910, the *Rogue River Courier* reported on a situation similar to the one pictured above. "Last Sunday while D.W. Mitchell was out driving he attempted to cross Louse Creek, driving what he supposed to be a good Democratic horse. But when the middle of the stream was reached, Mr. Mitchell discovered that the truant steed had flopped over to the Independent Party and would neither go ahead nor back up but sat right down in the middle of the stream." Below, a horse and carriage transport men to and from the ferry.

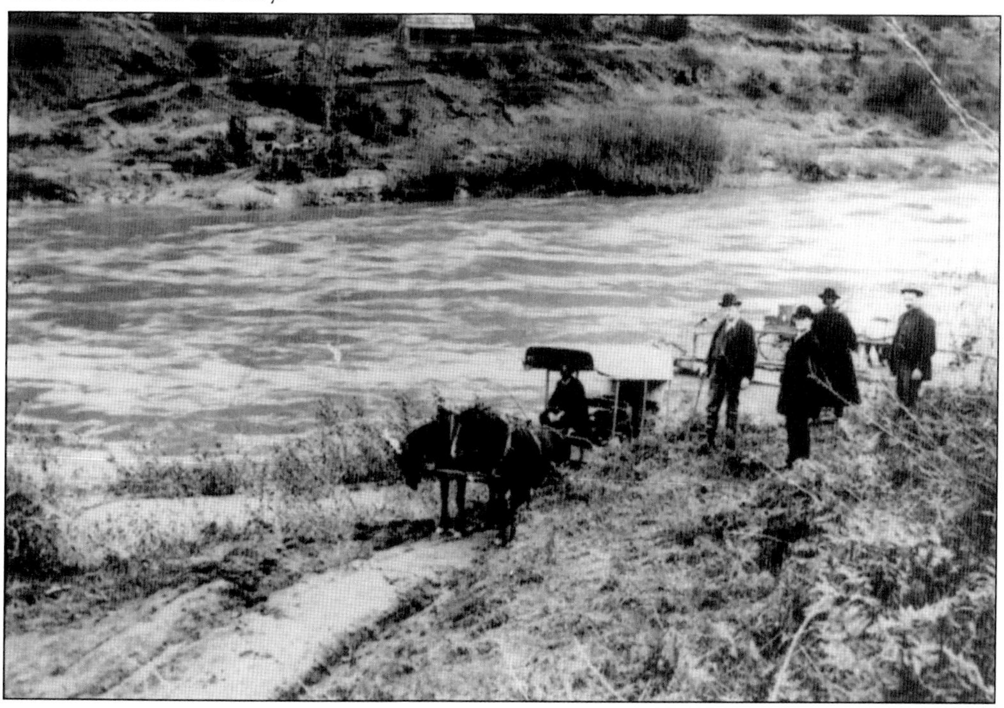

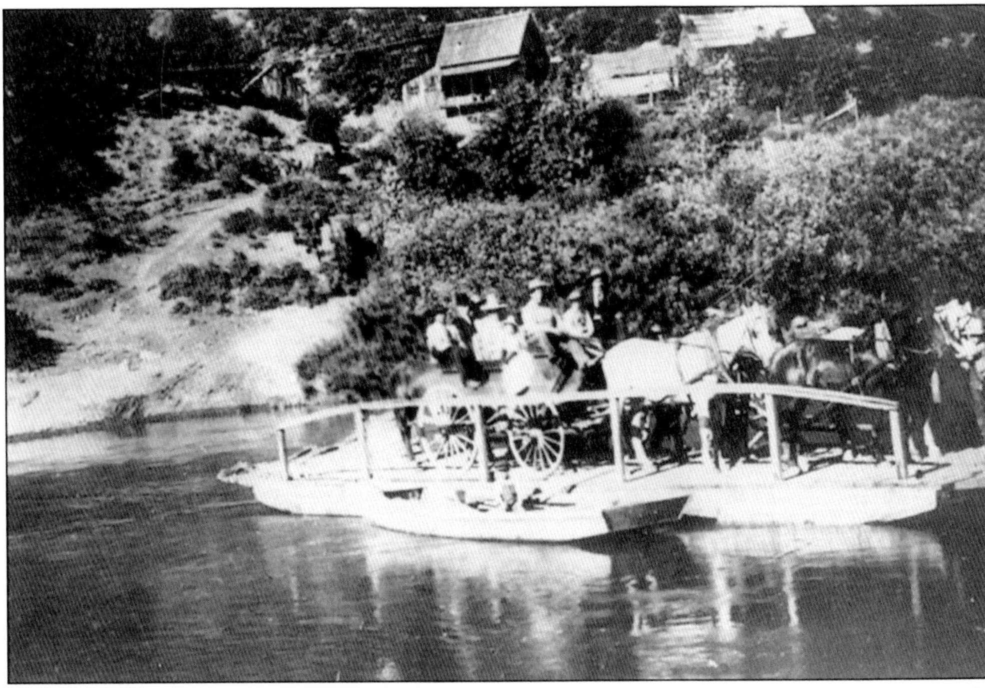

In addition to being a stagecoach driver, William Massie operated a ferry on the Rogue River. The costs to take the ferry in 1909 were: one person, 5¢ each way; one person and a single horse, 25¢ each way; or one person and a two-horse team, 40¢ each way. It cost 10¢ extra for each additional horse. The cost to transport stock or pack animals was 10¢ each way.

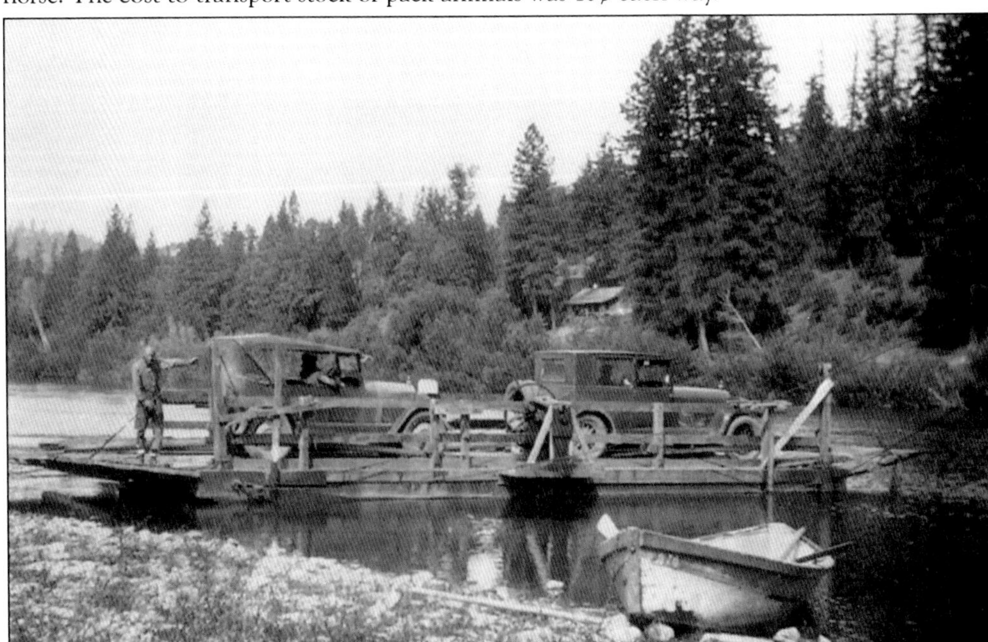

This photograph shows Willie Frankum ferrying two automobiles—an Essex in front and a Ford in back. Frankum's father had previously operated the ferry. In 1918, the residents of the area petitioned the county clerk to ask that Frankum be allowed to carry on his family tradition.

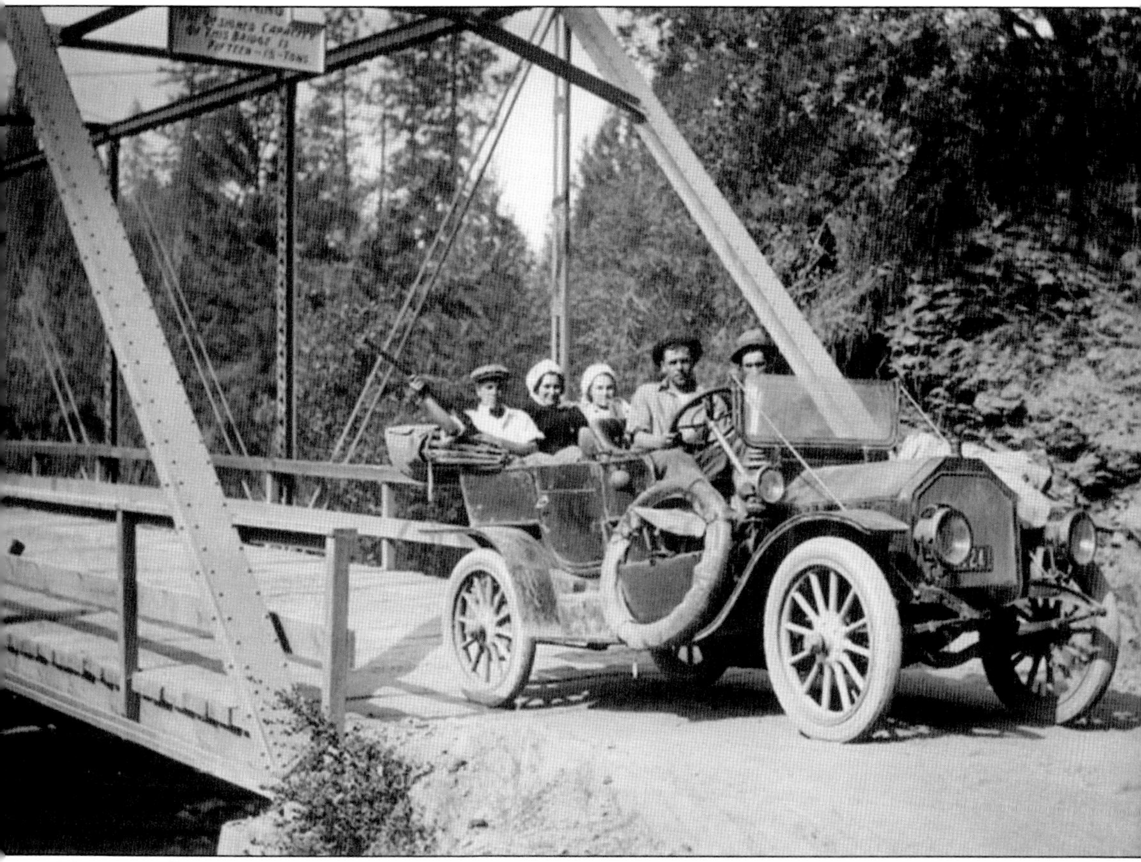

Not everything went smoothly when automobiles first took to the road. In 1925, the *Oregonian* reported, "In solemn indignation we devise laws, and more laws, for the curbing of reckless driving, which endangers not only the life of the motormaniac but the lives of all who use the road he jeopardizes. The laws are good laws. If rigidly enforced they would summarily correct the abuses at which they are aimed. But subsequent to their enforcement we appear to think that such laws should enforce themselves. For example, there is a current story of a California motorist, desirous of the empty fame of a speed record, who left Portland on the morning of a certain day and that same evening had traveled 500 miles. This was poor repayment for the hospitality of the state he had visited. More it was empty headed, dangerous disregard for law and life. To achieve this record he must have averaged, as he sped southward through Oregon, fifty miles an hour, this perilous speedster."

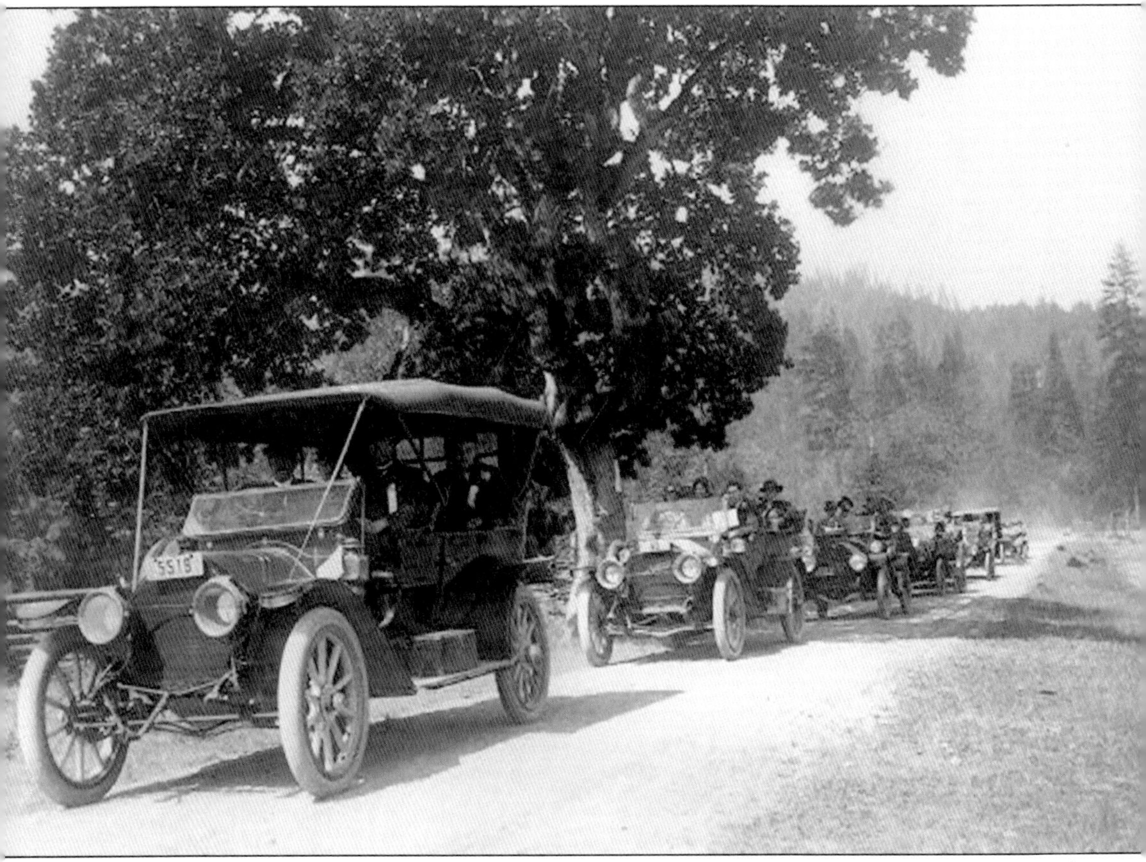

Pictured here are members of the Grants Pass Commercial Club. The club met once a month, and members were instrumental in campaigning for the completion of a road between Grants Pass and Galice. They advertised that they were "on the lookout for anything that will improve the town or county" and "ready to assist any worthy enterprise."

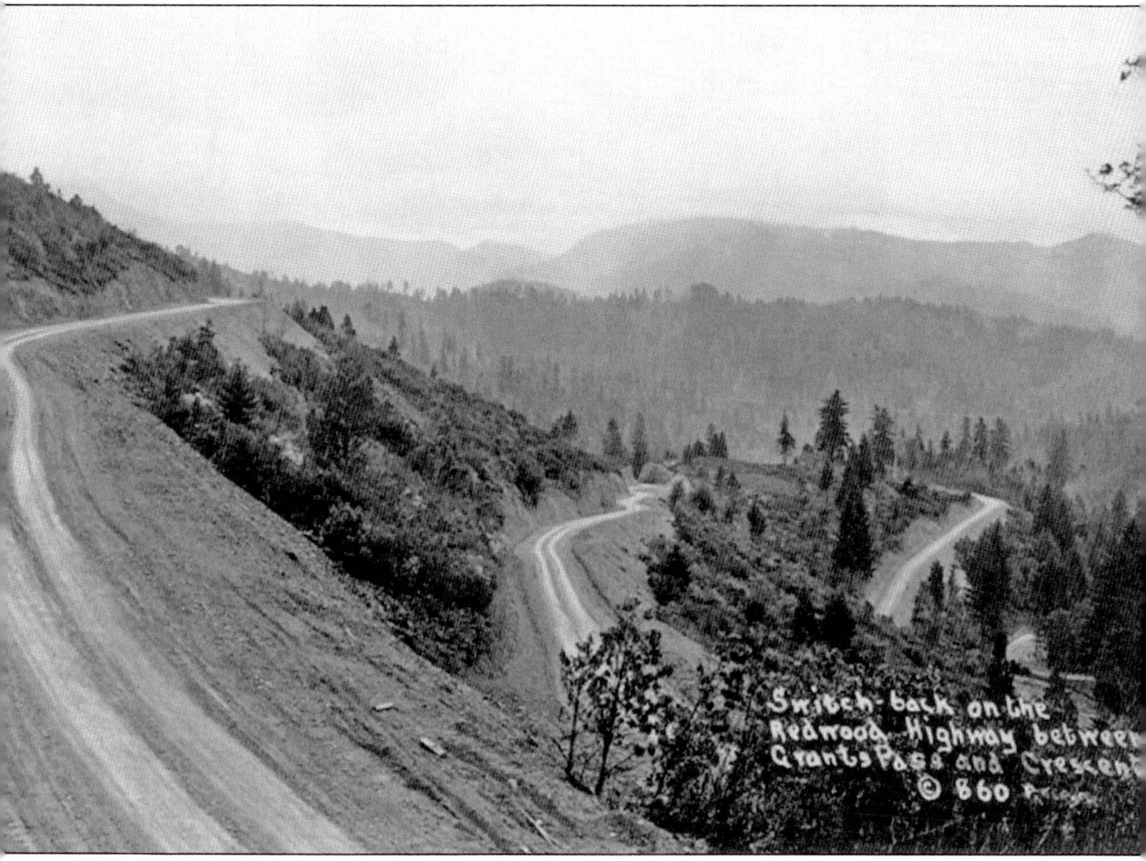

The McLean Auto Company provided service to Crescent City at a cost of $5 each way. One passenger described the service by writing, "With a wagon it is a tedious climb and much of the pleasure of the trip is lost in the inconveniences of the ever-upward pull and the necessary frequent stops in order to rest the tired horses, but in one of McLean's automobiles there is no such experience as the modern vehicle travels up the steep grade at the rate of 10 miles or more an hour and coasts downward at a speed which is only limited by the nerve of the driver and his ability to turn sharp corners where a skid of a foot or less would plunge the whole party down the mountainside to instant death on the rocks below."

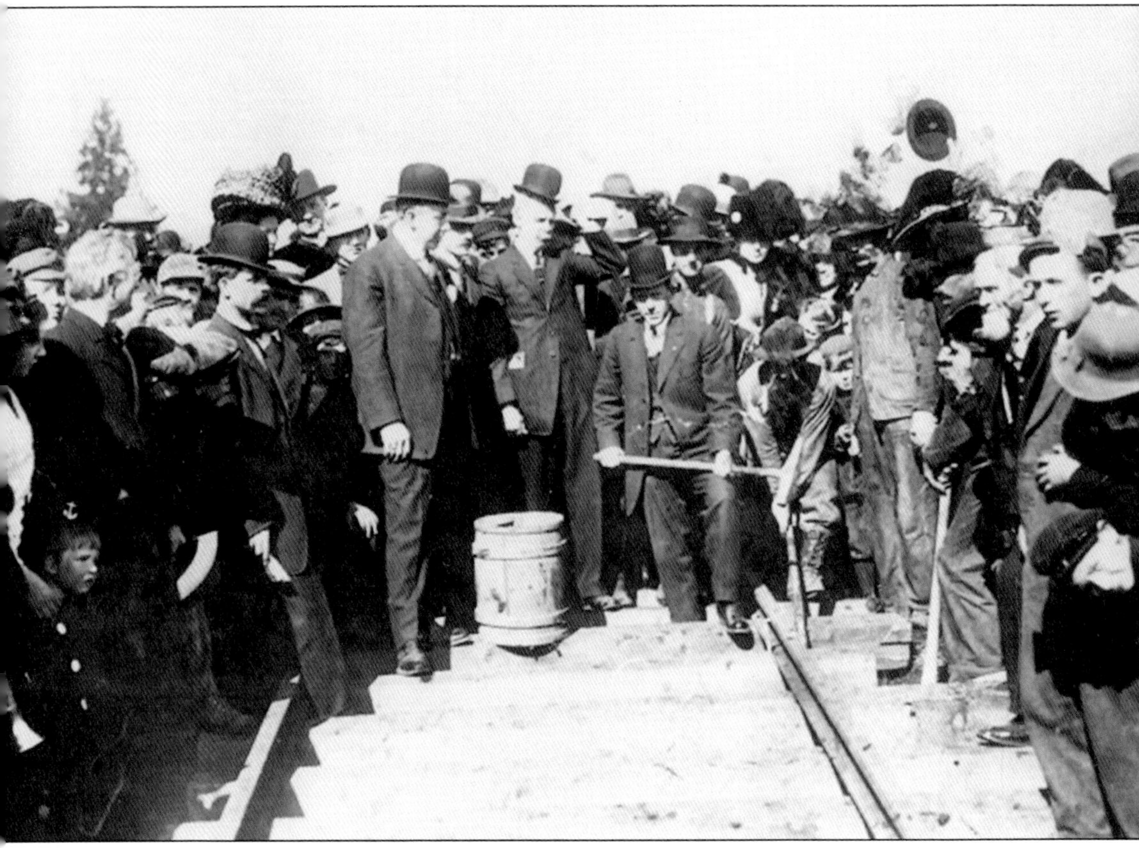

For years, the residents of Josephine County wanted a railroad that traveled from Grants Pass to Crescent City. Research showed it would be less expensive to use the railroad—as opposed to wagon roads—to get their products to a seaport. Finally, the day came. On March 2, 1911, all schools and stores were closed for the ceremony (pictured) surrounding the driving of the first spike of the California & Oregon Coast Railroad. The great celebration featured speeches and music. Another ceremony was held when a line was completed between Grants Pass and Wilderville. The first ticket was auctioned off for $115. Anyone caught driving to Wilderville that day was fined the cost of a train ticket—50¢. Despite many efforts, the train never made it to Crescent City.

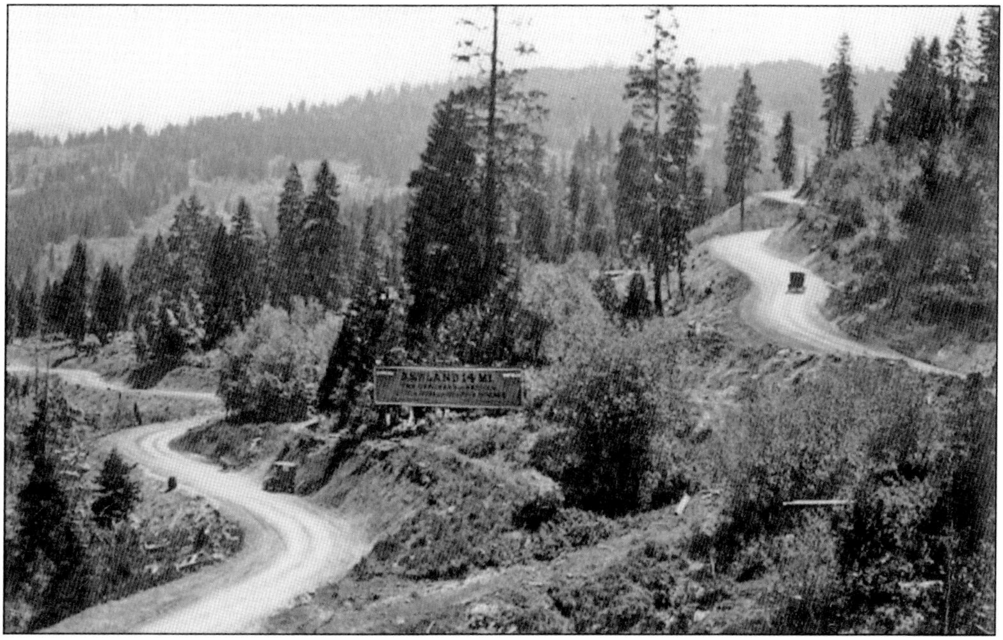

After visiting southern Oregon and northern California, H.H. Eling of Portland wrote, "They can say all they want about the terrors of the Pass Creek, Cow Creek, and Wolf Creek hills and canyons, but I want to tell you that the condition of the road between Portland and Salem is worse than anything found in southern Oregon, the canyons included. From Central Point on through Medford to Ashland and then over the Siskiyou mountains to California is the finest sort of a road. That new road over the mountains is a wonder and the beauty of the thing is that they are improving it all the time. The weather was beautiful and I want to tell you that those valleys in southern Oregon are about the prettiest sights that ever confronted a motorist."

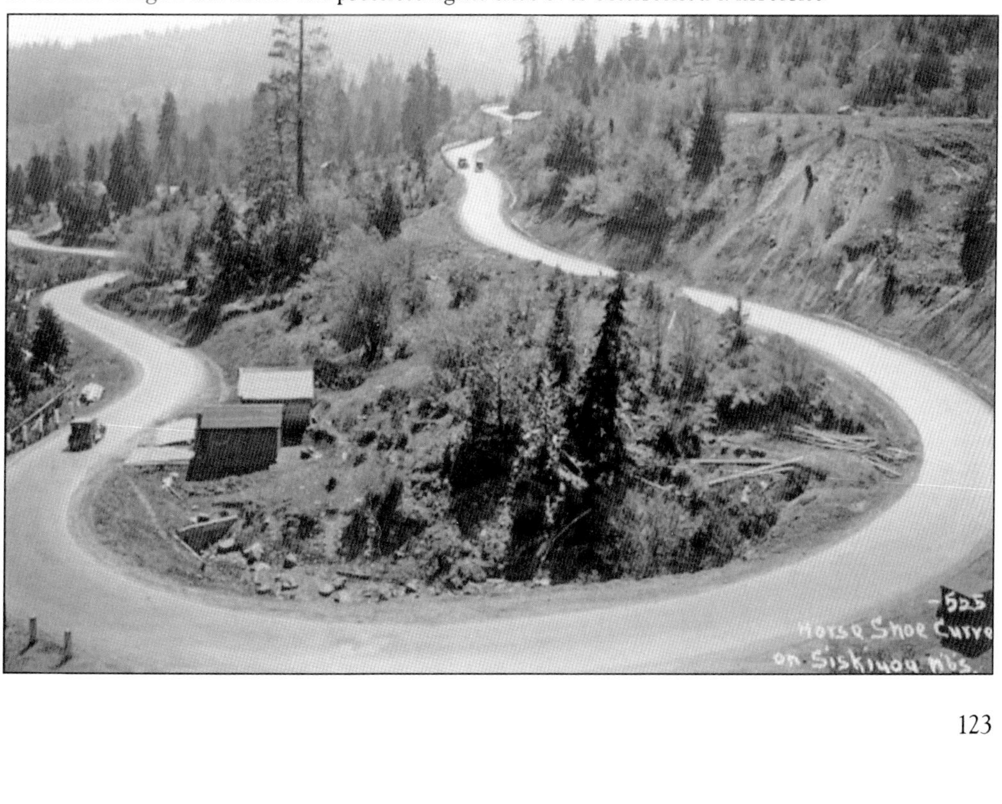

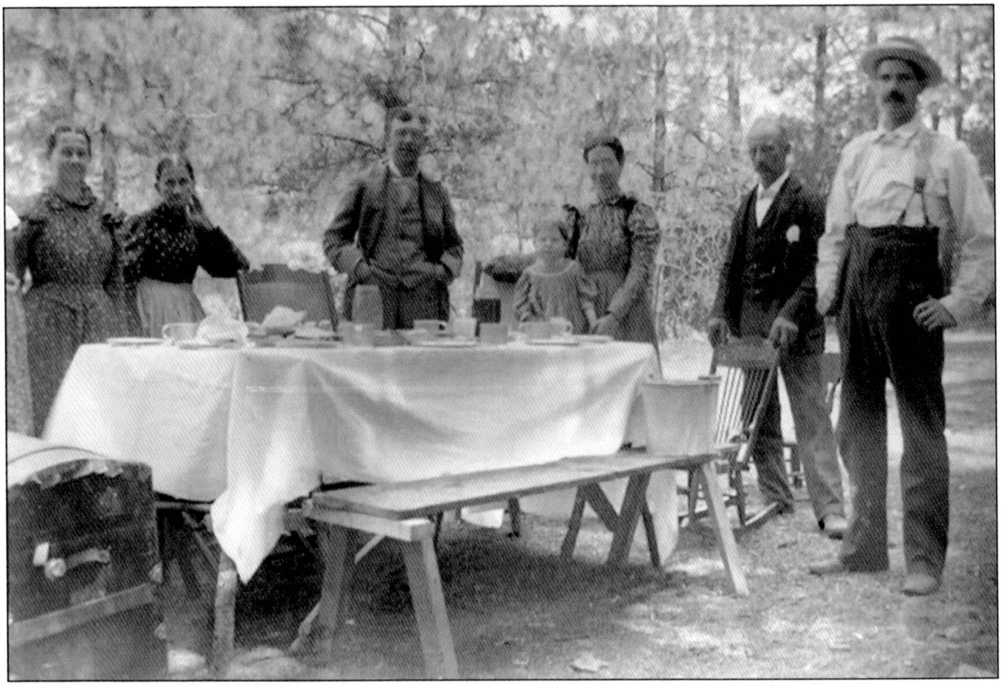

During the summer of 1910, the *Rogue River Courier* reported, "During the past few weeks the call of the wild has been answered by so many of Grants Pass citizens that the city has quite a deserted appearance. Business and household cares alike have been abandoned and young and old have responded to the clarion sound and gone out into the hills on camping, hunting, and picnic parties. With the exception of a few days the weather has not been disagreeably warm. It is good for the soul to cast aside the pressing cares of business and monotony of everyday life and mingle with nature and enjoy her countless blessings whenever it is possible for us to do so."

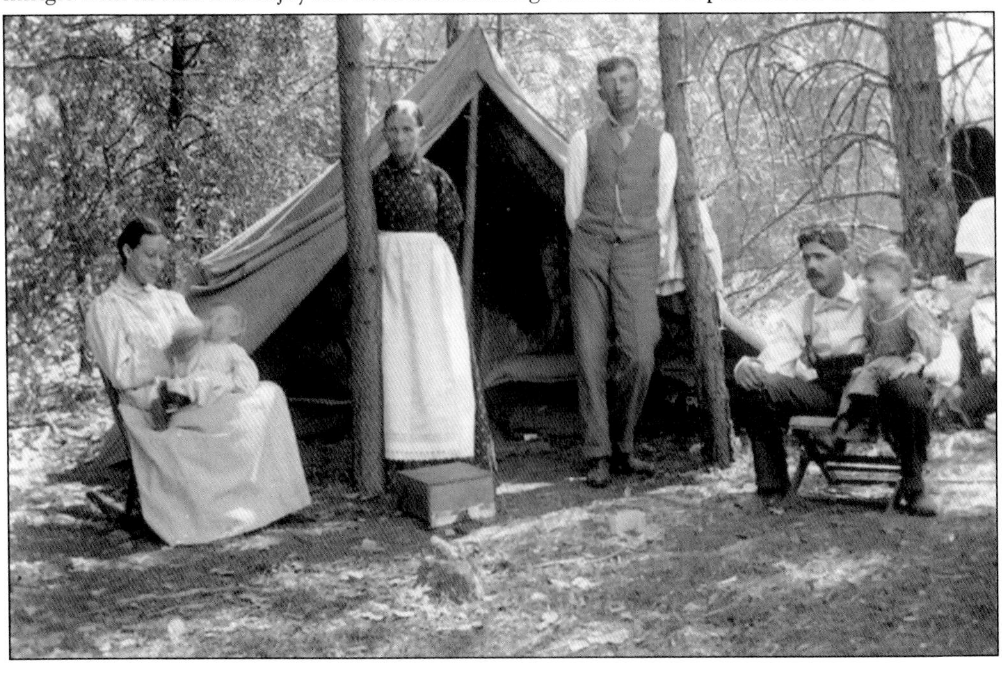

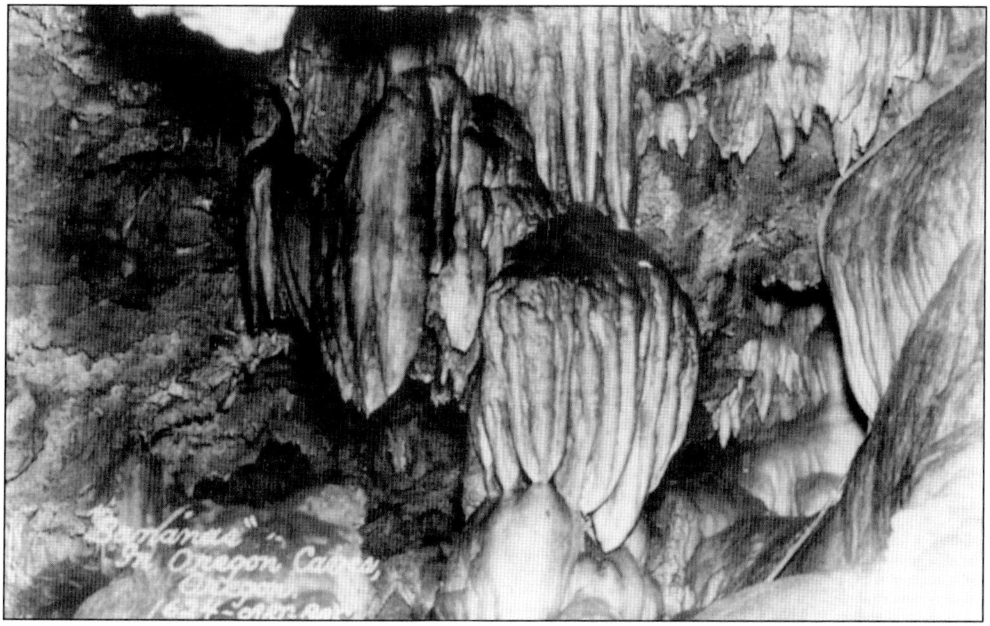

Elijah Davidson is credited with being the first person to discover the Oregon Caves. He came across them while hunting for bears with his dog Bruno in 1874. Early visitors took a dirt road and then had to hike six miles to the caves, though pack animals could be rented for a $3.50 for a round trip. At first, the area had no accommodations for meals or lodging. After Pres. William Howard Taft established the Oregon Caves National Monument in 1909, the US Forest Service (USFS) provided a guide who gave a tour every afternoon. The USFS warned, "Visitors planning to go through the caves should provide themselves with candles and overalls or old clothes. Ladies should wear overalls, riding trousers, or old trousers of some sort. Heavy, hob-nailed shoes will also be of assistance in climbing about in the caves."

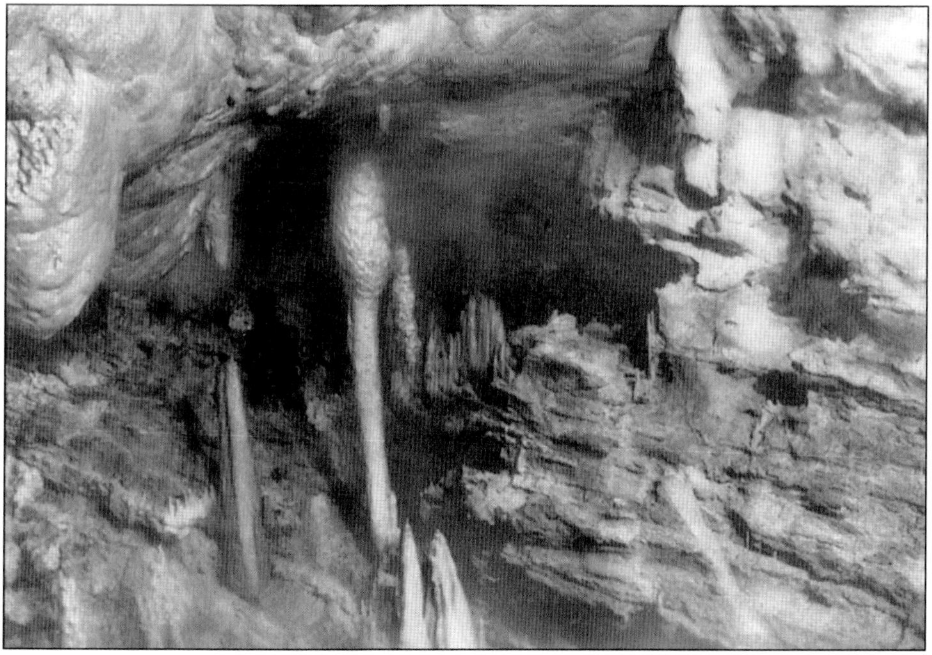

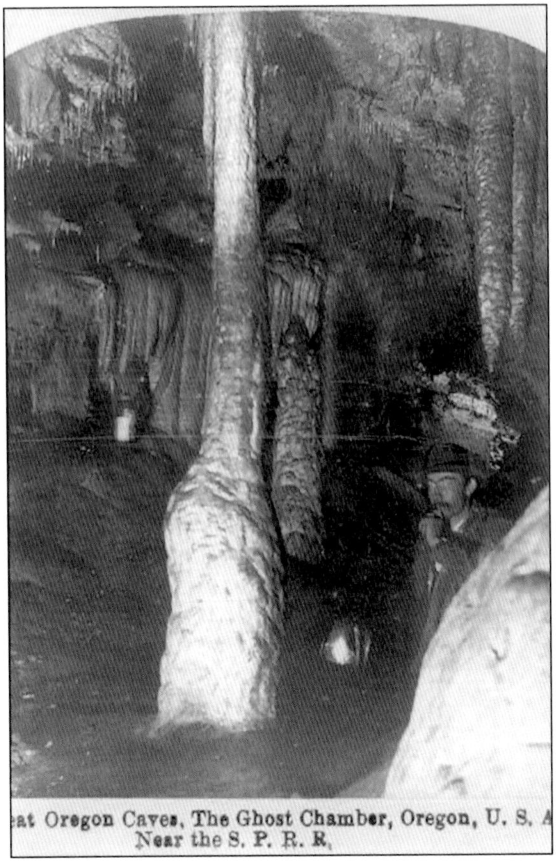

An article in the July 23, 1909, edition of the *Rogue River Courier* reported that "The *Portland Journal* of last Thursday published the following important news . . . 'the president has signed a proclamation whereby one square mile of land surrounding the entrance to the famous Oregon caves or "Marble Halls of Josephine county" is . . . set aside as a national monument. These wonderful caves are located within Siskiyou national forest, about 30 miles south of Grants Pass, Ore., in Cave mountains [*sic*], which is one of the peaks of the Grayback range. The mountain rises to an elevation of about 6000 feet and is of limestone formation. . . . The lime deposits take many beautiful forms; massive pillars, delicate stalactites of alabaster whiteness from the points of which suspend the crystal drop of water carrying its minute deposit of lime from which they are formed, and broad sheets resembling drapery with graceful curves and waves that seem to have been made by varying currents of wind." The first lodging at Oregon Caves is pictured below.

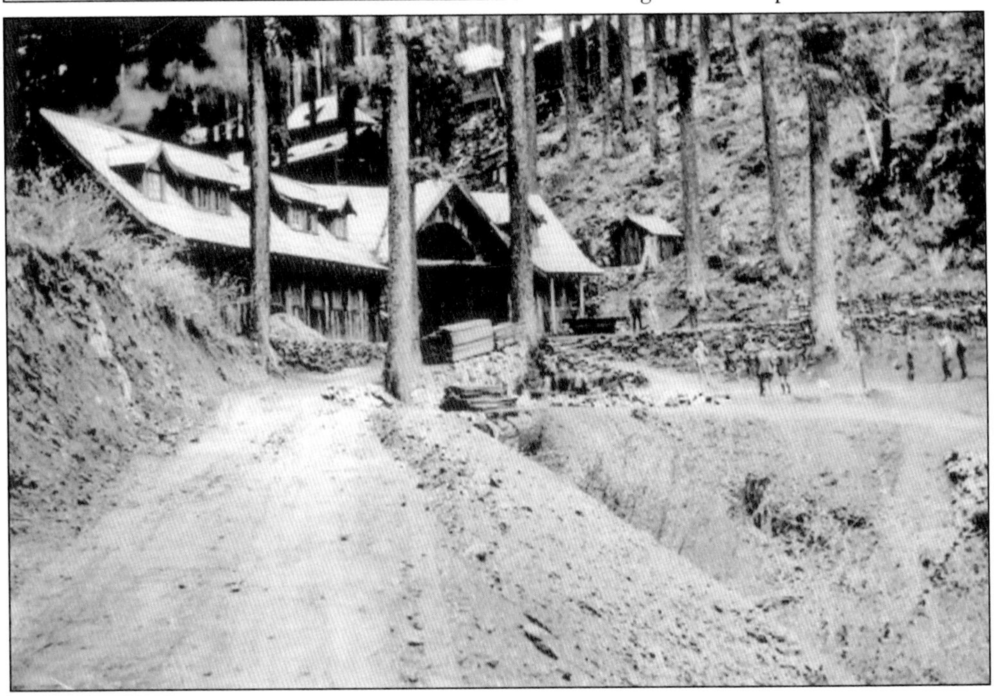

In the early 20th century, a trip from Grants Pass to Crater Lake National Park took several days. W.B. Sherman discussed this journey in an editorial published by the *Rogue River Courier* on September 8, 1911, writing, "We left Grants Pass Wednesday morning at 7 o'clock, went by the way of Gold Hill through Sam's valley and struck the Crater lake road at Trail creek." Upon seeing Crater Lake, he wrote, "The rim of this crater could be well likened unto a vase, being nearly round and 5 1/2 miles across, and towering about 1,000 feet above the table lands, . . . From the crest of this crater it is about 1,000 feet down to the water, which is as blue as indigo. . . . The scenic beauty cannot be told." Sherman summed up the trip as an educational, pleasant sightseeing adventure.

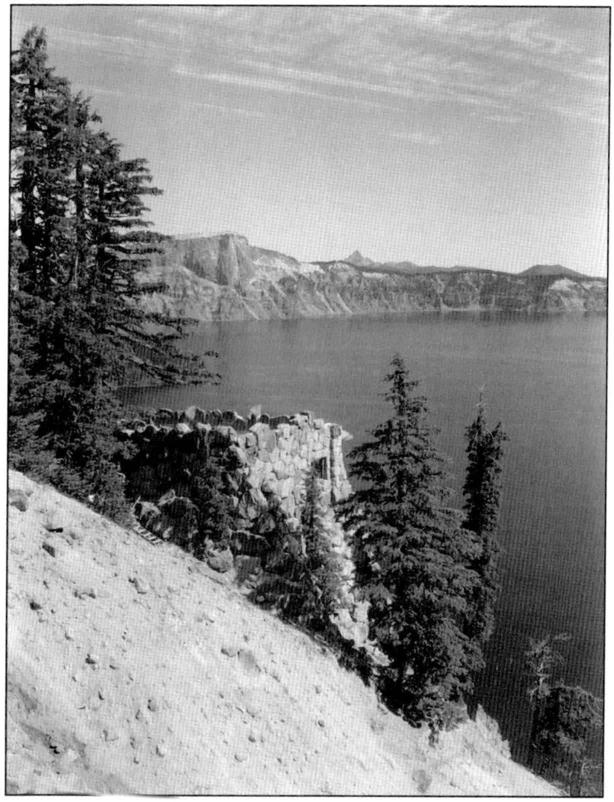

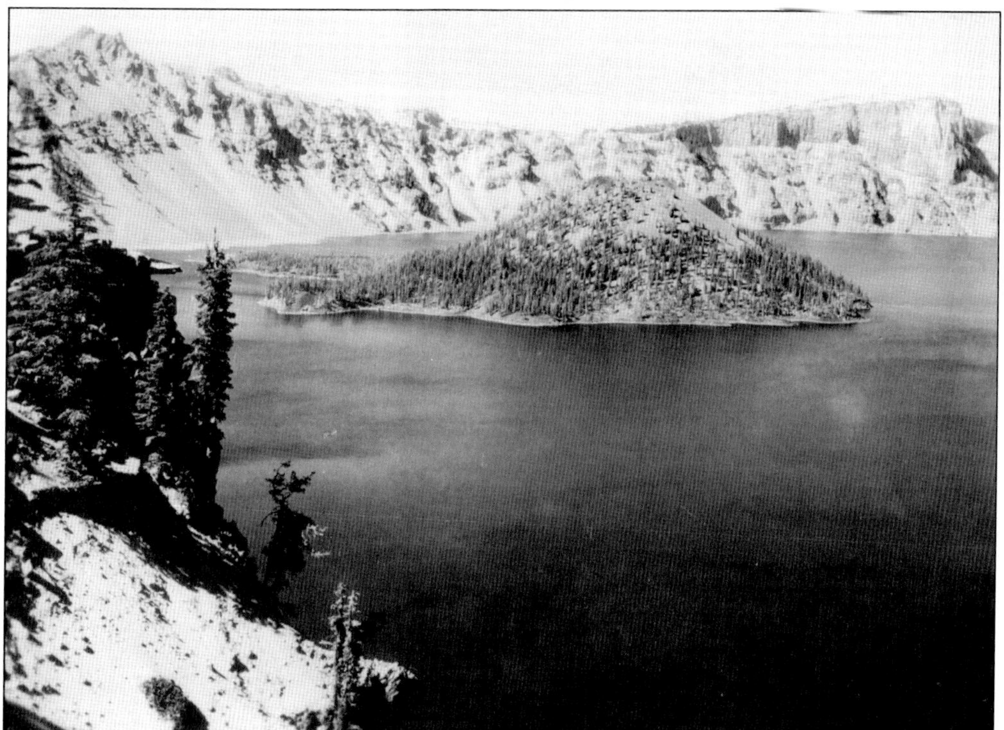

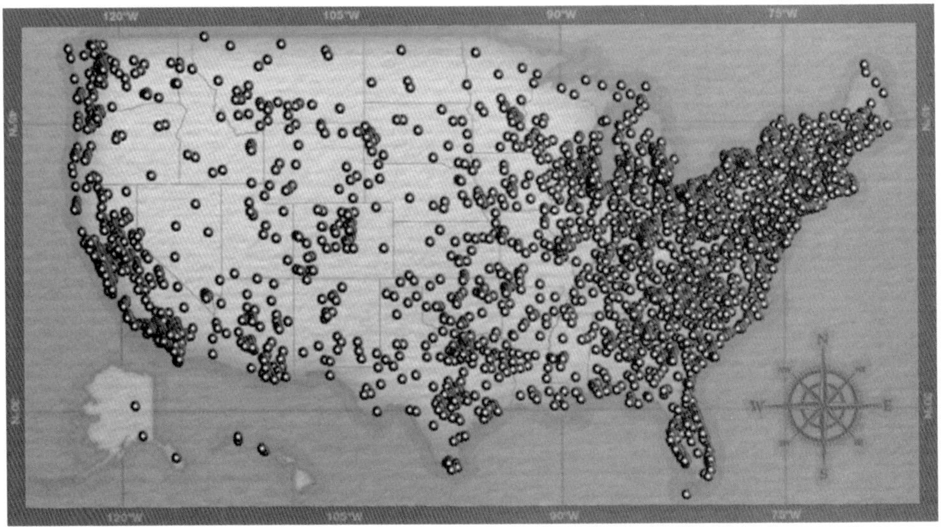